TEARS
OF
BROKEN
HEARTS

MALONG BAAK

These people cried from the bottom of their hearts, due to their humiliated dignity. They vociferously uttered the pains of their crushed souls and raised their voices about the inhumane treatment they faced. Yet it seems that justice is a myth under heaven for some enjoy humiliating humankind more than uplifting it.

A Note from the Publisher

The publisher wishes to acknowledge and thank Dr Douglas H. Johnson for his invaluable help and support for Africa World Books and its mission of preserving and promoting African cultural and literary traditions and history. Dr Johnson and fellow historians have been instrumental in ensuring that African people remain connected to their past and their identity. Africa World Books is proud to carry on this mission.

Dedication

I dedicate this book to my loving Mum, "the Mother of all captives of South Sudan" Deborah Adut Tong Khon whose courageous deeds count. To my late father, Baak Malong Diing, whose name did not appear in the History of the Sudan. He was a Freedom fighter who did not see what he struggled for. I consider all my brethren with whom we have undergone the same captivity.

Table of Contents

Chapter Two

Chapter Three

Chapter Four

Acknowledgments

Sincerely speaking, if it was not the persuasive encouragement from family members and friends, to write this book, I could not have worked harder to write this story. Therefore, in the first place I wish to appreciate late friend Gen. Lual Diing Wol who impeccably unearthed much truth to me on the Movement's 'All about'. Not forgetting also, the old friend of my father, Late Gen. Kawac Makuei Mayar, a great hero and a man of truth who frankly narrated all the darkest sides of the Movement to me. May their Souls rest in peace. I am thankful to my friend Mayuol Diing Mayuol who called these empty papers 'useful book'—I am still mindful to give countless thanks to my Kenyan friend, Maj. /Lab. Robert Gatata for his sage advice. I paid many thanks to my elder brother Cornelius Madut, whose imploring eyes set me to accomplish this impressive task.

FINALLY, I take thie sincere opportunity to recognize and to render my heartfelt Acknowledgement to Africa World Books Publishers Australia. I mindfully give my appreciation to the tireless work of Mrs.Elizabeth Gardiner, who edited this book. I am very much grateful to Peter Laul Deng whose nationalistic heart is obivous for us South Sudanese. Your support and concerned heart deserve much appreciation—without your efforts and wise guidance you have given me, this book won't have been pubished.

Preface

IN THE NAME OF OUR SUBLIME and Glorious LORD, Redeemer of humankind, Jesus Christ, in whose arms life is wrapped in celestial bliss. Amen.

I wish to preface this book by informing dear readers that we, the humankind don't have a human rights watchdog or insight-search on the dire life of human beings across the globe. The Sudan, even before its Southern part split, was a land which co-existed with many tribes, cultures, languages and beliefs. Political preeminence had already been hijacked by Islamic ideology, a religion which should have its demands checked. We, as Sudanese merely by birth, but deprived of its privileges and dignity, lived in a blocked world, a land where there still are no hospitals, schools, agricultural schemes, sanitation: nothing at all.

We are not like other countries of the world or peoples around us. We thought that we were the only people living on earth, if there could be other humans existing. We saw the Arabs as super humankind, who used to kidnap us for reasons we came to know as slavery. When lobbying for the successful progress of the Comprehensive Peace Agreement, the Former American President George W. Bush had this to say on our South-North dilemma, *"This is a fact of reality; "we must turn the eyes of the world upon the atrocities in Sudan"* he narrated that fact to the Americans.

Nevertheless, amongst the kidnapped Dinka lads; of whom some eluded capture on their own, others were waylaid, while myriad numbers remained captives therein up to today. Others were collected by Humanitarian Organizations, I am one. The truth proves everything—that is why I am not so much bothered on what my preface depicts. For the life we spent in abduction or slavery, deprivations, dehumanization and destitutions, we South Sudanese citizens were and still are going through, must be named violations: the ugliest violations of human rights. To name but few, consider the millions of South Sudanese citizens who live a horrible life, being threatened, molested, raped, robbed, forced to live outside their motherland and killed like animals. In addition, those who refused to leave their villages are facing acute poverty and starvation in their own homes up to today. Consider other millions of those who are now living in the shadow of illiteracy. We should consider the fate of being not educated; the rate of illiteracy is ninety percent (90%) of the population, not accessing their own privileges. The privileges could only be retrieved through the intellectualism of education.

This book titled "Tears of Broken Hearts" must function as a reminder and pathfinder. It will serve as an element that should warn my own South Sudanese Family of Nations. The compatriots, relatives and friends, and to open global eyes to the negligence we suffered from Creation times. Moreover, it should engender nationalistic spirit in South Sudanese hearts; and pave shrewd ways for the establishment of our beloved Country, South Sudan. I wrote this after a couple of experiences of dire situations, upon which we, the South Sudan flocks, are still in to this date. Sincerely speaking, whenever the issue of kidnapping is mentioned in my hearing, it always agitates my heart with stressful tension. It scatters my mind asunder. It leaves me a closed mind that could hardly recollect. May God forgive them.

Truth must be spoken; we were in the Stone Age. We are still Genesis people. We had no proper knowledge about the western world for instance: French, British, Americans, Germany or Italy. Something like world Organizations were unknown to us. For example, UK Anti-slavery or US Anti-slavery movements, plus the United Nations (UN), World Food Program (WFP), Food and Agriculture Organization (FAO), or the United Nations Children Emergency Funds (UNICEF), International Criminal Court (ICC) and The North Atlantic Treaty Organization (NATO) formed in 1949 in Washington District of Columbia (DC). In fact, when I grew to realize that human beings have created such organizations hundreds of years back, I was thoroughly disillusioned. I got shocked by the fact that there were already set laws that abolished slavery and the violation of human rights. I was not aware that there are laws adopted already that have forbidden human beings holding another human being hostage as her or his bought property.

We have never heard about the famous First World War that erupted in 1914 or the Second World War that followed in 1939. We know nothing about Aircrafts, Rockets or Gun-chiefs and the Navies, those Great War weaponries, used for fighting an enemy. Our situation was very ugly, terrible and unpromising up to date. We have not attained education on human development, up to date. Our kids still play with mud, molding cows, pieces of broken wood, grassy items, old bicycle tyres and live insects. As a result, they ended up bitten by poisonous insects from time to time causing serious illness or infections.

Truth must be spoken, a human being is an animal that once he/she is not developed, could mentally, economically and spiritually be a serious enemy and hazard to his/her own life. If we consider what Khartoum governments did in not considering the Southern side of Sudan with resources, but exercising sustained antagonism, toward South Sudanese. It seduced them to neglect us, their very own folk, from the privileges of citizenship rights. Our suffering is indescribable and its backwardness ugly. Our minds are poisoned, and this poisoning came with continuous civil wars which devastated only the southern sides of Sudan, exclusively sparing its northern side of Sudan. Where its roots can always be clearly noticed. The showcase is its tribal mindedness we still suffer up to now. Humans here are not fully human, whether you believe me or not, I will still repeat, we have totally a long way to go. That is why I have been trying hard to add a few images of great leaders from different continents and nations without describing either their names, lists of unbecoming deeds or exemplary good deeds which some of them did.

Introduction

THE HISTORY OF SLAVERY in Sudan, which has been witnessed, written about, heard and read by many better writers inside and outside this Country. Enough explanations were given on what inspired Arabs or any other peoples who aspire for human trafficking and abduction worldwide. Yet I wish to speak on what has left a scar in my heart for many years. It is about a tragedy of a kidnapped lad with his family including my Mum, plus others who had also gone through similar fates.

Our abduction story reflected extreme catastrophes, which South Sudanese citizens encountered in one way or another. Therefore, I wish to alert all my readers that this is a true family's testimony, which carries a real story. Therefore, I wish each of its names, places, words or quotations used therein to remain un-tampered with. True to say this, Mum being obsessed by this tale, tells it every now and then.

Okay, some may wish to know my full name, I am Malong Bak Malong—born by a woman who has occupied my writing,

Adut Tong Khon. I was born in a noble family background—our life trip started from the area known to be Marol Ajuong-thii village in 1986. Nevertheless, the acute poverty forced us to evacuate our home area in that year of 1986—and the only place where every South Sudanese used to venture for survival was Northern Sudan. The Southerners go to Northern Sudan for many different reasons; but no matter what those reasons were, still the main reason was for survival. I came from Yei on the 27th of August 2010, after I had attended a Leadership Conference which Bishop Elias Taban of the Evangelical Presbyterian Church invited me to attend. I spent few days with my family then I decided to quickly go and see my Mum and the rest of my siblings at Wanyjok, Aweil East. In addition, as I arrived home, every one of our family members including my Mum enthusiastically welcomed me.

And in the next morning, my Mum called me aside and said, *'Malong my Son, you are specifically unique amongst the kids I bore. Please my lad, I see in you greatness, courage, understanding and strong-heartedness. You also possess special abilities, what you wish to do, you always do. Please my son, don't forget your family, do not let us down'* Then she sharply looked straight into my eyes. Her eyes were telling me that, "we had survived the fate of captivity, yet let's not forget where we have come from." And for some unknown reason she left me abruptly. Those words encouraged me greatly and engendered gigantic strength in me and commitment to do something.

I realized that the time had come for me to share and record our slavery story. The importance of remembering the humiliation we have gone through and how big the mission I am going to accomplish chastened my soul! I realized that my first task was to jot down our tale adding a little history pertaining to South Sudanese's humiliated dignity. That is all I can do now. Since I came back with learned computer knowledge from Yei River County, it is therefore easy for me to get the whole history in writing. I picked up my computer and started to write.

I wish my readers not to think that I am ending by recording that we are forgotten by the world around us, but I wish you to know about and understand the extent of our life in captivity and concurrently the ideology of abduction in Sudan as a whole. My logical reasoning here is that we, after all the ugly humiliations; learn to establish capable and exemplary leadership after we were baptized into those dire situations. I honestly jot this book down with an intention to sensitize and inspire the would-be patriots for the facts of our supposedly national vision. I wished the "discerning citizens" with their "commonsensical leaders" that they should perceptively understand the call for momentum to retain mindfully of things passed. Not merely lured up in the bliss of the first fruit of peace, rather try to read the signs of the things still to come.

I embarked so much on the concept of nationalization herein, mostly in order to bring the realistic perception that can escalate our prosperity and pave ways for National harmony, security welfare, and peaceful co-existence amongst our massive tribes. Therefore, I argue that why not grasp the past along with us as many of learned lessons with their plentiful experiences, and benefit from those humiliations we have gone through.

Repeatedly, I wish to apologize in my preface for every wounding feelings, those my readers might encounter herein when reading this book. Nevertheless, this life-based book is jotted down also as fulfillment to those promises I made in my heart first to my Mum, then to Deng Yak and to all the brethren with whom we have undergone the disaster of captivity. I have also tried my level best to put down some important events on Sudan's story. I went searching about to retrieve realistic events and dates by grasping little portions of the history of Sudan here and there. However, if my readers wished the whole history of Sudan detailed, I encourage you to get books based on Sudan's whole history. Therefore, I deliberately wrote it to keep South Sudanese citizens aware, such that at least they should have something presentable to put their hands on and remind them of their rich history background.

Inasmuch as the parable that says, 'who could encourage the widow, if not another widow'? I appreciate my South Sudanese Martyrs, whenever I recall their uncompromised zeal; it used to bring me down to my knees. I love my Country! The Author of Creation spared my life from those rampant death fates; He saw my life as of a greater value and thus spared it. I saw to it that it is worth mentioning to give this testimony faithfully as an admonition bequeathed to coming generations.

To be honest, this does not mark that we have achieved peace, or that the wars between us and Khartoum Arabs are over. Rather

I am admonishing you that it is yet the fresh beginning of every plight. I will not forget to remember my compatriot Martyrs. If they did not sacrifie their souls, I would have been nowhere. Thanks be to them. Since I am a son of a freedom fighter I do highly value this. I am intensely impelled by their courage and vision. They have foreseen the potential coming of this Country from far off, and fought to make it tangible. They willingly died so that our land should not be exploited by our foe's wiliest deceptions. They died so that we live, and sacrified everything, so that we might have something. They were strong and patriotic, and their visions and wills were strong and durable. They gave us articulate examples on how one should stand your ground and claim your rights. I appreciate the martyred death of father Deng Nhial and Dr. John Garang Mabior for their God-given patriotism.

I also appreciate all the Martyrs of South Sudanese! 'Deng', 'Garang' 'Badi' 'Taban' 'Gatkuoth' and 'Zande' are my prerogative names! Their uncompromised stand humbled my soul. I will never forget to appreciate the American President George W. Bush for his tireless effort in prompting both parties, the Sudan People Liberation Movement (SPLM/A) and his ability to impose the mulish National Congress Party (NCP) to sign the Comprehensive Peace Agreement (CPA) making this symposium peace agreement that freed the South Sudanese, as a realistic task achieved.

I appreciate every Christians' prayer including well-wishers from across the globe.

Chapter One

1.1 The Importance of Events Before and After My Birth

To begin with, I am called Malong Baak Malong Diing. I was born in 25th of May 1982 in Rumaker village at Aweil East County. I wish to start introducing my birth by noting some few events—for our people strongly believed in events which occurred in certain times. We used to mention and identify certain events to remind us of time since we do not know counting of years as calendars identify their seasons. Thus, I wish to mention few events based on that fact.

I am a South Sudanese citizen. Sad to say this, I got into this life on my left leg as our old Jeing proverb used to say in misfortune happening. It seems as if I was born here in this world only to suffer negligence—everything opposed me on this planet. Things always declined to work out for me as if all the elements of this globe had conspired against me in defiance and taunting me without end. Life means struggle to me, with failures.Some remain to inflict my soul in a close pursuit of me in my life with resentments from the past. Whenever I expect good, evil comes my way. I have lived long enough to experience various humiliations which carry shameful disappointments..

People called me "the writer" because I used to write most of my times, but the fact is that I am not the one writing these stories. My hands only pickup a pen, then the stories themselves dictate my fingers to write them down .In addition, to precise how I was born, my birth was so intricate. My father was a "gorilla man" and he could not spend much time with his wives. Moreover, my elder brother Mou spent four year old still breastfeeding. And my father left my Mom without weaning the child before a new pregnancy. He went on his military mission for years. My elder brother Mou sucked the breast of my Mom for four consecutive years before he was weaned because my Dad overstayed his return. In addition, when my elder brother Mou was weaned, it became so difficult for my Mom to conceive easily due to some unknown reproductive disorders. Therefore, she spent another two more years without any sign of pregnancy—which thoroughly annoyed my father perpetually.

. Moreover, Dad sent for his aged uncles such that they could come and say their words. They came for their ritual of saying the word. Within a half a year, my Mom did conceive. My Dad became so excited that he gave me the name Malong before I was born, exclaiming that 'when this lad would be born, his name should definitely be "Malong" after my father Malong Diing'.

2

And he strongly commanded his elderly wife Anyiet Anyuon saying, 'never bring a man in my absence as midwife in the birth hour—for my wife Adut Tong might kill my son in fear of seeing a man putting his two hands in her bosom'. In addition, for sure, when my mother showed symptoms of child labor, Anyiet never left my mother to deliver in any other human beings' hands and Anyiet became the midwife.

My father came back from another mission, when his baby boy Malong was born to him. He shot countless bullets in the air with very joyful heart. He called his neighbors and comrades to celebrate the birth of his beloved Son, and a very big bull was slaughtered. Again, it was said that before the year in which I was born, a certain great Sorcerer called "Deng Ajakleng" rose performing mysterious miracles. The meaning of his name 'Deng' means 'God' and 'Ajakleng' means great surprise. Because it was believed that Deng was a great god who ascended to heavens long time ago mysteriously, so now he had decided to return with doubled virtue of powers as Salvation Messenger to Jeing people. He used to identify some people who happened to be wizards. They had made the community members as their hideout and used to bewitch such innocent people with spells. Therefore, everyone disputed over the examination, such they could point out who could really be the true sorcerers. Countless girls, women, including old and young men brought their critiques before him to be identified. Many girls, who were identified as associated with sorcery or bewitchers, lost their relationships with young men to whom they were engaged.

3

Thus, many rueful songs were composed by the then girls who lost contact with their loved young men due to their devastated social relationships, as young people shy away from one another in avoidance, fearing one might also lose his or her social belonging. Because any young girl or man who was identified as wizard were never married again. Their boyfriends or girlfriends withdrew from their promises of becoming forever life spouses. The identified women from the other side also lost their families because their husbands put them away as soon as they heard about them being with magic from the great Deng Ajakleng. He (Deng-Ajakleng) alleged that he simply came to save the land of Muonyjang (Dinkaland) from the act of sorcery, saying that his powers saved like an omen for a peaceful and zero wizardry life to the Jeing community.

He ordered that all children born in his time should be named, 'Makom, Nyanciek, Maciek, Magot, Agotand so on. He stated that any child born in his time should be given those names in order to mark his own period and season. Another event that occurred also was the story of the two (gods) animals, the he-goat and the dog, which came from where the sun rises to the Aweil community. The he-goat and dog gods were celebrated in adoration wherever they happened to reach any community. They also demand eight most beautiful virgin girls and young men to remain as hostages for the period of their stay until they decided to leave those communities and go to another location. They were to be escorted also by those eight girls to the other community to which these gods wish to go to. Then they let go of the girls and young men of the community they had just left. So, they were escorted to Aweil from eastern communities and as usual, they were welcomed with celebration of adoration by the Aweil community.

As I had already mentioned, they demanded eight girls (they used a certain man as their interpreter) which was accepted with feigned interest by the Aweil community. Moreover, unfortunately, some radical gunmen fired at them killing the he goat but the dog escaped its death and it was not shot. Many communities blamed the Aweil community, stating that such reckless deeds provoked a curse. They blatantly said that Aweil crops would not yield a good harvest in the coming years due to the committed sacrilege and provocation done to the great gods. Some came to believe that the terrible hunger that afflicted the Aweil community in the late 1988 was a result of what happened some years ago.

Another event occurred when I was six years old, when my mum narrated to me a certain story of the lost sun. She told me that the sun was lost for almost three hours—people were in total darkness without a single sunlight. Those who were found in the fields looking after the cows in the forest were stuck there because there was no light to show them the way back. Everyone who used to go to the neighborhood begging for food (Mom said this intentionally to warn us from begging for food in our neighborhoods) in some other people's homes were frustrated because they were blocked therein. Therefore, after she finished narrating the story of the lost sun, I asked her saying, 'mama, what was the reason that make the sun unable to shine or who prevented it from shining? In addition, what would have happened if the sun did not appear again? 'Mum in response vehemently exclaimed saying, 'Keei! Keei! She said in our tongue. In addition, as she raised her two arms out, meaning 'the entire world' said, 'Malong my son, we would have perished at once. All mankind would have died miserably.'

She went ahead telling me the complete myth as: "once upon a time, the sun was a Son to a great god, his great god-father used to tell the sun his son that he wished to destroy the entire human race. And his father entrusted him a volcanic hammer'. In addition, he sent his son the sun down with a mission to destroy all humankind on earth. Therefore, on his arrival to earth, he saw how peaceful and innocent humankind was. Therefore, he was convinced that they did not hate him as his father alleged. He felt compassion on them and did not kill them. When his evil-hearted father saw such a deed, he counted it as an act of treason and he wanted to either kill or arrest him. And he began to chase after him all his life time until he could get hold of him and take his hammer back from him again.

Nevertheless, the sun on the other hand, did not want to give back the volcanic hammer lest his evil-heart father might at once use it against us, by killing such an innocent human race. That is why Malong my Son, you can see the sun rises up early every morning before his bad father gets hold of him. Nevertheless, unfortunately, one day the sun slept too long, when he woke up, it was too late already, and his bad father managed to get hold

6

of him. In addition, his bad father arrested him in a big luok (rural hall); he prevented him to get outside. Therefore, the sun thought critically, then cunningly deceived his bad father saying that he wished to go to urinate, which was permitted by his father. There the sun escaped through the window and managed to dodge again his bad father's intention towards the human race.

That was the end of the sun story, but my heart remained fascinated, pondering the story deeper. And from that time on, I used to wake up every morning early and looked at the sun and began to encourage him not to sleep too much so that he couldn't be caught by his evil-hearted father, such that he might not fail his mission of saving the human race. Every day I consider the importance of sunrise and sunsets.

Yes, to come back to emphasize on the point of my story. Sincerely speaking, my life history is one of those stories to whom the word "unbelievable" is true. When I was born, my people were already undergoing a deterioration of life due to Arabs of the north who coveted our land. There were so many civil wars between Dinka and Arabs, including fratricidal revanges amongst tribes. On the other hand, different militias were murderinging the people due to the refusal of food items and cow meats, including tensions over chiefdoms and low lands. Raping of both women and young Dinka girls went on.

Life in South Sudan became more adventurous and perilous. Experiences of disaster after disaster engulfed the entire Jieng lands. Raiding was rampant, especially from every side and people exceedingly begun to die daily. My parents lived in desperation and were enraged by such ugly turbulances. My mum asserted that she could stay all the time with us in the bush while Dad went spying. We could expect my Dad to come back at least with little news of changes to bring hope. But Dad could solely come with signals telling mum let's take the kids there, or let's shift to another jungle not back home .Muraheliin Arabs were fiercely incinerating our huts each time they came, such that people gave up thatching their houses since they would be set on bonfires again. Dad tarried all the times spying on the Arabs accross the villages to see whether they ceased from passing by. Yet he would always come back frustrated and discouraged when seeing their perpetual coming. We were kept in the bushes until the late hours of the nights because our home became precarious to live in. Hunger and thirst were not our major dreads but Arabs of Khartoum and Muraheliin were our enemies realistically

Another factor that added more suffering in our conditions was that my dad Baak Malong Diing was one of the prestigious member of insurgents since the first insurgency known to be 'the Anya Nya One' up to the 'Anya Nya Two' and finally now the SPLA/M insurgency highly ranked. Thus his frequent visit to us with both him and his men in uniforms made things worse. Because such were the ones specifically the Khartoum government were hunting down. All the villagers dreaded to hide in the same jungles with us when they realized that the most sought after people were the armed black insurgents. The worst thing was also that the Khartoum government was hiring some gullible people within some Dinka community members, to spy the whereabouts of the rebels. In fact, these spies could know the whereabout of the black insurgents dwelling with their respective families. Our lives were in a perilous situation!

As the situation deteriorated every day, some people were impelled to escape to northern Sudan, some to faraway jungles, while some gentle men and women who were persuaded by this situation to join the insurgency as a result, joined it. But some preferred to remain with their firm decision that they will die in their lands. Many of them were homicides. The screaming of the young ladies undergoing molesting, the pains of sodomizing together with screaming children, leaving their mothers sobbing embitterdly and their husbands massacred, could be heard in the distance. Everybody was a coward. It became common that whenever the villagers could hear screaming emanating from ravished girls, that they could nonchalantly ask whether it could be another attack, or killed victims. But if the answer would be a lady 'undergoing ravishing' they could normally come down saying, 'not bad if she is still alive'.

Those families whose homes were incinerated in bonfires and had their livelihoods destroyed were just comforted with a few words, since what mattered most was life not food or cattle. Every villager was looking for safety or secured places out of the reach of Khartoum Arabs and Cattle raiders, yet it seemed as if the Arabs raiders flooded everywhere. There were no secure areas and every bush had become like open fields. They set our home on fire five times burning everything our parents had had. They used to come sometimes from Warawaar market, a place which the Muraheliin did burn over and over and over every season they used to come unexpectedly. They came to Marol-ajuongthii, our village, and raided our goats and cows, leaving our parents empty handed. So, those losses caused by a lack of cows and goats in our home and we ran short of food as well. And in the next year somehow, in a short while, there seemed to be temporary peace which lasted only for four months in the place and what mattered then was hunger now, but it was a shortlived respite. We had been left with no hope to make better thatched houses to begin with. We had got one hut and another small store that was made in traditional type; it was our traditional warehouse.

1.2 Baak Malong Diing's Birth, Zeal as Freedom Fighter, and Death

My father Baak Malong Diing was born in 1908 in Warapath village, Wanyjok. In addition, in 1933, his father Malong Diing took them to stay in Nyamlel at Magot-dit village. My grandpa Malong-dit (Malong the great) and his others two stepbrothers Akoon Dorjok and another Malong left at night when they felt that their elderly brothers had envied them. Magot-dit village is our grandpa's motherland Nyigut Deng Gar. They stayed there until 1945 then they moved to Maker-Anei village the current Aweil North—they stayed there until in 1948. When he was 48 years old, he joined the Colonial government's military. From there he went to so many trainings in different places. In addition, he was promoted to rank of sergeant at his graduation in Wau. Then again, he was promoted to Sergeant Major the same year.

The Officer Baak Malong possessed strong Military disciplines with an energetic spirit. Though he was illiterate and war-like, yet everybody admired his morals, which engendered him trust especially in the Military sphere. My father Baak Malong spoke oral Arabic, oral English and Dinka. This unbecoming negligence of him not to have gotten education, which pushed him backward, he repeatedly warned his sons about it saying: *'my sons, don't be late to go to school, you all must go to schooling. Please, he continued, "you must join anything your age mates used to go to, or do. He continued saying, "You will not be valued figures in the eyes of others you have seen now with your own eyes how far I strongly fought, yet I didn't reach where I am supposed to be'*. He always said that with a rueful heart and sullen face. I wish if my father could be here today, to see how those academic abilities which refused to add credit into his dignity, how his own son had really excelled over alphabets, of those languages once disdained by him.

According to the Hon. Lual Diing Wol, told me that my father had many friends. They were as follows. Kuol Makuac Kuol; Senior Paramount Chief of greater Abiem was my father's friend. Deng Akuei Ajou of Bac, head of regional courts; Chief Mawein Diing Akol Paramount Chief of Ajuet was also his best friend. Arop Kuot Nyiuol, Paramount Chief of Makem community (Gok-Machar) and Chief Aher Arol Kuon, head of regional courts (Korok) were his friends. The business person

Athian Athian, amongst his sons is Pastor Garang Athian and AkueiAthian—and Commander Kawac Makuei Mayar including Hon. Abel Alier, the first Vice President in the Khartoum government. In addition, Lual Lual Madeer, his old soldier comrade who defected from Ariath. Lual Diing added that he (Baak) and Salva Kiir Mayardit (the incumbent president) are cousins and so they were amiable to one another. The Madi man Agiri Jada and Ali Gautalla from Equatoria were also amongst his beloved comrades. My father Baak Malong defected from Wau in 1956 with a rank of Sergeant Major—and joined Anya-Anya one, whose location was in Tiit-Adol. Then from there he was sent to Owinykibul the first Training Centre for Anya-Anya One where he was assigned to be one of trainers to the new recruits. Amongst the first recruits was Martin Mawein Agokrial—who became the Chief Commander of Bongo Training Center of the SPLA. Baak Malong was thereafter promoted to a rank of 2nd-Lieutenant, after they graduated the group. He remained to be one of the Anya-Anya One's stalwarts for his strong fighting tactics which increasingly begun to add to his credit every time. Some from those who defected included comrades Ali Guatalla, Madut Chan who defected from Torit—beside others who had defected from different areas of the South.

In 1972 when the Sudanese President Ja'afir Muhammad Nimeiri allegedly called for South Sudanese peace and reconciliation of Addis Ababa, all the Anya-Anya One leaders came in response to the call. All the politicians were told that they would be given their right positions, which was just a deception to get them, trapped. Our father realized this, and Marcelino Tong, the father of Chol Marceline, also having understood this pledge, silently resigned from Khartoum government and went to his private job of being a physician. All the officers were o degraded. Amongst them were Maduok Akot Aru, who was degraded from the rank of captain to 2nd Lieutenant, including Kuach Wol whose nickname was "Kuac-Madiir", from a rank of l.t colonel, degraded to a rank of Major.

Such mistreatment faced all the Anya-Any one movement's Military Wing to both soldiers and their Officers. Baak Malong, was a Major, but was demoted to a rank of Captain. When he saw things had fallen apart—nothing was realistic in all the agreements. So he went to the outskirts of Aweil town at a faraway village called Marol Ajuongthii. He (Baak) has begun to take his personal commodities to Wau market for selling. The Wau County Commissioner by then was Isaiah Mabior Kulang, as I said earlier, that Baak Malong's family had prospered on cultivation and cattle—which made him a recognized and famous man to those who used to go to Rumaker, Ariath and other markets areas and to as far as Wau.

The Khartoum government was searching for him, because the government's plan was to have those defected officers killed or arrested—Baak Malong did not know that such danger would overwhelm him. He was to take a visit to Wau for two purposes: first, to sell his groundnuts and secondly, to visit his in-laws Edward Lual Deng Khon. In that year of 1979, after he decided to take his groundnuts to Wau market by a Train (though his journey was secret, yet the security men of president Nimeiri heard of his whereabouts), not knowing that the Khartoum government's notorious security organ was following him to arrest him even in Wau. Moreover, when he reached Wau, his arrival was noticed. He was followed by notorious security organization that took him to Juba where he was arrested for two years by the orders taken from President Nimeiri. The years were from 1979-1980. Molana Abel Alier was the Vice President in the Khartoum government by then. Therefore, in that year of 1980 by good luck, the Vice President Abel Alier paid one of his visits to Juba— where he saw the man Baak Malong whose hairs were completely white but young and good-looking in the face, being escorted by the military police to the dining hall. Alier was curious to know who such a man could be.

Abel Alier was told that it was Captain Baak Malong, from Aweil, who was arrested through the orders from the President Nimeiri. Thanks to Abel Alier's courageous deeds, Abel Alier ordered his immediate release without hesitation. Following his release, the Khartoum government took him from the Military section to the Prison Department as a prison officer. Then he was sent to Aweil where he served until 1982 when another underground movement was boiling down there. The Khartoum government on realizing that Baak Malong would defect again, immediately got him arrested right here in Aweil. Luckily enough, in Aweil the Khartoum government was not very strong to resist the ethnic spirit that sought to release their beloved son, Baak Malong. In addition, in 1983, a certain riot broke out in the

Aweil market and some violent police quickly rushed to where he was detained and broke off the locks, setting him free.

Baak immediately armed himself with weapons and asked his younger brother Daniel Deng Malong to leave Aweil to go to the bush. He defected from Aweil in that year of 1983 April— and joined his colleagues in Bongo where the SPLA/M was located under Dr. John Garang De Mabior Atem. Baak Malong and Dr. John Garang Mabior were already familiar colleagues; Baak was warmly welcomed into the movement. The SPLA movement's vision was very clear: freedom, the human rights of all Sudanese people regardless of their ethic or religions, democracy, equity, prosperity and Justice for all. In 1986, Dr. Garang De Mabior sent all Chords whose tribes were mostly from Bahr El Ghazal to go back and start their offensive operations against the Khartoum regime. Therefore, in response to that order, he returned to Bhar el Ghazal until 1997, when he died in 23rd of March 1997 in Nyamlel, at Magot-dit village. That he was assigned by the C-In-C Garang Mabior (Commander In Chief) to the Wildlife department at the rank of Alternate Commander (Major) that is.

1.3 The Initiative of Going to Northern Sudan

And it came to pass, that in March of 1986, in one of its nights while in the compound, I heard my mum telling my elder brother Madut in their conversation, "if we can go to Rumaker now, we can stay there until the land back here beomes safe". Mum

15

continued, "or if we will proceed North, we will still find for ourselves a good Arabic man whom we can work for and earn food until we come back next year" she said. But my elder brother Madut retorted with enthusiastic heart saying, "I will go and work for the sake of my young brothers, in order to make them survive, of course I am no longer young to do so". He spoke superciliously as to prove his manhood. They negotiated this issue at the one side of the fire place while we were playing on the other side of the fireplace.

Three days later my mum decided to go to her brothers and sister in Cibiliek at Marol-Ajuong-thii village. After she went there, she called Ngong-matuong her elderly brother, including her younger brother Atak-Macharkuei and Anok Tong Khon, her junior sister, to a meeting. My mother's face looked a bit weak but she was determined that she could start the talk. Her face could demonstrate that she has fully given up living in the village. "I have been sick all this time in my knees, I did not cultivate for my children and I have no Dura as food for my kids, as you can see that my husband did not dig the garden because he is a soldier on the move every day," said mum. But her younger brother as he looked at her in the face with stern eyes, realized her pledge. He said in reply, "And what has come in your mind to do now?" But without halting my mum said, 'I want to take the children to Rumaker or I might proceed to the north'. North! No! He argued, "I will never accept this plan of yours" said the younger brother of my mum. It was seconded also by her youngest sister Anok. But their elderly brother Ngong-Matuong

16

as he was leaning on his arm against a traditional wooden chair, in his wise counsel said, "What will you give her with the children seeing that what she said is realistically true?" He continued, sincerely speaking, I allow her to go but her elderly son Madut will not go with her, because if she reaches there in peace, no problem, but if some misfortune happened to her and the kids on the way, we will still have our sister's blood with us in her son namely Madut.

Her elderly brother Ngong-matuong won the meeting by his sound statement and it was accepted by each one of them including my mum. Then finally my elder brother was sent away the day after the meeting in the company of my uncle Atak Tong Khon. While Madut was still away, we were told by our uncle Ngong-matuong to leave before he could come back. He concluded saying, "your son Madut is a radical boy, and he might not accept our pledge of letting him remain behind here with us". Then on the next three days, he called us aside for a traditional ritual, since he was the elder in the family line, he woke up and poured water on our feet saying, "Go my sister with your children, nothing will harm you on the way, your husband's dowry were brought to us satisfactorily" may the gods of our grandpas and grandmas protect you, Amen. And my mother took us to our Dad. She took us there in order to discuss with my dad the issue of that severe starvation. When my mum reportedly told my dad that she needed his support, my father replied frankly that my mum is a strong woman and she could survive with her children. He declared that his seldom concern was based upon his other weak wives and orphans whose mothers died. For my dad had married more than one wife. After we bade goodbye to our father, my mum took us next day straight to Wurkuot village where our grandpa, the elder brother to my dad namely Diing Malong lived.

On arriving at his house in the evening, he asked my mum worriedly, "Adut, where are you taking my kids?" But my mum replied his question flatteringly that we have just come to visit him. Okay, he said as he pushed himself backward on his wooden chair still with suspicion in his eyes, as to what is the real aim of my mum coming to his house with the children . In the late night my mum told his wife Aluel Wol separately the entire story of her leaving to Rumaker with her children and how she told her husband that there is no food. Her husband had released her with the children to leave to the northern side namely Rumaker for the survival of both herself and the children. Since there was no alternative, in the morning my mum told Diing Malong the fact that we were leaving to Rumaker and that she was also released by her husband. This pledge has fully been accepted by everyone including her brothers since there was no alternative at all.

Rumaker was considered those days as one of the northern villages when it was under Khartoum troops. Bewildered by this case, my grandpa looked at her face with observant eyes as her lips moved up and down, nodding his head in every sentence that mum could utter. My mum told him that she had come to him with his sons so that he should not throw blame on her for taking the children without informing him. My grandpa in his acceptance said, "Since our rich family of Malong Diing has now

18

become as weak and destitute. As such; we have no choice but to restrain those leaving into exile for their survival".

In the morning my mum arranged for our departure. The kidnappers, Arabs used to be lurking in the bushy road to Rumaker. It was known by every passing-by Dinka people who used to sneak to the north for survival. And therefore my mum was demanding my grandpa's blessing on us before we leave. She went down on her knees kissing his hands and feet to bid him goodbye as a sign of homage given to the elderly one in the family hierarchy. Our grandpa cried ceaseless tears before he could say anything. But our grandma Aluel-dit vehemently retorted saying, "why did you do this to your own kids, how will you manage to bless them now as they leave? Don't you know that if you do it without a pure committed heart that they will never penetrate through those merciless kidnappers?".

So as not to make the situation go bad as grandma said, my grandpa calmed himself down. And in blessing us he said: "*You my ancestors, and the spirits thereby, I entrust my kids into your unwavering care; I command their way to be cleared from the way-layers Muraheliin, I wished none to touch my children on their way, so shall it be*". Then abruptly he quelled his sayings by sprinkling us with water mixed with charcoals and oil. And with his right thumb, he rubbed on our foreheads and feet, as he marked them with oil mixed with charcoal. Then he immediately turned his back to us. In order now to bid us goodbye, as he remained with his back turned at us still, he said, "*You may leave now, with a weak and rather broken heart*". *As he heard our feet tapping with movement of leaving, he broke into tears and begun to say loudly that "Is that is my doom, that my children could be exiled to the land which is not of their grandpas?"* my grandma Aluel Wol in an attempt to rebuke him to stop weeping, found herself deeply broken hearted too and they both gathered to one another wailing badly. In seeing this, my mum brought us back again sobbing and said, *"There is nothing in my hands to do for the wellbeing of your children, if there were other choices to make, I would have done it to avoid taking them to the north"*.

On hearing such convincing words of my Mom, that my grandpa vehemently restarted his ritual blessing again with tears still on his cheeks—saying, "go my younger brother's wife, you have been so faithful to me and to the entire clan of Paliuel, (our clan) may the gods of our ancestors protect you on your way with the children". He poured water to the north, east, west and south directions saying his words. And finally as we were leaving again, his uncontrollable sobbing and groaning could still be heard clearly such that we both broke in wailing, my elder sister threw herself flat alongside the grassy road questioning that we supposed not to leave to the northern side at all! In seeing the sun was rising while we were still bound with chains of love. His elderly son Deng Diing persuasively drove my Mom on her way telling her that the sun is getting hot and it will affect the children on their way. My mum started walking off promising my grandpa saying, *"believe me, I will bring your sons back again safely....and if I don't, then you will have something to bother about....I love you my father! I love you! It's only the situation that forced me to do this,"......then she ended up sobbing without finishing her last sentence.*

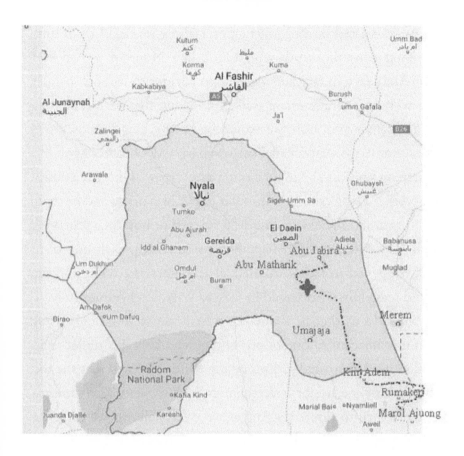

1.4 The Tragedy of Kidnapping

a-Our journey started from Marol-Ajuong

b-Then we headed to Rumaker

c-We left Rumaker at our left toward Kiir Adem

d- We reached under big tree after two days where we were divided

e- We went towards Abu Jabir el Madina

As we started on our journey, everything seemed like dreams, thinking what the north would look like. None of us had ever seen Arabs face to face and we were so curious to see such people. We were so energtic as we walked knowing that we were going to a different area, how we would be having new friends, wow! We screamed as we walked. I surpassed my elder brother Mou in a scurrying walk and he in turn came and surpassed me. My youngest brother Deng could ask his sister to put him down and he started to run, and my eldest sister leap frogged us both in a scurrying walk. My Mom was just happily recommending each one of us that happened to have surpassed all at a scurrying walk. And she could tease him who would be lazy to walk faster humorously.

She told us that in Rumaker, where we were going to stay, that it is adjacent to one of our uncles who kept our millet sacks which were entrusted to him by my Mum. She said that she did that in case we might have them as food security any time we could return to Rumaker.And as we were walking, we took the journey easily; we were still playing the games of 'who walk faster'. And our mother was still teasing those who could not walk faster than the others, promising the one who could walk fastest for a plateful food when we reach our location. So each one of us was struggling to be the number one, so that he could merit a 'plateful of food'.

But after a long walk until noon, I got tired and begun to cry questioning my mum, when we will reach Rumaker such that we could stop and rest, drink water and eat food…?! While on the other side, mum begun to stumble arbitrary and clumsily as we walked before we couldn't see anything bad or good, though she knew that such an abnormal stumbling was an augur of bad fate, yet she managed to hide her alarm behind the veil of courage. After a short while, we began to realize that our mother was hyperventilating and perspiring. We realized that such abnormal eeriness was depicting beyond doubt that it was nothing else but would be death spreading her ugly wings over us! To make it worse, my elder sister said, 'Mom, I smelt something like modern aroma'. But my mum told her to keep quiet, telling her that there was nothing she smelt at all. And she began to pull us to herself more closely each time. I saw a spasm of change on her face with wrinkles from sincere worrying. She eerily began to breathe as if she was wrestling with a lion. And after a short while, we saw strange people armed in uniform and some in casual clothes speeding toward us with their hands on triggers, shouting at us saying, "stop right there! Stop right there!". My mother started to lament saying, 'haa Nhalic, ye kiya, na acoga yiin eya kagam—meaning "O God! is it like that? Would you also really accept such happening".

But without much wasted time we were unfortunately waylaid by Arabs as captives. One man called Ahamed rose his sword intending to kill my mother because he said perhaps she might later on escaped away with the children. But two men, Mahammoud and Khamis held up his hands from killing my mother and rebuked him to stop it. Mahammoud said to him, 'these children she has will slow her down and she will make it nowhere, so we don't need to kill her'.

We were too young to resist. We were three boys and one girl. Then they took us to a bushy jungle where they were hiding. In seeing us suffering from thirst, they offered me green water from their small jar-can, but my mum groaned secretly for warning, "no, this water is poisoning Malong my son, don't drink it". They realized this and tried to explain to her that the color of water was changed by millet which was poured into the jar-can, but my mom ignored any explanation as to what had changed the color of the water into either green or yellowish color. They used to absorb the wheat and eat it after it had been softened in water, in order to sustain them in their days of travelling. We heard flies' noises emanating from far off before we could arrive.

On our arrival to the jungle, we found all the slave men's hands tied tightly backwards. The male slaves were sighing badly with swollen legs and hands those which were tied for a long time. Women were helplessly crying bound in ropes repeating the names of their children and husbands saying, 'will we really meet again?'. Some of the men caught with their women going to Rumaker market and their children left back at home, were questioning their Creator directly with stress, 'why our Creator did you allow such a catastrophe to befall us? What would be the future of our children now?'. Young ladies who were sent with some raw materials for sale in the market, but unfortunately they were caught on their way, were crying ceaselessly and uncontrollably.

Our Mum was told by one of them, 'take your children far away from those tied men'. We sank in real fear when we saw such a horrible disaster. After we arrived, they scrupulously questioned Mom as to which area she was from and why she looked different even her children were clean and good-looking. They asked my mum whether if she was one of the insurgent's wife, or whether she was from Aweil Town resident. But mum by her subtle technique answered saying, "I have never seen those insurgents of either John Garang and Anya Nya or even how they look like, I was born in Aweil town and that was where I used to live with my family. And ignorantly they simultaneously affirmed it even by saying, "you looked so beautiful and brown, are you from Jur (Lou tribe)?" But Mom declined and said nay, I am from a real Dinka lady.

Though their questions seemed to had been answered, yet they remained suspicious murmuring amongst themselves that this is a aristocratic family without any doubt, they exclaimed this, but Mom gave them no loophole to prove it. In the evening I saw them all lining up uniformly, with one man two meters ahead of them all. And as the first one man bent down, and bowing his head even to the ground, as he did anything, they all did the same. To my surprise, I questioned my mum saying, 'what are they doing like that Mom?' but Mom responded and said, 'they are praying to their god Allah'. And as they were still praying, my Mum cooked a little food quickly.

When they finished praying, my Mum asked them cunningly, 'Mohammad, here is food for you and your men, but please I beg you untie the hands of these bound men, you may tie their hands to the front so that they could manage to eat food too'.

My Mom continued, 'because food is for all as Allah said' mum convinced them because she was trying to help untie those tied men. They first looked at one another, because they sensed the mood of royalty in my mum's bold approach manner, but as it was toned with polite wisdom, it gave no ground to prove their doubts. She was accepted.

Each one of them nodded his head affirming to his doubts that this is a real woman of a general Dinka man, because they realized how the lady was neither afraid even from guns nor alarmed in the way of their appearance. And in the mid night, those men in ropes were badly suffering from being bound for four days! They began groaning saying, "God! God! Why should we not die as soon as possible and rest from all these, we could count ourselseves favored by you. Why are we allowed to suffer all this? For we are done away with". I heard their desperate words and I became fully disturbed and grieved in my heart badly. Amongst these men were Deng Yak who was from Malek-Alel resident, from Panoon clan and Atak-dit, from Peth-Atak resident, from Parek clan.

And it happened that in the morning early we started off—but our companions Atak Malual-dit refused to come with us. He said, "I had never been to the north; but if I happened to be waylaid like this today, I prefer death a hundred times over, than to yield to go to North". An elderly man called Mohammad, knew the dialect, heard the man saying this, so he commanded his men saying in Arabic, "whua aba achan yejei ma'ana, aktulu heni" meaning he refused to come with us, kill him right here.

26

Before he could die; he was telling us with humor that it was him who used to go against the other tribes with whom they used to fight, (fratricidal wars) and he could kill one of them. As fast as a Cheetah, he could overrun them to the place where his people would be lurking in wait. And as I saw his head tilted up, and his eyes becoming wildly red as if it was by reason of strong wine, quoted his war quotations which goes:

"The bull I brought up myself, you Malual-thon (redish bull)!, Like blood are your eyes in those thick eyelids,handsome is your long tail that you uses to wipe yourself with;your hump smoothly bends aside";

Your horns are sharp and sorely pointing, because I sharped them by my own fingers; You suffered me on sharpening your horns every now and then. Due to your aggressive horns those love to stay stained in the blood of your enemies always;

Both the youth and aged men of Peth-atak know very well my sharping talent, yea. From your infancy my bull, I skillfully endowed you with the culture of war;

No bull tampers with the mare that you desired to follow yes. They quickly shy away from you by the reason of your alarming hissings. Both males and females exceedingly dread to look at you in the eyes, because of your wild conduct;

Your heart is fierce and fears nothing, that is why I believe you're not just a mere bull, but you're a great Oxen that belongs to no man else besides me, I, Atak Malual-dit (Atak-The-Great-Redish) alone".

Atak Malul-dit was stating frankly that the only heroes born to Dinka clans those who could be considered with this word 'courage' in the entire Jeing tribes, should only be him and his best friend Majok Deng. He believed that what he can do, only Majok could do the ninety-nine per cent of it, not even all of it. He was telling us that it was he and his best friend Majok, were the sole Dinka men born with hearts immune to any fears. They are the only men who can make it, yes, even to the maximum bravery, but not anyone else beside them. I then saw him as he gently looked but in a fierce way, looking all over the trees with stern and searching eyes as if he was extracting a new thing in how the trees were patterned. The man was bidding goodbye to the earthly life. Gradually, gradually, he began to pull back his eyes from trees as he groaned in an exagerated hissing again and again in a manhoodly bass-tone. Then he finally declared that he woud never be dragged along to the North Sudan by these little dogs of un-tattooed men. "I have never changed my word ever since I was a lad, and it won't be in my ripe age that I could do such a trivializing thing. As my soul still lives, so shall my word be" he said.

But my mum earnestly cajoled him not to take such a deadly decision; but after he lifted up his eyes, he first looked at the trees again, then unwaveringly in his reply said, "for everyone, there must be a destination to stop therein, and once its time has fully arrived, dodge it not". He continued, "but for you my lady, take care of our children, for it is a big responsibility". Both the words of my mum and others who were dissuading him, were simply cut short by his heroic words. He removed his dark-green long jalabiya and threw it to Deng Yak, and told him to use it instead of being torn by those dogs, with their sticks. As they were beating him, he was still handsomely reciting his quotation with a loud and clear tune as proof to his heroic manhood. He ignored their strength by even asking, "is that all you can do, you sons of strangers?" Our hearts melted with mixture of agitation and cowardice, being stunned at such upheaval and havoc. We couldn't do anything, had we appeared even gloomy, that alone would had concluded our lives.

We remained inwardly agitated for watching our great hero dying while we could offer no help. In him I saw the real strength of integrity, liberty and the power of dignity, mulishly refusing to yield to any sort of humiliation. Nevertheless, he welcomed death rather than living under somebody else's command. When I saw how mercilessly, they were killing him, as I was hiding behind my mother's legs, I could not withstand to bear this disrespectful humiliation. Nevertheless, wild statements gushed out of my broken heart. It was too strong to resist, remembering it now. It goes like this: *"Beat him, beat him until he dies—molest him as you would like. Kill him in a taunting and aggressive manner as you deemed in your eyes. But remember, as you have not shown honor to my aged man—so I will do this to your man too when I grow up!"* In addition, from that day, I hated Arabs for their barbaric deeds.

Like wolves devouring their prey, they crowded on him with sticks and beat him to death. All the slaves were heavily laden but stripped of clothes and tied by a long rope which connected one person to another in a tightened string which caused swelling of the hands of everyonebut that was something never to be complained about. They ladened my mom but they did not tie her

29

hands, because they believed that she couldn't make it away, for her little children are enough string to for her two legs.

We started off by turning east-north leaving Rumaker six Kilometres behind. And after almost six hours walk, we started turning again west-north toward Kiir-Adeem. Because they told us that the rebels had ambushed them at those sides near to Rumaker Market fearing that they might be attacked by rebels which they might not manage to safely defend themselves against and the slaves.

They told us that we are safe in their faithful guidance, and that there was no need to panic. I can still remember when we were taken by them, I saw three men sitting under a bushy shadow with their backs against the tree as if in deep sleep. I asked my mother childishly 'why are those men sleeping there Mum?' My mother rebuked me in our language to be silent! Don't you see that the Arabs have killed them, she said. Then immediately they commanded all the slaves to loyally keep going to where they were taking us without tarrying. Though we were in a very catastrophic situation, I still hear my mother reasoning our situation with her daughter (our elder sister) on capacity and how we could escape later on. "Mou is mute, I don't know whether he could really manage to escape from them?" such were my mum's stressful questions. With an upset faced she gazed at me. I was the focus of her greatest concern, for she believed me as the only boy among her sons whom the Arabs would quickly slaughter due to my unruly habits. She mutedly spoke about her daughter, because she knew that her situation was worst, for poor Dinka girls were used (heinously raped) by these cattle Arabs when they became mature. These cattle men don't marry them but after they use them, they're eventually given Dinka slave males as wives. Mum never dared talk about her youngest son, because she feared that they could take him away from her too.

I did not know really the life of these cattle men, though the slaves' number could double them three times, yet we all were very, very afraid of these cattle men. Not everyone of them had a gun, yet our souls were incredibly alarmed and captivated by their brown color, Arabic dialect, white jalabias and towels on their heads, primitive weapons like daggers, spears, especailly their being on horses with few guns ingrained formidable fear over our impoverished and ailing lives.

Walking with torn clothes, half naked in torn underwear that left both males and females' buttocks outside. The clothes we wore were ingrained with dirt, we suffered cruel mistreatment and heavy loads. The road was very long and walking was hard, yet none would bring trouble on himself or herself by requesting for water and food, leave alone rest. We looked very skinny and destitute in a terrible situation. I did not know that these cattle Arabs were human beings like us. I saw them as very different, and to make things worse, everyone of our people, considered them more powerful and above everybody or thing else.

As we were walking with them and the sun begun to scorch us severely; I began crying from the very hot sun—and also we were hungry because we had no food and no water for the whole day and a half walk. And as I was walking with eyes in tears, I could

31

not see the grassy road; I stepped on the hand of one of the dead people alongside the road. My mother screamed loudly "No! No! Don't you see that dead person my child" because there were couples who tried to escape from the camp of Reziegat Arabs, but they were caught on their way and shot to death!

When we were suffering in that hard journey, I saw my mum look straight at me then to my two brothers and sister with a broken heart. I saw her with tears rolling down on her two cheeks saying, *"Hiey Nhailic (Oh God!)! I hospitably served the strangers, I have not disrespectfully fought over well water with elderly women. I dearly uphold both the young and the aged in total regard. I have kept myself from abomination, never did I ever know man untill the day of my marriage. Then, why Madhol (God), why did you allow this tragedy to happen? What have I done since in the virginity of my childhood that deserved me all these? Why Aciek (Creator) did you allowed such tiny children to go through this worst catastrophe? What has brought my bad luck—or what guilt have You found in me? Yin Raan koch caath puoth (Oh the great Judge of all humans who search the hearts). What should I do now our Lord? Ha, remember God, that these kids are not mine alone, rather they belong to you God, and to that clan of Paliuel and to everyone else under heaven. Do not therefore wipe off my descendents from the face of the earth in a day!!"*

Also my elder sister with tears in her eyes said, 'are we not going to die Mom, yea…we aren't going to die? Where are they taking us now?" But Mom told her, "do not panic my daughter, we will be alright—just carry your younger brother well". My mom was carrying very heavy materials on her head those things which she was made to carry by the kidnappers. And my elder sister was carrying my younger brother which she could hardly manage to, because the boy was very heavy and no one would help her. And my other brother was made to carry many empty jar-cans. And my younger brother was also crying because he was thirsty and hungry too. I was very small and there were fire-drain grasses on the way which begun to cut my legs as I was walking bare-footed. Some amongst us who complained saying "we are tired, we need to rest", were just slaughtered as simply as that. And when we arrived to Kiir-Adeem, watery low land—but we unfortunately found its water all dried except mud that was mixed with the animals' urines left. Yet we started drinking from it like that. My Mum instantly rebuked us that we should never drink too much because the water was very dirty. And again we started off our journey.

Carrying slaves to different worlds was not an easy job, in his book titled "From Slavery to Freedom," John Hope Franklin has also described that the African slaves who were carried to the western world, suffered severely on American voyages. These small voyages were too narrow to carry even more than one hundred, yet they were forced to carry more than 350 slaves in such small voyages. And as result, some died of severe diseases, and hunger. Others who endured all the fatigues of rough chains for those who remained bound in chains, both hands and feet for quite long time, could only reach the American beaches crippled, thus unable to do anything. Some who saw such suffering but did not want it, quickly decided to commit suicide by jumping into the sea.

Everyone suffered in slavery, even the slave-traders. They faced diseases, strikes and hunger. They also saw harsh retaliations from those who did not wish to go to western world, so both the slaves and slaveholders eventually fought one another to death. After a short while, my elderly sister's stomach began to pain and her skin was itching! She began complaining from those sever pains, but my Mum quieted her. Again after another short while, my Mum began complaining from same stomach pains and itching of skin. But this time one of the kidnappers said, 'it was the urine of the animals which you just drank, because camels drink there too therefore it is the camels' urine which caused your body-itching and stomach-painng'. And finally he concluded saying, "and beside, you are not allowed to complain too much".

This group of kidnappers consisted of two great tribes, Messiaryia and Reziegat, though there were often clashes between these two tribes, yet for fear from cohorts of SPLA those of Tuek-Tuek and Nil battalions of Murmur who had flooded Aweil lands in 1986, they pledged for a joint move. The Messiaryia tribe was an aggressive one unlike Reziegat. Messiaryia's notorious men were harshly mistreating the old men, women and children captives along the walk. And after two days walk at noon, we arrived at bushy trees.

We were commanded to sit under a tamarind-tree. Then their elders made their way to a nearby tree. They began eating their food; their food was from the meats of the birds they just shot as we were coming. But we didn't have food to eat for those three days. Therefore, after they ate their meat, then they called Deng to come to bring us their remnants. Their remnants were cleared bones. So we all pretended to be looked eating 'good food provided' to us by 'good people'. They went on making their respective meeting in which they were plotting what to be done with us later. And after they ended their talk, they walked to where we were sitting and stood before us with fierce glaring. And four of them fired guns into the tree where we were sitting .They kept bombarding for almost seven minutes until our hearts melted with true fear in that day! And then the elderly one walked forth and addressed the captives with real toughness, "here is where you all may die or live. If you attempt now or later to escape, you will surely die! For we will hunt you down on the way and you will be made like those ones. He then pointed his fingers in the bushy road where six dead bodies laid alongside the bushy road which others had been shot dead the day before our arrival. And he then finalized his words saying, 'you all are going to be divided, but I don't wish to hear any debate on that.

There was a man called Deng Yak in our midst. He was kidnapped twice by other different mercenaries, in those times he managed to escape. Deng having known a little Arabic orally, got up abruptly and requested to interpret the whole speech clearly to us in our native language. They permitted him to do so, because they knew that it would change nothing in their intention.

After he finished explaining it, he then added saying, "my people! My own people! We are already exposed to them by God! And now we are in the mouth of death, therefore, let's be loyal to them no matter what they will do with us. Let us save these children amongst us, perhaps if we stay calm, it might go well with us and survive from this tragedy, we may live and later on some of us might report back what had happened to the rest, if we all die, these little kids, he pointed at me, that they may live and be our survivors. I promised Deng in my heart on that day that I will reportedly tell all these catastrophes if I could be even the only one left alive! But the elderly one with snapping called, 'Deng! Deng! What is that all?! No! No! No sir, I am just explaining to them that you are good people. I told them that you are not like those Anya Nya rebels. I said that you are taking them to a place where there is enough food, water and everything. Deng convinced them.

In response, the elderly one said, 'in exchange for that loyal service, you may live but not die. Death was the only guide for our journey as, "if you don't behave nicely, death will lick your soul, or be loyal in everything as exchange for your life!" The Reziegat were to take their portion of slaves harvest leaving the Messiaryia with theirs; but before they could do that another Mercenary of real tough kidnappers arrived suddenly before we were not yet divided. These were the Arabs who castrate males and disable their legs. They greeted one another. Then they asked our kidnappers to sell to them some of the salves harvest. And sure, some from our companions were sold to them. Then they instantly began flogging them mercilessly; cutting off the ears of some and gouging out the eyes of some.

My Mum in seeing this, got disturbed and exceedingly troubled. She turned her eyes towards us looking in a wide motion, and she warned us in our native language saying, 'my children! My own children please listen to me, don't attempt to escape all of you from either of their camps. No matter how badly they will mistreat each one of you, if I am not dead, please don't do that. In this area, I wanted to stop for a moment and bless my mother: *"Mum, God bless you! God bless you my Mum ! I acknowledge your concerned heart. You proved to me individually and to all the sons in the entire world you have given the examples of motherly love! You gave a clear challenge to the mothers of the whole world. Your fearless and motherly love had become my testimony today. Your brave and bold approaches are worthy of immense appreciations. "*

With that the Misseriya tirbe departed with their slave harvest. We were taken by Messiaryia. My brother Mou, whom they named Sa'alehi, was given to Mohammad Dade, my younger brother Deng, whom they named Mohammadon, was taken by Mohammed Khamis, our sister Nyigut, was named Rakia and she was taken by Ahamad Pa'aruk. I was called Ahamad and was given to Sa'alehi. Our Messieriyia lords collectively took us first to their Medium who had been their spiritual fortune-giver whom they believed to have enabled them, for the successful acquiring of slaves. They passed by their Medium before they dispersed. So to sharpen my point, we arrived at noon at the first camp made of tents where their strong sorcerer lived. The villagers of that small area rushed out with an outpouring of ululations and shouts of joyful hearts. They called to Allah, as they were welcoming their heroes who were coming back from the south with such a bulk harvest of slaves. They sang a heroic song of triumph, they went running around us singing: "Where is Garang Maboir? You the slaves who know the heroes of Arab's strength. Ye too will be brought to this cattle camp of Arabs one day, you will take care of our calves". We were convinced that they would truly bring John Garang to their cattle camp in chains, making him look after their calves. Fears were engraved into our hearts.

As they were gradually slowing down, I saw our custodians ritually bowing their heads down as they were queuing up. And as soon as they remained with their heads bowed down, I saw the great Medium emerged out of the procession with water in the plate. She started to sprinkle her triumphalists with water using green leaves of a tree after she dipped it in the water. Our custodians were just silent with their heads bent down like idols in homage for her as she was passing by saying her words. We were abysmally seized with fear seeing such a unique woman.

The Medium was a tall woman; she walked energetically in a divine and noisy manner. She wore reddish max that allows her shoulders to be obviously seen. She was a woman of one breast with beard at one side and the moustache like that of a man. Her eyes were blue-brown. She had a stern and sear looking eyes habit. Her voice was toned with mixtures of both masculine and feminine simultaneously. Though she was a little bit old, yet years had spared her skin. And as she was still sprinkling all of us with water, she addressed both we and those who called themselves 'custodians' with authority saying, *the black Dinka of the south are your Allah-given slaves, the Allah will be keeping your hands strengthened against them whenever you would be launching raiding every time you wish to. She continued, "They have no choice, because if they attempt to resist you, they will still die of hunger eventually, those insurgents of John Garang and so-called Anya Nya II will do them no benefit, especially to these little kids like this, (pointing at me directly) as she pointed at us with her stretched fingers. She continued, "Go ahead, and bring more of them, because by doing so, you are sparing them from both hunger and forceful robberies they are undergoing from their own militias".*

As a child I absolutely got alarmed. I started questioning myself how did she came to know our ugliest hunger and the merciless robberies from the two insurgents groups of Anya Nya II and SPLA, including other militias who had no food supplies. The people who used to come often to every house of our villages including our home demanding food, meat, soups and Dura, as they used to call these things "rations" in Garang Maboir's terminology. All the SPLA cohorts of Tuek-Tuek, meaning wood cutter bird, Muormuor meaning brown ants and other wings of Anya Nya and militias who used to come wildly, knowing neither day nor night demanding food ceaselessly. All Dinka inhabitants were severely disturbed from such turmoil. So, recalling those perils, I asked myself how did this woman knew everything in detail about us, even the misfortunes from those pursuing us closely from behind! I came to understand the sorrowful song our Aunt Akon Bol which goes: *Nhialic Aciek Madhol (God the Creator) how did Akon Bol end in shame. How did a woman whose breaths once breastfed a child, now became a dried bone? What wrong have we done Madhol, you gave us a very wide land that does not have an end, but what would a fugitive woman have to say now—since we are not finding rest in this land. Nevertheless, the Arabs of Khartoum are coming here with their gun, Baggara (Cattle keepers Arabs) and the rebel militia coming here with his gun and the hunger also, is coming therewith its gun. What shall we do? Our big land had been narrowed into a small fence, my heart! My heart! Why do you cry all day and night? Who will consider your vexed soul? You have none to comfort you, but you refused to be quieted, because your kids are no more!*

All her two children were forcefully mobilized by John Garang De Mabior's soldiers to Ethiopia to be recruited as SPLA soldiers, for an unknown time of return. And as I looked down, bolls of tears rolled down on my cheeks I was completely convinced that our abduction had a hidden reason, as to why we must pay for such a costly and severe price. I concluded that something was wrong somewhere. And after their Meduim finished addressing them, she was charged with five slaves; two men and three women, that is. We stayed only for almost one hour. We were given frayed meat of sheep and aseeda made of millet. After quitting the residence of their Medium, they started dividing us and gave us Arabic names. As they were still hugging themselves, I felt a gently push on my shoulders and a voice said to me, "Let's go" in a smooth and a rather dictating manner. That was Sa'ahli, the man for whom I became his rightful slave boy.

Mom realizing that the man is taking me away, she gawkily stood on her feet trying to call me, but she remembered how we were instructed and restrained herself, she observed me sternly with balls of tears on her cheek saying, "My creator, follow the lad, protect him from their rigid molestation and restore him back to me again". She called, "Malong my son" and as she wished in an attempt to warn or give me some comforting words, but her lips refused to. She put her hands upon her mouth sobbing quietly as she watched her dear son taken away.

As we were walking for about six hours, I remained behind my custodian, weary from such a hard, long walk. As he was snapping at me to hurry up, I saw him walking lamely, awkwardly in front of me. I blinked my eyes at him wondering. I said to myself, "is he really a lame man or is it my eyes troubling me?" I looked at him more closely such I could come up with a true analysis and truly I sensed beyond doubt that he was really lame. He was not pretending. I argued agitatedly in my heart saying, "how could such a weak man kidnap me! I began to ask myself, "My people are humiliated by such as weak a person as this? I continued, why are we easily threatened by their coming to our villages"? And my heart vehemently begun to tell me that "why should I not kill him when we would be asleep, and finish it all"? But my mind whispered within me telling me no, for I won't find my way back, and maybe other Muraheliin might encounter me on the way and they would surely either kill me or kidnap me again.

There are four major tribes in these areas namely Messiaryia, Reziegat, Ma'alia and Humor, each one of these tribes has her habitual conduct i.e. Messiaryia go hunting for the Dinka of the South to kill or make them slaves, but Reziegat on the other hands, they kidnap the Dinka girls and boys and transform them into their tribal men and women, while Ma'alia dislike coming to the South but buy from the Messiaryia and Reziegat those slaves harvest brought from the South, and Ma'alia take those who come for work to their gardens and handsomely cheat on them by hiring these Dinka workers to work for certain amount of money, and slowly, slowly they begin to bring some little salt, sugar, oil and dry fish, but when the time comes for the Dinka workers to receive their wages, they could only be told that "you had already finished borrowing your wages on salt, oil, fish and sugar"

You know what, amongst my brethren I was the first to be taken and then my elder brother, followed by my sister. And after my mother spent one full month with her youngest son in the house of the two brothers whose mother was called Fatimah; the Muraheliin man who was given my youngest brother was restlessly looking for an opportunity of taking him in the absence of my mum. My mum used to argue by herself frankly in their hearing and adamantly declined saying, "this is the only one little boy left for me and if anyone wishes to take him, let him take my life first". But the man who wanted the lad refused and tried to use force against her, something that which did not help, but worsened it more. Mom was young and an energetic wrestler, and violently pushed him away. Then he cunningly pretended to be good and peaceful, but after another three days, he hijacked him while my mum was fetching water at the well.

My Mom stated that her heart begun to beat seriously with fear and doubts as to what would be happening with her lad at home now. And she accepted that some bad fate might have happened, so she took her jar-can and rushed back to that house. Unfortunately she saw her lad on the horse with that man running away with him. My mum was a fast woman, she ran very fast and when she was about to pull him off the horse, the man removed his long dagger and was about to hurt her. Fortunately that old Fatimah also rushed after her screaming saying, "no! No! No Fatimah (was a given name to my mum), because of that only one child, you accepted death and leave all your other children?" "Let him take the lad", she continued, "after all, Allah loves everybody, he can't accept somebody else to take a child that does not belong to him. He will bring back all your children and one day you will believe me". Thus my mum stopped and threw herself down wailing ceaselessly. Fatimah came and took her to the house comforting her not to lose heart saying, "If you give up or in now, they will take them away for good; but if you remain calm down in patience, Allah will provide you with a way out".

As I said earlier that I was taken first before everyone, when they were departing and dividing the slave harvest. The man who brought me from the south was young, but married to two wives. After one and a half day's walk we arrived at his house which we reached when I was completely tired. In arriving at the house of his young woman, I threw myself flat on the ground tired and hungry too. His wife welcomed us with an exhilirating ululation and gave us water to drink. As she remained waiting for her husband to finish drinking the water in the cup, I saw her as she could look so often at me and back to her husband. I was worried about what she thought of me. The interesting part is that it was my first time to see Arabic woman! I was glancing at her long hair as I was sipping her sweet aroma which was so sexually seductive. That exhilarating fragrance of hers made my heart relax in a rigid silence. I looked at her with searching eyes observing her beautiful lips, eyes, laps, long hair and seductive buttocks as she showed them at her husband. After her husband finished drinking the water, she questioned him about his journey to the south and who could this little lad be.

Her husband spoke up with arrogance and in response said, "It is my lad, I got him from the south after a fierce struggle with Anya Nya of Garang". And she quickly rushed to where I was lying down and helped my head up. She began to look at my body sternly as if she was measuring my entire skelton. Her husband was a bit disturbed by such a thorough look. But he convinced himself saying, 'since he was a boy, he is harmless even to a chicken'. And at eight o'clock in the night, her husband went to the nearby neighbour where he spent more than three hours conversing with that family. His wife warmed me water for a shower. And as she called me for bathing, I saw her white teeth in the moon light with those bright eyes as she was waiting for me in her sexy clothing, With soap in her right hand, she was like a demon. I dawdled to where she was awaiting me, groaning from tiredness of a long walk. She told me that she was there to help wash my back with soap. As I started to take off my torn and dirty clothes for bathing, she abruptly began to pour water and rub my back with soap, and teasingly said, "Don't let your little penis disturb you, for you are too young for this", then she gaily laughed waiting to hear from me a reply.

The poor Dinka boy could hear Arabic with difficulty yet let alone how to reply in it. I was fully convinced that a woman from hell was rubbing me at the back. Moreover, after she finished washing me, she prepared for me food to eat, then let me rest on the wooden bed. She slept right behind me and begun to breath in a lustful tone asking me to turn to her. She kept murmuring saying, "you will be my boy, for me alone, you are young but a good-looking boy". She remained glued to me till when she heard the tapping sound of her husband's feet coming from the nearby neighborhood. Her husband prompted her to bring my bed closer to where she had prepared for him a bed. She scurried and did it quickly. Then I slept on my bed and remained with my body wrapped in an old blanket.

After almost two hours, they thought that I was sleeping. In addition, I heard the sounds of the heavy wooden bed pressed down and up each time; it was my master with his charming woman. Moreover, bit by bit I begun to hear a smooth and sharp sighing of the man in a high climax and the woman stuttering in a gibberish that a living soul could rehearse. She was in coital climax with her husband. The pillars of my heart were heated up with uncontrollable forceful beats—my throat ran dry, sometimes I could swallow almost nothing. My eyes, without my notice, rebelled against me and started to open wider and wider each time and doggedly refused to be closed up. My eyes remained blinking under my old blanket, though I pressed them together. My mind got obsessed with its own verbose inquiries as, "which humankind are the most beautiful ones?" Moreover, I hinted answers on my own as, "maybe... maybe... maybe the Arabs or no...no...maybe the kawajaat (whites) or, no...no... maybe our Jeing (Dinka)". Alternatively, maybe...maybe this is the place where such beautiful beings are born, yes. I got stuck there. My confused mind refused to admit that this charming young woman had already assailed it when she was breathing from behind me moments earlier. In the whole night, I remained awake with my eyes blinking. I tried to sleep but I could not sleep throughout the whole night.

Until the next day, my heart kept visualizing that act and I comforted myself saying, 'that something would happen that could grant an opportunity to...to... to...had I not been boxed in by my physical youth, the story would have been then in the opposite. Moreover, in the morning we took off to his extended family. We left the young and seductive wife's sad questioning that why should not the lad stay with her, but her husband declined. We came to the house of his first wife where I was also welcomed happily. That woman spared now her dear lad, sending him and began to send me to any place her heart desired. They discussed amongst themselves that this lad must be Muslim such that he could qualify to eat normally with his child. It is an Islamic ritual, so that I might not defile their child "with my paganism" they said. They coerced me to be a Muslim.

When it was the first time for the mother of the house to adopt me as her new slave boy (the writer), she was not properly prepared in how to handle me, and sometimes she awkwardly used to handle me fairly. It was not really the way the slave boy was supposed to be treated as they saw to it in their well-known way. And so, sometime she could make mistakes by ignorantly preparing a food, then she happily called for her dear son Dawood and for me too to come for food. But when she could see both of us puting our hands in the plate to eat food, she could get disturbed and roughly order me to go and wait outside until she would call me. And slowly and slowly she begun to dislike me more. Even if she could see me playing with her son Dawood, sometimes would disturb her giving her unrest in herself. Because she strongly believed that for a slave boy to play with her son is a great worry to her.

In the first time when we arrived, it was the month of May in which the cultivating season was just the next month, June. And so we started to go early to the family garden, the father of the house could use a hoe for digging and we come after him sowing the millet seeds. And when we went to the garden the following week, I was given my own hoe which I did not managed to use properly because it was heavy, and it cut my toes several times causing swelling of my feet. But despite that they saw my feet swollen by the hoe's cut, yet they could still order me to come to the garden so that I could still sow seeds calling it as the 'slightest work'. The mother of the house wished me to go from her house, though I was made into a Mulism boy. Yet she was not satisfied with that. She could still see just the Dinka boy, yes, the slave one. She was very happy when her husband decided to see me off, yes, to disappear from her sight. Her son was sent away in

47

order to not know what had happened to the slave boy Malong whom they nicknamed Ahamed.

1.5 I Was Sold to a Tyrant Man For 500 Pounds

And as soon as we arrived to his extended family's house, the first thing done to me was separation, I was isolated. I was ordered immediately to sit under a certain platform, that was how slaves were treated. The slaves were not supposed to be treated as equals with sons and daughters of the family. Because the slaves were believed to be without any dignity, they had not any integrity or regalia on equality. And as a matter of fact, we were not allowed to use any plates or cups of water that they have used. Another deprivation was the law of non-speaking-your-mother-tongues here. We were not allowed to recline at the same fireplace with either of their groups.

They used to sit in three groups: women, men and youth groups. We were restricted to speak in our dialect, and any mistake of speaking in our own dialect was considered to be a big offense, followed with terrible punishments. The normal punishments known were: humiliating insults, lashings plus prolonged work. Those rules were the difficulties set to cement down our feet in fears. We could never ever attempt speaking in our own dialect, which did not work for any goodness. And to make it worst, it became too difficult for both of us (we the salves and those who held us hostage) to interact.

I saw them as my real enemies, and sometimes I wished to

escape, but I still could remember the instruction of my Mum that none of us kids should attempt to escape. Because mum stated that we could lose track of getting each other again—and that the consequences of escaping would be more costly too. Moreover, in the same family, there were other slaves, two men and four women whom they had brought from the South a couple of years back. These slaves were already ironed into the submissiveness they wished—but struggle came with this young lad who seemed to be from "a different world they didn't understand". A world most of their times called "jana bita kabiir metamadiriin" meaning a son of great rebel commander. Because they didn't see any immediate fear or change in my behaviors at all—which made their proof concrete on naming me so—which was undeniably true.

But they didn't stopped bothering me, sometimes; I could give into their rules in order to avoid hearing insulting languages only—which they could ignorantly consider as obedience and vehemently they felt happy. I could get shocked and disillusioned sometimes, when I could see how horribly they treated other slaves, it was too bad. And after not very long time, the thoughts of speaking my own dialect begun to scourge my mind—but the set instruction on not to speak other languages with severe punishment following also were strong enough to shut my two lips up. And, one day, as I was to light the firewood that belonged to men side suddenly I found myself happily and freely singing our favorite song "in dinka dialect".

So, one day I forgot the instruction of "do not speak in your dialect rule" with those severe punishments following such offense. Nevertheless, the love for our Dinka songs and dances begun to lighten my heart with joy to sing—and suddenly I was so exuberant, and vehemently thought that people around me were enjoying my dinka language and its good song. But the opposite was true, I saw those slave women rise to their feet, and slave men were almost to cover my mouth with their hands if they were not at distant from where I was sitting. Poor young boy, I did not realize that I was committing an offense, the offense of singing in my own dialect.

I hated such a fear, I disliked it. Then suddenly a booming voice mingled with cascade of haranguing, cut me short. And fear of punishment—alarming consequences that I will be facing sooner moved my heart terribly! The house husband rebuked me saying, "minu ghalek tita kalam, wala tagunna, ba rothan dengka hini?" meaning who told (allowed) you to speak or sing in your Dinka dialect here? And fortunately, I was not punished but seriously warned not to repeat that again.

Whenever they wished to send me they resorted to using gestures, signals or visualizations as if they were talking to a deaf person. To make the matter worse, they were impatient with me alot, to learn their tongue. They expected me to learn their dialect quickly, though I set my face in close attention to observe their signs and visualizations, yet I couldn't make it to their urgent demand of "this slave boy must know the language quickly". Therefore, beatings, insults and slapping me became so rampant, but that did not conquer my unruly heart with its unyielding spirit. All their threatening language could not bend my head, and to their surprise, I could sometimes refuse some of the works which I termed "feminine work". No matter what everybody else said, I doggedly refused to repeal my words. We got shocked every now and then, for we were born with impunity to be slaves to no one.

For if any of their children attempted to raise their voice over us—it was reciprocated with very fierce tune and red eyes from us. This shocked their parents over and over again, because they expected loyalty and submission, nothing more than that. They always tried every now and then to remind us where we really belonged and who we were, but to no avail, because the types of persons they wanted us to be was an impossible expectation. We normally sat freely anywhere with anyone, which was considered a great offense and was a punishable act. We did it. Slowly and slowly, they got used to us. They finally gave in, and eventually rendered us open ground to chat, eat and slept in same places without any frowned faces. But to the rest of the slaves, that act was considered as great privilege. They considered it to be a rare miracle. And the topic about the newly brought slave boy whom they named Ahamad, skyrocketed and it became of a greater interest.

Everybody could come from far villages only to see such a mulish boy. The goats I was ordered to take care of became victims of my retaliation on humiliations done to me. I completely hated these people for treating me like this as if I was not a human being. The act of depriving me of my loved ones (Mum, sister and brothers) including my own language, those were the things ringing in my mind. There was no chances for good relationships between us, no matter how much they tried.

1.6 I Was Sold Again For 400 Pounds to the Worst Man

After we arrived back at the camp, I spent one week and again another man came who looked more polite and cheerful than everyone else in the entire world. He requested my guardian if he could buy me from him. That was not easy because my Arabic father told him that I was bought by him recently from a man who mistreated me. But that man deceptively said, 'no! No! You should not worry about me or how I will treat him since he is a 'khulam' meaning lad, and eventually he persuaded him and possessed me as his bought slave. And my custodian told me that I should not be worried because this man will not be like the other bad man who took me first. Finally I was sold to him and he took me with him to his camp. When I arrived, his lanky old mother greeted me with humor saying, "*is this is the young lad you bought with 400 pounds?*" she continued, "*will he really manage to shepherd my cattle?...I wonder if he really could*" she said that and abruptly went back to her tent. In the first two days I was given a worm aseeda to eat which was cooked from millet. And from that day onward I ate only the remnant food of yesterdays' which were rotten.

After that I was made to shepherd a great herd of sheep also. Looking after sheep was extremely bad. For as the habit of sheep, they don't accept to walk a single step when the rain is raining or in stormy winds. And whenever the rains happened to get me in the bush with them, I was obligated to remain there till the rain had ceased—even if it took me up to the late hours of the night in the bush. They used just to gather themselves together in one place. And I must not be tempted to leave them, else the wolves and hyenas come to consume them straight away in the bush. O my God. I always had to wait in the rain until the rains stopped, throughout the rainy seasons.

And after nine months later, I was ordered to look after goats. Looking after the goats was extremely frustrating. These animals called goats were different, unlike sheep, the moment they could see the rain coming, they just run home. But looking after goats was completely humiliating, because they snuck into some people's gardens and I was lashed for those mistakes. All those two years of me looking after the animals of that man, were like as if thousand years had passed by, to my young age.

After four months they made me look after camels. Looking after camels was a very hard task, because I had to use a male camel to ride upon, unfortunately the one I was told to use was a very ferocious one. It could roughly throw me off its back and tried to toss me under its feet on the ground to death. But I did not know how I always escaped this, so it was by God's help that I could manage to still roll away from under its feet and survive. I told my custodian that this male camel is not good, but he simply declined saying, 'because you are not yet used to it, but later it will be alright'. But it happened, that in one of the days we both rode on it for a short trip, and it started as usually, by jumping up and down rapidly and wildly till it threw both of us off terribly! Being disappointed by this, he got up and slapped me severely on my face with cascades of shoutings, 'why didn't you remain stuck on the camel?, why did you not have control of it, why? why?" And he slapped me again.

I really saw humiliation at the hands of this man. Yes, truly looking after camels was not an easy job because the camels use to eat much grass and leaves of trees and beverage, lots of water. So, as young as I was, I had to take them to where there were good pasture and trees' leaves. Then after every week, I must take them to ample water for drinking. And one day, after I finished taking them to the water, as I was bringing them back, the camels refused to go and tended to rest. I lowered my camel down and I went under a thick tree to take rest also. I slept. When I woke up from sleeping I found all the camels missing. My eyes became like a fountain of water with ceaseless tears rolling down on my cheeks. I sensed the severe flogging awaiting me back in the camp. What shall I do now? Gasping worriedly I went searching for the camels until in the late hours of the midnight. My entire body was dripping with perspiration and my old jilabia (short garment) got torn as I was passing through thorny trees.

When I thought of getting back, I realized that I was lost because I knew no way back home. In this thick jungle alone, I was terribly confounded. I started searching my way back to the camp and fortunately after a long search I saw a very tiny glimpse of fire. Quickly I went there straight. But it was a different camp and as soon as a certain man of that camp saw me, he got scared and was about to shoot me. But I quickly screamed, 'I am a person!' so then he welcomed me, and I found that it was a camp of the Arabs who knew the man for whom I worked. Then I was directed to the camp. I came back to the camp when it was already eight o'clock in the morning. Of course, that night was too bad to mention, because it affected my life. Being alone in the night and especially in the jungle was tremendously scaring. That night was full of alarming consternations. I was young and without enough strength to defend myself against any wild animal or ghosts of the nights. The only thing I could remember about that night were the "abnormal shock and worries which covered my hopeless face".

I cursed it up to now…. *"Darkness! Darkness! Darkness! You frighten your victims with quaking of consternation. You pale the real heroes' faces; you cause their hearts to pump too much blood in an abnormal speed"*

"You make someone submit and surrender to your forged lordship; You have a terrorizing habit that arrogantly exaggerates your alure. You make your believers vehemently believed that there is something real in you."

"You disarm all your victims and chain them with irons of dread. Your cunning is from old. You have your own language, The language which you had stolen from the abyss; you took the teeth of death and wielded them against your victims in the dark. You cause your members to goggle their eyes recklessly due to your fierce whippings! You know very well how to coldly deceive the hearts of your poor victims."

"You are a cheater! The scales you use in balancing are mockingly crooked! It bites me! It bites me! Your victims scream always. After my long pondering, acquaintenceship and sighing of my breath, I understood that you are a liar. And all that you wield are fakes!"

The moment I arrived, my master, the owner of lost camels, took his dagger, attempting to slaughter me when I told him that the camels were missing. Fortunately his old father intervened and I survived. In that same morning, I went again looking for those lost camels till evening. I came back to the camp thirsty, hungry and tired. But I saw the camels resting under trees already in the camp. I knew later that someone who was their relative got the animals.

The other day I took the cattle to the forest. I was still upset and terrified. And at around the same afternoon as the camels were grazing and others were resting under trees as normal, I mounted aloft a nearby big heap of ants that was between two trees. My eyes were alertly observing everywhere such that I should not miss another animal and be punished for that drawback again. But suddenly an imaginary phantom flashed before my eyes. I saw as if my mum was coming from far off, she was getting closer to me almost through those thick trees.

This phantom became clearer such that I begin to swallow the saliva with difficulty. Something I didn't know began to call me clearly, "Malong! Malong! Nothing will ever hurt you my son!" I looked everywhere, but I saw nothing. Then my heart burst into an outpouring questions saying, *"where is my mum now? Where are my brothers and sister? Where is my strong father with the rest of our family relatives? Could my armed father be of any help to me in this bush now? I remembered how my father trained me on all the military tactics of turning round, marching, rolling and attention. Will I really see my homeland such I could play with my little boymates and girl friends and make fun? When will this tragedy end?"*

I cannot fully describe the brokenness of my heart at that moment because it was so deep. As I was questioning myself with these questions, a live image of my mum stood clearly and more distinctly in my eyes. My heart broke from the inside and my stomach hopelessly cracked asunder. Fountains of water mounted to the brim of my eyes with a broken heart. I cursed the day I was born. I hated being what I was. I lamented, blamed the Creator for having me allowed to exist on earth. I roughly said, "It would have been better if you hadn't moulded me in the womb of a woman, I could have considered myself favored!" I grew weak and lanky from day to day's resentment. Malaria and yellow fever scorched me every now and then. The taste of food became flavorless and worthless in my eyes—nothing was important to me any longer. My eyes grew dim, reddish and gloomy in their sockets. My white and handsome eyes completely turned red and continuously painful. They used to question me every time I could return from looking after the camels saying, "Heeey, what is wrong with you? you look sullen and gloomy?" I could only fib either happy or that I hit my foot against a bad stump of a tree just as I was coming. That was how I reply to their questions. I could pretend happy, masking that I was not fibbing.

After seven months, I was told to look after cattle. I was given a horse to use due to long distant grazing lands. Getting on the horse was not an easy job to me since I was young .Using the horse caused a lot of wounds between my buttocks because the horse got frightened and suddenly bucked me off which got me crushed down on the ground badly. I got bleeding scars between my buttocks from every day sitting on the horse. I could hardly sit properly or directly on the horse-back. And as I used to sit on a oneside buttock on it, that caused me more falling down from the horse due to that painful injury. Despite those severe challenges I could still take the cows to distant places for good pastures and I got to take them to drink clean water. But when I could come back from those distant water places weak and tired, having two or four cows missing, my custodian could slap me on my face severely. Then he told me to get back and bring those missing cows immediately.

I was still proud for one reason, namely the brown bull which was good to me. It proved itself to be my true friend such that I should not neglect putting it down in the tale of my pastoral life. It happened that whenever I was with the cattle, that brown bull's help became undeniable at the cows' grazing fields. I had faced startling attacks from some fierce cows which did not wish humans passing by them especially when they are with new born calves. People had to stay far away avoiding getting near them for two to three months. And as my habit, I didn't like this frightened manner of running away from anything threatening whatsoever, human or an animal. I was almost run through by their sharp horns several times. I survived through the help of the young brownish bull I brought up myself. For whenever it saw me undergoing an attack from kubej (pink colored cow) or ghdra (green colored cow), it rushes very fast with a roaring voice that was enough to make the aggressive cows run away for theirs lives. It never accepted to see me humiliated by either of the cows. When I could be back home from long and tiring forests, it controled some aggressive cows those which used to sneak away stubbornly. It ran against them roaring until the cows ran back inside the rest of the herd. I could walk ahead of the cows reluctantly and proudly because of its help behind me.

But still there was one temptation, whenever we met with other cows of slave mates who had bulls within their herd, my young brown bull used to run away from their bulls those which emerged out for fight. I felt so harrassed and melted into real frustration of humiliation several times! I shouted at it each time and rebuked it interrogatively saying, "Don't you know that you represent me, and that when you run away, that it is a great embarrassment? And one day I was completely fed up from its cowardice when another white bull chased it for a long time without turning to fight the bull back. So after the fight I ran against it and began to beat it terribly. It never expected to receive such rough treatment from its father who loved it dearly. Though I beat it terribly for a long time, it never attempted to fight me or even showed any sign of aggression but it ran away from me gently in a lowly manner. When I became tired, I left it, sat under tamarind tree and wept. The bull stood at a distance watching me as if it wished to tell me why. Then after that it went back to grazing. But stopped abruptly and looked at me again for a while wiping itself with the tail, then it resumed grazing. And shortly again it raised its head from the ground. The bull kept itself at a distance doing that for three days and on the fourth day it disappeared. When I came back from grazing field that day, the owner of the cows did not realize that until next day. He asked me, where is the bull today Ahamed? I replied, "The bull ran after other cows of a certain man who was going to the east and maybe it will come back tomorrow" I pampered him. But inside me, I was trembling as to what direction did the bull take and when will it come back or what might happen to it. I went looking for it but couldn't find it. The owner of it went on his own searching but he did not find it either. The bull disappeared for one and half months from my sight. After it was almost two months, in the early morning I heard its deep and startling mooing at distance. I tried to understand the direction from which its mooing was emanating yet it was difficult to detect that. And in the morning as usual, I took off with the cows to the forest, and I came back in the evening. As I was making coffee for the family members, I tried to tell them that I heard the bull's mooing in the earliest morning, but I said to myself, this man will beat me for the drawback of that lost bull and so I kept quiet.

The next morning I heard its voice again, Its voice was launched with real confidence as self-proof. I realised that in tears. But it was still at distance. I took off that day while my heart was beating seriously, but I ddn't understand why. As a habit of little cattle boys, we always make our cows gather together and watch the bulls as they fight and when your bull is beaten you are mocked seriously as if it were you whom the other boy had beaten, and that provoked me to anger perpetually. Finally I saw it as it came pushing through branches of the bushy trees on its way in great fierceness, aggressively as if it was reportedly telling every bull that he had received a hard training in the art of war. He is immune now to anyone. After it came out, it stood at a distance looking. It looked very dirty and full of scars on every side of its skin. Tears rolled down on my cheek as we both stood looking at each other at a distance. I tried to go to it but it went back in to the bush, declining to meet me. I felt sad and sorrowful.

Next morning as I reached into a deeper part of the bush again, I saw branches of trees reeling as it approached. It eventually appeared to me, yet it stood still at a distance pretending that it was grazing but it was not so. But this time I threw down my small ax and the rod and went to it showing to him that I want him back beside me and that I missed him for a long time, and that I am coming to apologise for beating him. I never dared fear what it could do to me. But it stood looking at me in the eyes, and never moved away. This time until I felt on its head I rubbed its body in complete love quoting to it that I missed you my bull. I missed you! After I finished rubbing its body, he went back into the bush. And in the next afternoon when the cows were drinking in the pool as I was still telling my mates that I saw my bull yesterday morning, abruptly it came before I could complete my speeches, hissing in an aggressive manner.

It came chasing away every cow that was drinking the water. But it was a surprise to those great bulls which had never run away from him. Seven of them came running and stood in a group against him. My young and energetic bull hurried against them directly, wasting no time. They saw to it that my bull will stop when it could reach them, but it came in an aggressive manner fearlessly. The bulls realized that it was coming for its revenge. It attacked all the bulls, and mercilessly tore two of them terribly until they ran away on the spot bleeding abysmally.

Those which held their ground surrounded it still and attacked it again. But the bull became so expert in handling their horns and dodging each piecing of their sharp-pointing horns. It tackled all their striking and repetitive assaults. And within a short moment another two bulls left but with ugly bleeding. After another moment other two more hastened away roaring seriously wounded. We all stood at distance scared of their rough movements, some of us climbed in the trees. We were shocked from such terrible war, our mouths remained widely goggling and dumfounded from such a wild jungle bull killing the bulls mercilessly. My mates began to harangue me that I will pay for these savage battles. Yes, so costly for their wounded bulls. But I ignored all their statements and remained nodding my head with a big smile on my face, saying in clear words "that is me! That is me!" and arrogantly I refused to look at none of my mates' faces. Tears began to roll down on my cheeks as I was watching him doing this to the bulls. I felt valued.

Finally it tore the one bull which remained to fight back eight times on the spot so terribly that the bull fell down roaring for its life. And after the last bull died, I took both my little ax, the rod and walked away warning my mates that none should attempt to follow me. I groaned back that it was a mere fight between the bulls. I continued, but if any of you wish to fight me, then come after me, if I'll not gash anyone who would attempt to do so. Since we knew each other better, none dared to risk his life to follow me.

Silence swept over the place. My bull kept mooing again and again fiercely looking with its merciless eyes. Now he has taken complete ground amongst the entire clans of *Awalad Ogulah's herds*. My bull became the husband of every female cow we all herded. And every bull had to shy away from him as soon as it saw one. None from those Arabs asked compensation for their wounded or killed bulls because it was a taboo to do so. I became so proud of it, telling my bull that now you had really represented my strength. To conclude, I was not happy when I left looking after cattle, especially him. I missed him untill now. I love that bull, for it has lifted my head up. *"Yea, my brownish bull, you have become a man like me. Yes, my brownish-bull, after you returned from the bush; after you have eaten leaves from the tree of heroism. After you sucked milk from the bosom of the goddess of the jungle, thus your heart waxed magically fearless! You have become a man like me.*

"Yea, my bull. You came back with my own heart, the heart of a barbarian—though the bulls of those who vehemently despised me for long arrayed themselves against you for war. Yet your heart waited confidently

with your war skills; because you trusted in your energetic feet and sharp horns those work havoc when they operate. Pride became your necklace. You made me smile today my bull; you made my heart swollen and engendered with joy of victory. For when you pieced them to death, they screamed like girls in pain of ravishing, I heard this with my own ears. What ailed you to cry like women? Had I not told you this?

You become a man liking me. Your jokeless eyes and rough habits proved your manhood and made you great; Your dining thus shall always be with Emira (Muslim princes), your real seat shall be amongst the valued Chiefs of our Dar (village).

You blessed my heart my bull, for when you returned back from where trees and long grass are many, you had gathered along the prize of a regalia for my glory, of course you had quickly introduced them to the wrath of my vengeance;

For vengeance is mine. Now they will consider my name they won't forget me as from today, they will always remember me whenever the sun stands where it is now and forevermore Amen!

1.7 Then My Mom Escaped

My Mum stayed with them for two months, so one night the father of the Arabs for whom she used to work, called her with five other slave Dinka women, who were kidnapped too. Those women were asked first to sing their Dinkaland songs and dance their Dinka dance. The elderly ones called the rest of the family to come, so that they 'enjoy Dinka culture of dances and songs' if they have to present one. Immediately those women started to sing their sorrowful songs. They sang a song of someone who escaped Arabs' merciless clutching, who described in his song how he managed to jumped over a big thorny fence, and escaped from a dangerous and tough situation.

Those five women started jumping up and down in their real Dinka dance styles—describing the dodging tactics of a man escaping the Murahiliin (nomad Arabs) grabbing. They silently watched as they sang and danced happily, but these women ignorantly thought that they were exhibiting the interesting parts on their good culture, but things went to the opposite. The master was already disappointed with what he heard, because the song depicted some mocking, insulting, blaspheming and friable language against them. After a not very long time they were told to stop it.

My Mom was next to sing her Aweil town songs and dance—because Mom in prerequisite declined that she was not a rural lady, rather, that she was Aweil town resident. Therefore, when her turn came, she sang a song that described the cohesiveness in Sudanese as one people—and that their leader was President Jafir Mohammad Nimeiri. She started to wipe in the air with her spread two hands showing that she was greeting the president of the entire Sudanese tribes coming out of his very splendid presidential plane. In addition, she danced in an urban dancing style, she moved here and there cunningly with a big smile on her face, which engendered great joy in the hearts of everyone including her master.

They all stood on their feet and started to dance collectively, as people of one Country under the same President disregarding religions, colors, languages and cultural barriers which stood as an antagonizing bulwark, separating the oneness of Sudanese people, who were supposed to share rights, because they inhaled and exhaled the same oxygen and are described by the same Identifications. Her song checked them in their norms, for it had exposed their lack of respect to the Sudanese Family of Nations whose harmony deserved respect. They loved my Mom and respected her perpetually, saying that Miriam Dinka is really from Dinka of Aweil town residents. They thought that it was just a coincidental song not knowing that my Mum had truly met with President Mohammad Nimeiri face to face in his first visit to Aweil in South Sudan and that she even poured on him her sweet perfume.

They didn't even know that her husband was a big man with a rank of captain in the Sudanese Army, and that he was even arrested one day when he defected from the Khartoum government so the President Nimeiri ordered his arrest in Juba, and he was arrested for two consecutive years when Abel Alier was the Vice President. Moreover, if the Vice President did not coincidentally see him as the security personnel used to bring him to the officers' eating mess; he wouldn't have been released. The Vice President Abel Alier admired my father's white hair for he saw him too young in the face, but with completely white hair. That was an amazing feature of my father's. Moreover, my mother remained with those family who kept her hostage for four years these Arabs for whom Mum worked were from those who kidnapped us because she was not sold. And so, the next day the master of the house sold those five women to nomad Arabs who were passing. She was afraid that if she would be sold to different people that she could lose track of her children's whereabouts. Because she believed strongly that if she stayed with those people, that she would one day find the rest of her children. If she was sold, then it wouldn't be easy for her to meet her children again. And fortunately, they did not sell her. Nevertheless she was disgusted with the long wait.

My Mum loathed everything and even preferred death when we were taken away from her. She became weak and lanky from stress because she missed us for a long time. Besides, she was made to cook, wash clothes, sweep the compounds of both women and of men, because men used to stay seperately. And in the morning, she could rise up earily and take almost twenty to twenty five jarcans of water to fetch water and she must come back earily also to make tea, and small breakfasts for them. She never got rest even in the late hours of the nights, because she must also get their beds prepared for her masters including young boys and girls who wanted to sleep comfortably. At midnight my Mom could grind millet—she ground millet fo two years. She was called here and there to do this and that. In turn they could decietfully applaud her saying, 'you are a hard-working woman, Mariam Dinka'. Nevetheless, she could mask her face with fake smiles, pretending that she had appreciated their praises. She became skinny from such hard-work and restless long hours of staying for almost the entire day and nights without closing her eyes in a single respite. She wanted to see her children, but that alone was something absolutely imposible to happen. Every time she happened to have prepared the food, she could decline staying near her Custodian and sneak away without eating her food. She lost all appetite for food. And any time she could see her masters watcing her when she was eating from afar, she could pretend eating happily, but secretly, she could throw away each morsel without their notice.

But, and amazing to say it, the old mother of the family knew all her tactics of refusing food and the mask my mother had had on her face. This old woman was not happy about what had befallen my Mom, and she was looking for a chance to talk to her. The old woman was called Fatimah. The then Fatimah having sympathized with Mom's situation, and hating inhumane acts done to my Mom, impacted her heart. And one day, she subtly asked my Mom to escort her to forest to 'collect fire wood' as she put it. And after they reached the forest, she properly narrated to Mom what she should do and the way that would lead her to Abu-Jabir el Medina where the Judge lived. She told my Mom that even if the Khartoum government was behind this suffering of Dinka people, still that my Mom should know, that the Judge is never bound by the system's politics. She encouraged my Mum to escape and to go to open a case against these merciless people if she wanted to. Then she seriouly quoted this saying, "for if all the four children of yours are amiss, what sort of kids would you bring forth thereafter, than those first ones? Or why would you dare the jeopardy of death and live childless when somebody else held your kids hostage?" And she concluded saying, 'whenever I see you seated alone with sullen face I couldn't forgive myself for this. I can't withstand the cascade of guilt those condemed me for my Sons' inhumane deeds.

True to say that, Fatimah's words strengthened my Mom's heart, she became strong and determined. And after that, she sneaked away from the camp for nights. I appreciate my mother's boldness, when she escaped from Arab's camp; she left in the dense darkness. And the God of Heaven protected her from being held back by any of those who would follow her. The dogs which were in the camp never barked at her: what a great favor of God. The Jehovah bound the watching dogs, they just stayed licking their lips in silence. As she was walking in dark night on foot, suddenly two Muraheliin men who were late in the market to make it home appeared. But my mum quickly rushed behind the bushy tree and kept silent. The one in front began to shout, "You! You! Heeee! Who are you?"

But my mum remained quiet. Eventually fear visited their hearts hey my Mum melted down on the road and with tears of broken heart, prayed saying *"Ah! Ah! Nhialic Aciek ku yin dhel Arek! (Oh! God the creator and you rod of Arek) Arek whom she mentioned i.e. (Arek was a woman who believed she had seen God's help in such dark nights as this. Moreover, she was buried in the road as "road covenant", thus she owned the road forever. In addition, we are relatives to her, for our grandpa's mum was from that same line) "Listen to a cry from a woman whose soul is crushed like me. You know that such a desperate woman like me has no help elsewhere beside you alone. And you the road of our ancestors, do not turn me down, do not let me be encountered by any human beings again tonight. If there is someone who would wish to use you, let him or her use you tomorrow."*

Then she took a handful of sand from the roadside and threw some to the left, to her right, to her back and then to her front as stigma of binding off anyone who would attempt to come by this same road, and she continued her walk. When she reached Majaj market, it was still very dark and she started wandering from one platform to another and big Lorries which were packed, looking for a place to sleep. Finally she decided to go to a house adjacent to the market and when she left, a woman who was urinating outdoor screamed miserably! She was one of those women whose children were kidnapped too. but did not prefer to go to the Judge, for she feared that she could be arrested by the Judge. The man of the house rushed outside with his finger in the trigger to shoot, but my mum screamed, "I am a woman, I am a human!" Thereafter the man realized that she was one of the Dinka women who had escaped and he welcomed her in.

In the morning, my mother boldly went to the court of Couty Court Sub-judge that governed those Arabs in Majaj. The Judge told my mum that she should be sworn in if she was really speaking the truth. The Judge was too serious as he questioned her saying, "Mariam Dinka, if you have agreed on certain deals, then these Arabs refused to do what you both had agreed for, then let me know". And he went on saying, "but if they had really gone to Dinkaland and kidnapped you and your children from there exactly—then please tell me if that is the case" And he added saying, 'for if you lie to me that these Arabs have brought you and your children from Dinkaland and it won't be true, know for sure that the knife (authority) I have, I will definitely turn against you, for there is no market of human beings". He exclaimed that as he knocked on the wooden table terribly.

My Mom began to clear her throat in fear. Then she accurately told him exactly what had happened. She said, 'Bany (my lord), if I am lying, may the Allah of heaven slay me, if I say these people had really gone to Dinka land and kidnapped me with my children therein!' The Judge, as he observed each movements of her lips, hands, face and the entire body, gave him a complete clue, he precisely asked, "and now, what do you want me to do for you"? In reply she valiantly said, 'I wanted all my kidnapped children to be returned back to me, my Lord the Judge'. The then Judge took his pen and wrote an immediate warrant of arrest against those kidnappers. And by God's help she succeeded in presenting her case to the Judge concerning her kidnapped and enslaved children.

After that the Judge told her not to sit back, but that she should go looking for them and if she sees them, she could report to any available policeman, that she could see they should be arrested. And she remained in the house of a certain Dinka chief who happened to be one of our relatives too. He was so much stressed also concerning this issue. So both my Mom and the Dinka chief waited for the kidnappers to see if they might attempt to come looking after her at Majaj market. One of their relatives was a policeman, and as soon as they came next day, that policeman sneaked to them and reportedly told them just to run away from Majaj market! And sure they ran away. When the Dinka chief saw them sneaking off, he shouted at the policemen to arrest them, but it was too late. The Dinka Chief vehemently attempted to run after them. He was almost to grasp one of them from the back, that man removed his long dagger and was about to pierce it into the chief's heart. Everyone began to shout at the chief to stop. Which he did eventually and the renegades managed to disappear into the bush.

When they escaped from the Judge's first arranged capture, he wrote another tough letter and attached it to the arrest warrant to whosoever this warrant falls on his or her hands; he or she was ordered to execute the plaintiff thereby acoordingly. The then Dhein county Judge wrote the verdict of confiscation to those who would not show up, ordering the return of the four children to their mother and that they should be compensated for their wrong deeds or else they could face serious offenses. He stated that in default of any police officer or chief, who receives this warrant, In whose place these renegades will be, if he or she compromises to execute its directives, that person would be held responsible for the kidnapped children and he or she, would face the law. The Judge advised her to go in search of these men in Abu Matha'arik, Abu Ja'abira Al Medina and Kha'arij markets, such if Mum could hear about them in any place. So when she went to a small town called Kha'arij on its marketing day, she was met by some Dinka women whom, after they introduced themselves to one another she found out that they had same dilemma.

They were also shocked when they heard my Mom state her

problem differently, because she ended her tale by adding that she had opened the case against those renegades who kidnapped her children. One of the then women valiantly faced her saying: "NyanWunda (the girl of our nation) Adut Tong Khon", that was my mother's real name, she continued, "As you had heard from me that I myself did lose my children, but did not think of going to a judge to ask for my kidnapped children. Seeing that they are very same people, I meant one tribe and one government with same ideology. Please my sister, I love you personally and I hope the rest of these women do, please, you are still too young to start your new life—seeing that you are a fair and hard-working woman that every man dreams of such woman like you". However, my mother rebuffed that and, in her reply, said ,"I know that I can restart a new life, but with whom?" She continued, "Knowing that I loved the father of my children I know also that I can bear other new children, but will they replace the love I had for my lost children?" Then she finally said, "My sisters, I don't wish to lie to you that I have no other choice, for I can't live without them. I will try, and try and try until I die if that could be the fate of my life or I must get them back. I am only prepared to get them or die because I am fully convinced and determined that I cannot live without my children".

Moreover, on the next day she went to Kha'arij market where used to take their cows for sale. As mum went on searching for them in every market. One day she fortunately saw some of them in Abu Jabir el Medina. And before they could see her, she secretly gave the warrant to one of Dinka lads who was selling water. She told him that he should go quickly and directly to the judge of that area and give him this warrant. Please, she continued, "do it for the sake of your brothers who are kidnapped, for these baggara have kidnapped my young children". "Do not be worried", said the lad, "it is my responsibility now, I will surely deliver it to the judge of this area, of course I know him where his office is".

When the custodians suddenly saw my mum, they excitedly welcomed her, questioning her "why have you done to us all this? You know that your children are all fine". They said, "all your kids are doing well. Ahamed, Rakia, Sa'ahli and Mohammadon are all fine". Then they questioned her saying, " Fatimah, We saw you talking so much with a conspiring face to the lad, have you opened a case against us?". But mum cleverly denied and vehemently told them that she came back only to stay with them for good, and that she realized that being with them she was far better off. So they joyously laughed and thanked her for coming back again for them with such a friendly heart. They promised to give her many gifts as presents for such her return. But abruptly a voice retorted from afar off, "don't move you and he, if anyone of you make any clumsy mistake by running away, you shall be shot dead. Stay where you all are."

They begin to question my mum saying, 'is not what is happening now no different from what you have just told us Fatimah?"they continued, "Are you coming to arrest us with your warrant? Why Fatimah? We have been so kind to you and your children, did we ever attempted to mistreat you? Or have you even heard about one amongst your kids was hurt? Please Fatimah, we urge you, talk to them in order not to arrest us, and if you want your kids back, we will give them back to you.""I don't really know where they are coming from or even who sent them" my mum flippantly denied. But she was paining in her heart badly for her kidnapped children. And so, they were silenced by the arrival of the notorious policemen who arrested them all except children who fled away.

When they stood before the Judge, he called out, "Adut Tong Khon! Adut Tong Khon" Then mum answered, "yes". She was called in. Then the custodians were asked by the Judge, "do you know this woman?" "yes", they accepted. "Okay", said the Judge whose eyes were thoroughly reddened from the serious warrant that was written by the other Judge. He moved his head up and down as a sign of asking them whether they had her children with them or not. He said, "And what is next that happened?" "Tell me", he shouted at them. And so they quickly told him everything. He had them properly flogged with 40 flogs each except the women. And he (Judge) made them to swear that they will bring all the children to their mother. They swore an oath. The Judge did not stop there only, but he sent for their Chief to come. And when he came worrying as to what the Judge summoned him for, he was given that serious warrant instructing anyone to whom this plaintiff dealt with that he has to get the children from these men by himself bring them to their mother. And that if he fails to get back all the kids to their mother, whosoever, he or she, the penalty will be death. Death will surly lick his or her life!, that was what the Judge's warrant dictated.

The Chief was called Musa Abdallrahman. The Chief Musa Abdallrahman was sworn in to bring back the kidnapped children . The Chief was then ordered to leave the office thereafter a serious warning from the Judge. He left the Judge's office alarmed, swearing rapidly that he will suppress them all. He said, "I will not be held responsible or die for what I didn't do". The Chief Musa Abdallrahman was a great warrior whose fame threatened every soul in their area. He was tall with long shoulders. His eyes were handsomely fearless. His teeth were healthy with none missing. The beard was totally white such that it could be seen from afar off like a towel folded on his cheeks. He had all the weapons to fight with i.e. guns, ax, spears, big sticks and so forth. He mounted on his speedy mule and started to go to their camps, one after another searching for them, asking to get him the kidnapped children.

When some of the kidnappers declined aggressively in disrespectful hostility, he called his son to come with him such if it means fighting, they were ready to. And one by one he took us out of their custody. I was the first one to be brought to my mum. I was so lanky. The first time I saw mum also, I could not recognize her, because she looked very thin and dark. She did not look like that brown, energetic and beautiful woman as I used to know her before. And as soon as she began calling me, Malong! Malong my Son! Then I quickly recognized that she was the one, but I was still wondering why she looked so weak and unbeautiful like before! I talked this to myself saying, "Maybe the Arabs had change something in my mum. If it would be true that they had changed something in her, I will never forgive these Arabs for sure, else I will kill them when I grow up" I concluded. Anyway my heart relented peacefully for one reason or another, since I have met my mum, nothing now is impossible. Mum made a tea for me, but when I took the tea, I starting vomiting blood! She cried out questioning me "Malong, have they beaten you then they brought you here just to die in my arms?" tell me quickly my son! But I said, "No, I have just fallen down several times off the donkey—maybe those fallings risked my back and chest bones". Yet after hearing me, she screamed louder such that the Chief rushed to our place questioning what might have overtaken us in his fence. And mum told the Chief that, "my son is not okay, he has terribly vomited blood!" But the Chief having been briefed and bribed on this issue, (by the man whom I came with for fear from my Mum, he says she is a radical woman!) soothed my mum saying she should not worry—and that she should trust his ability to handle this issue.

Then the Chief sent for a Medium who was said to have powers of healing. When she came, everyone was made to stay outside the hut except my mom and the Chief. After she made me l lay down on the mat, she started to mark the areas of my broken bones with ash—beginning from my chest then to my back bones. She then began to look at the marked parts of my body, seriously and quietly for a few minutes then she helped me up. That was her magical surgery! But my mum being disturbed by her simple way of alleged healing, complained saying, "will this old woman by her simple way of healing make my son really well?" but the Chief retorted with great confidence by shaking up one of his hands saying, "none from both Dinka, Reziegat and Messiaryia tribes has powers to do what this old woman is doing right now, no power could be compared exactly to her powers!" he exclaimed. Mom being dumbfounded at what the chief said dropped in silence. After the old medium finished, she began to rub one of my shoulders teasing me in humor, 'you are a handsome lad, 'how do you feel now?' Mom being moved with worrying questioned me still, "Malong my son how exactly do you feel now? tell me, for I am your mother. Do not fear to tell me the truth". She continued, "I have permission to arrest anyone who mistreated you". But I said, "No Mama, I am alright". Then she thereto believed me quickly because she knows very well that her son doesn't tell a lie.

The medium went outside and came back quickly with milk and aseeda made of millet and gave it to me. But my mum refused saying that she would be the one to get me food, and cunningly told the Medium that the lad's food was already ready in the kitchen, and that she was going to bring it. But the old woman seeing her suspicions, told her that she should not worry about this lad, and she added saying "I can see this little lad of yours has a great future, and nothing will stop him". Her words dropped my Mom in silence again. I and the Medium both exchanged words boldly, I began questioning her about some black beads she was wearing on her neck. Everyone was afraid of her except me in the room. She looked at me in the face seriously without answering to my question, then rubbed my back teasingly, "You have a strong heart, little Adonis". Then she bade us goodbye and left.

After three days later my younger brother Deng was brought too. He did completely not recognize my mum at first, till he screamed saying. "I don't want Dinka woman!" The Chief in doubt, questioned my mum, "is he really your son?" Absolutely yes! Mum answered without halting. And after another two days, my elder brother Mau was brought. He lost his Dinka mother tongue and almost forgetting his kindred, but quickly rehcognized his mother. My elder sister was brought after six days. She was badly beaten by the Muraheliin man who held her hostage. That man was about to kill her; three weeks before she could be brought, he took her to a remote place and attempted to murder her, but fortunately a certain Faki heard her voice crying in ropes! The Faki found her as she was strangling her in ropes! The tale of my sister is worthy mentioning for couple of reasons.

The Chief Musa Abdurrahman declared a celebration, saying that it is worthy celebrating for Allah has given him strength to gather back all the lost kids to their mother. He began to disperse sweets, tea was there for the taking, a he goat was slaughtered also, and he invited so many people to the banquet. Then three days later, the Chief reportedly wrote to the Judge a letter stating that he had gotten the children, he continued: *"I have suppressed the kidnappers, now those kids your Majesty ordered me to unfold them from the renegades' hands are with me".He continued, 'rightnow I have Malong whom his custodian named Ahamed, Mou or Saahli as his*

79

custodian used to call him. Nyigut whose other name is Rakia and youngest boy Deng whom was named Mohammado, all of them, exactly as your Majesty dictated. Therefore, I hoped now that you can trust me, please, I beech you, I wanted them not to go elsewhere, for I discovered that the woman whose children were kidnapped is a consanguineous to one of my Dinka friends called Malou Malou. Therefore, I will foster her with the children till when the south attains it peace, she will depart then if she wishes to".

Yours faithfully,
El Chief Abdallrahman Musa
Na'azir of Abu Jabira el Medina, Dhien.

We were getting news from those who came from home that the hunger in the year 1988 had heinously devastated the land with starvation, Dinka people of the South were said to be preferring bondage of kidnapping rather than that merciless hunger. And as we eventually stayed under the 'care' of that Chief for a whole year, my mother now tried to tell him in the other year that she wanted to leave with her kids; but he nonchalantly replied, 'where? for you are to stay here with me until the south become peaceful!' My mother got upset! She realized that we are under another cold bondage of that Chief. The chief told my mum that once my sister grows up, he will give her to his son in marriage! And with those statements, my mother optimistically realized that another cold bondage had come, s o she decided secretly to escape with us. And sure she did escape with us in the dense darkness with the help of a certain young man who was staying in that area. She sent us away in conspirancy with the young man at night around 12:00pm midnight on a Thursday. And she remained behind cunningly pretending that the children were around and went on washing plates and then clothes. She did that so that Musa, the el Na'azir of Abu Jabira el Medina should not realize that the children were not around— and avoided being asked as to where are the children. She cunning took empty jar cans to leave at the pump pretending that she was going to fetch water—but the woman left for good. She reached where we were in the afternoon full of dust as she was coming from a dusty place.

1.8 Malong's Lamentation

And when I absorbed all these things there was no spirit left in me. I cried sorely saying:

"*I am captive. I am enslaved. I am brought low and humiliated. My people are well known for poverty and losses. We are done way with. Oh Jehovah God. For how long will you be angry with me? Remember that we are but dust, and back into it shall we be returned. Our punishment is much greater than we could bear Oh Lord God;*

I am scattered all over the world, I am coerced to go to places I never know, and speak languages I had never spoken. I adopted cultures those were not my own, my punishment is greater than I can bear.

Those who found me, mocked and scoffed at me. Take away from me such ugly chagrin and make me a person. Raise me up and make me a nation, turn to me with your tender mercy and love. My enemy began torturing me since I was still stone man, when I was puny. Truly I am infuriated and lament. Bite me, torture me, throw me into your pits, rule me with tyranny as you wish, kick me like a dog as you desired, husk me of my glory and expose my nakedness as you say, but remember that THE JUDGE OF ALL MANKIND HAS SEEN YOU DOING IT. Be afraid, perhaps he might come and grant me my full right and establish my Cause.

I have cried to the Lord! I thoroughly uttered my voice to the Throne of Justice the sighing and groaning of my soul The Almighty God will judge between you and me. HE will perfectly stake out whose land is this.

You said in your heart that you will annihilate me from the face of the earth; you arrogantly marshaled for my extermination, in order to sweep me off from the land of the living. Because you knew that I am weakling and vulnerable to withstand your deadly fists. You fought me mercilessly and was about to terminate my weakling movements because you called for more and more merciless nations like you; so that you could do a team work against me. So that you could take my green lands; you want to snatch from me the fruitful and fertile grounds, so that you can make it a heritage to your sons leaving mine wan and helpless. You longed to foil my destination and curved it with your tactful mind. Cursed you are.

You make me lay your bricks and build your splendid houses for your well-living. You made me dig your grounds until my hands became full of scars and backbone paining. You made me crash my toes with the hoes when I was digging your gardens in the dark hours; poisonous snakes bit me as I was walking bare-footed making you happy with trembling. You killed my own children, and had my wife ravished as I watched you *doing it; and chastised me severely with merciless flogging until I could not be recognized as a human being! You made fun of me and laughed at me as you watched me dying.*

You never considered me as a human being; you cared not about me, for the Almighty God has allowed me to pass through those disgraces because of my many sins. Oh God! Have mercy on me! Pity my life and gird yourself well with a girdle of a great warrior to attack, come down and break the legs of my adversary.

You kept me alert all nights protecting your cattle; you made me bring you fire wood for your animals; you called me 'heeeey! Heeeey!' because my name is not so important to you. You had enslaved me.

You pulled me by my beard, you gushed out one of my eyes and have my ears cut off; but I am like a ram ready to be pruned. I cannot say any word; because anything I could utter would only cause the remaining life to rudely ebb.

You sent me into dense darkness to bring you the things you desired, regarding not that the wild animals might consume me. You made me take your cattle to the distant water to drink ample waters, and I came back to the cattle camp skinny, pale and sick; yet you struck my face and called me 'you stupid' You have become rich by my sweat. You ate the product of my blood; yet you showed me no appreciation. But the more I served you, the more you despised me. You burnt with seething against me with no vital reasons; you harshly rebuke and humiliate me publicly without any clear mistakes I made against you that have offended you. May the Almighty God considers this humiliation of mine, and give me my rights and bestow me his peace.

You dragged me along to the bushy places and there you slaughtered me, my blood poured down with none to tell you stop it. I rot hanging with nobody knowing that I had rotten hanging up in the trees. My enemy doesn't care about my dying children or serious sickness: and when I ask him to help me, he would respond angrily 'please go away from my presence; I don't have any medicine remedy to work for even one child's treatment'. Oh God. You are a God of justice, strike him down. For he was furious against me with no reason. You longed for a long time to terminate my life, for years you wished me dead.

My enemy has no respect in his heart towards me. When he calls for me to serve him, he shouts angrily and arrogantly saying 'come and serve me!!' and when I want to do something, I loyally request to. I am enslaved. I am not considered as a man even by their own women. Remember me Oh Lord. Make us wise and learned. Make me shrewd and tactful. Give me courage and excess to boldly stand my ground and speak out clearly who I am! Favor me.

Give me grace in the eyes of all the peoples of the entire world! Crown me like a king. Give us our monopoly standings, yes, we deserve it Yes it is mine. And bring me back home safely from my exiles and captivities. Gather me back from all my immigrations. Repatriate me from all the nations where I was scattered to. Send dispatches officially with strong statements to win me back from those who adopted me as their own. Amen!!

Make me laugh and sing songs of victory and joy and turn your wrath against my enemy. Pay them fully back for their evil deeds those they intended against me! Let my people feel your embraces and words of comforts. Let me see the downfall of my enemies. Let me behold your goodness and awesome deeds Oh Lord towards these poor and multifaceted tribes of South Sudan, for we are your own Servants.

Remember no more the sins our fathers transgressed against you and provocation of their idol worship. Oh Lord be pitiful to us and guide me into the ways of peace. Remember that dark color you bestowed upon me, remember the blackness of my skin. Recall my name. Remove me from the hands of my strong foe, liberate me from the obnoxious clutches of my adversary Amen.

For a long time, enemy forbade my young men and women to express their decisions, meetings or activitate those that gather people together. For years my people were chained and held handi-capped to expose and send off her fragrances! NO! NO! AND NO!

I am a human being. I have the same blood as you do. I breathe as you do! I am created with dignity. I am black by nature and you are brown by nature .I have human criteria; I eat, drink, laugh, dance, sing my own songs, walk, run; jump up and down with all human activities and creativities those of mankind. Why do you want me to copy you? My names are 'Deng, Garang, Abuk, and Achol. I am called Lado, Uchala and Kuku. I am Uliny, Gatkuoth, Mugga and Makur; Lakatar, Bude, Takei, Adah and Oyiaare my names! I am a black being. Really believe me, I can't change.

Rejoice as you welcome me back home. Let my eyes shine with peace. Let me feel peaceful. Let me work my ground and till my land, and let it yield for me rich fruits let me drink its juices. Let me eat my food to be satisfied. Let me have abundant crops yielding. Make me strong and wealthy, peaceful and without rumors of war.

Let our government be very wise and concrete. Raise me up and make me the trusted Father of your entire Universe. Let our children be brilliant and excellent minded. Let my trees send off their sweet fragrances and bring forth sweet fruits. Give me tasty meat from healthy rams. Give me a healthy body. Let my paths be without fear and straightforward, and let me walk even in the nights with no harm to overtake or threaten me. Let the spirit of haughtiness be far away from me, even the dullness that lures a man into erring by neglecting your Right standing, yes, the demand of Your Wisdom; and allow my heart not to stagger off or be hostile to You God of all Creation to the shame of my own face. Rid me of pride and regard your creation entirely, let me wisely perceive your purpose in creating everything you has made, the reason in making them.

And though You raise me to power, still keep in me the spirit of faithfulness, and allow not the puffed up attitudes to tour your lad's heart; give me an audibility and due strength to be the solving key and remedy to your people's dilemmas. Let your people be nourished at my bosom, keep your lad at your holy bosom and purify him from those unforgivable sins O God I pray Thee Amen!

Make us kings but not slaves, Let our vision stand clearly even to our kids those who will come after us, oh God I pray You. For I humbly heeded your discipline, I accepted the rod of your punishment for my wrong deeds, I call you my discipliner and my teacher for You Great Jehovah God, has taught me very well.

Therefore let my Country be termed as "The Faithful Father of all Nations" Crown me instead, make us as Supreme of your entire Universe; give me the absolute Freedom in the eyes of the entire world; for all my life, we were enslaved. Make us the head and never the tail again. Do not allow my Country to be dragged along by the hands of unfaithful peoples again allow nay my Nation to be allocate in any sort of such shameful disgrace again; but be my fortress forever; be our immediate Defender for ever more Amen.

Allow me to come to your heart and fulfill the demands of your will, for I humbled my heart before you, I lowered my soul before Thee alone Oh God. Give me my heart's desires to its satisfaction. I promise you, O! Lord, that I will serve thee with all my heart I will never look down on your ways and wills. Therefore be the Banner of your Son's Land forevermore Amen. Keep my candle burning and my wells streaming and abandon me never, O Lord.

For I am abandoned for long, I am murdered mercilessly for long. I stayed poor and weak for long. I have served nations for long time, I tasted all different sorts of bitterness of lives for long I am mocked and scoffed at for long. Come therefore with good tidings to me, for I am deprived of good news for a long time Oh Lord God.

Yes, the Lord is able. God will see our dead bodies, yes, hear me O Lord. My blood is crying under the grounds of many nations. My bones are sighing inside the bottoms of many deep seas. Ugliest hungers struck me; I am crushed by its obnoxious teeth. The wild animals ate my flesh to their satisfaction! I am truly crushed; I am not considered even by the smallest tribe in the entire world.

I look wan and weak. I served everybody in the world. My enemy considers me not, he sees me like a tamed animal, yes, like even a barking dog. He never gave thought to me for good, but when he thinks about me, he craves for more evil against me!

Yes, as truly as I call upon Him, the Jehovah, He will undoubtedly harken unto me, and he will set me apart as He did set Jacob apart. I am black I am black. I am black.

You looked at me with contempt and trivializing eyes. You filled your mouth with heinous insults against me that I look dark and black, you called me ugly. Yes, that is the color the Almighty God bestowed upon me.

Oh God! Forgive him not; show him no mercy, for you are a God of Justice even of vengeance! See, my people are tortured by the hands of pagan peoples. Merciless men and women are making fun of me every- where due to my dark skin that I am black. Wait. wait you peoples, wait a minute, for the Almighty God made my color that way. Look at me in the eyes and you will know who I am, I am black and dark.

Oh. Lord, develop my Country quickly. Give my men wisdom and insights in building my ruined Landmake our houses to be built with concrete buildings .Let our carpenters be expert and excellent. Let our songs be full of joy and thanksgiving to the Almighty.

Let my blind walk peacefully and confidently, let my kids shriek in giggling laughers of play let my old ones use stick nay to support them- selves with by reason of their good healty bones. Let me rejoice even in my ripe age Allow me to be called "granpa" because thou has exceeding- ly extended my days.

Let my youmg ones romantically love themselves, and make weddings of the heartfelt joy for an everlasting life bliss marriage Amen.

Let those who love me rejoice to see me thrive let them be blessed with me too. Let the entire world bring in their tithes and taxes because of the honor you bestowed upon me Amen!

Let my ministers be wise, strong and discerning minded. Let my priests be devoted to the Great Jehovah God. Grant them wisdom and your Holy Ghost and let them have the knowledge of the Holy Scriptures in the good measures, Amen. Let them be willing men and women who will serve you diligently and lovingly, O Almighty God I pray you.

Let all the templeguards and all believers be completely committed and loyal with no violence amid them at all. Amen.

Oh Lord, let our children be loyal to their parents, as real and devoted believers to the Almighty God. Oh Lord. I pray you! Let our temples be your dwelling places, so that when we come and seek you there with our hearts bowed down, may we find you.

Let my Country be given this title 'THE LORD'S OWN NATION' Amen. Oh Lord God. Never again forsake us now and forevermore. Amen.

Give me partriotic souls, let me love my precious Country thou has given us. strenghten my feebleness. Let me be united and harmonious.

Let me know what to do, or when to do it and let me be bewildered never, escalate and make me stronger than all my enemies. Amen!

Let the light of my new Sun rises everyday with rays of joy with a new hope and victory. And when it sets, still keep watch on me O God.

Yes, know this my enemy, that because of my Blue Nile's abundant waters; I will cut your head off! Because of my Red Sea's abundance and salty waters; I will rudely hold you by your throats! Do not be tempted to go to the Lol River or stand by the sides of my Black or White seas; for I will not be halting to grasp you by your neck. Be far away from my Niles' waters;

For I will not debate you on that. Stay far away from my Rivers, for these are the King's properties. Be far away from my Forestry. Let not your heart crave that, let not your legs dawdle there;

For I am a man I will not be halting or hold back my weapon, to run you through by my deadly sword. You craved greedily my son's own petroleum; you long to exploit it as your own; But I warn you only once, stay far away, for this will rise me up into a quick and merciless wrath and I will pour on you all my burning and incurable hatred of an old time.

I am black by nature. I am a South Sudanese Being. I am a Son to this Nation. I am born here; my Umbilical-cord was cut here. my Placenta was buried here. Yes, I know nowhere else but here. O God who upholds great causes, bless my Country and bless it forever.

Amen!

Chapter Two

2.1 The Kidnap of Tong Deng Lual in El Dhein

THE STORY OF TONG DENG LUAL, which he narrated to me, Tong whose mother was called Thiecjok Dut Anei — Thiecjok which means "asks the gods" such a name, always carries reasons behind it. His story shocked me the first time we met. I was living with an attitude that the only children who were kidnapped could be my brethren and me, the only family suffered could be us. For I believed that, it was only my mother who merited a worldwide global prize for her courageous deeds. And that she could the only woman who suffered. Because she stood firm in a wrecked situation in which no woman could second her. Nevertheless, after I finished telling my gruesome story to Tong, he looked down for couple of minutes, so I thought that he was deeply sympathizing with my gruesome tale but I had only reminded him of his own story.

Tong was born to a family of normal life. His father was a catechist whom he said was transferred to Dhein Parish, his father took them from Khartoum to Dhein to stay there with him.

They were five born to their mother and father. Their mother was still pregnant with their youngest sister Akech. Arek was the first born girl followed by Akoon, Tong, Aduany, Abuk and their last one was Akech (girl) who would be born months later after the Dhein conflict. They were four girls and two boys. He stated that they stayed there for couple of years before what is known to be the Dhein massacre of 1987 occurred. Moreover, according to him, Tong stated that they had heard some rumors on Thursday that three people were shot by police in which two were saved but one passed away instantly from the bullets which pieced through his chest. No one knew actually, what the cause was behind the incident. Tong said; some Arabs who sympathized with the situation advised his family to go to the neighborhoods for protection and leave our home. So his parents took them to a certain neighborhood for hiding. In addition, when the situation grew worst on Friday and Saturday their parents thought it wise to take the children into an iron train house that was not very far from their home. Nevertheless, to their surprise, we found it almost full of Dinka people who had already sprinted in the same train rooms' hours back.

There were three more train rooms of wood, in them there were over one thousand to one and a half thousand people. In addition, one Arab man went to the market and bought fuel. He started pouring it into those train houses in which myriad number of the Dinka were. The Arabs who were holding their guns with their hands on triggers ready to shoot those who would attempt to escape from the train houses burned these people in a bonfire. In addition, to make it worse, the government was aware of all of this but refused to intervene to save its people due to ethnic racism. Tong continued saying: I heard the burning people singing a song in desperate and contrite voices—each one of them cleaved to the other as they were singing one song in the three houses of the train in one spirit. Tong in continuity said, 'that song, whenever I could remember it, makes me cry because it used to bring a painful resentment in my mind' to confirm what he said, both he and I found ourselves deep in uncontrollable weeping. He continued, 'and when the fight against Dinka tribes grew worse, and the Arabs were approaching the train houses, the Dinka who were in the same train with Tong locked its door from the inside. Nevertheless, the flame of fuel's fire was mercilessly rushing into our entire train room; no one knew what to do. In addition, Tong's mother in an attempt to save us, begun to lower her children through the train window and Tong was lowered down first through the window. Tong' father was immediately killed when he made an attempt to defend us—another train was leaving from Dhein station and some Dinka persons were squishing their way through it in an attempt to escape. In addition, my father's cousin was in one of the train houses when he saw the father dead, he jumped off from the train and came running in great rage, killing four Arabs with his spears, then he was shot to death. Moreover, when the

Arabs fighters saw that a young Dinka boy was lowered down through the window, they sent against me their young boys with knives in their hands in order to stab him to death. Tong was still running away from those little Arabs' boys who were pursuing him with sharpened knives, when I managed to look behind me. He saw two sisters Aduany, Arek and brother Akoon were lowered through the window also. Moreover, all Arabs who were standing outside the train, kidnapped them. He never saw Tong's two sisters, for they did not meet again. It was by good luck that our brother Akoon was found, of which I will explain it later how he was found, chasing him seriously for his ulterior motive.

The man eventually got hold of Tong at the end of the other corner and put him on his back. In addition, as he was leaving with Tong on his back, a certain man also came filled with rage and fiercely tried to beat Tong off with a big stick from my custodian. This was not allowed by the man but met a harsh resistance from him. He (his custodian) stated that "This boy is mine; He belonged to me right now, from now onwards, I will allow no molesting against him." He named me 'Muhammad' the name Tong was no more The rest of the Arabs who were watching them rebuked the man who was trying to kill the boy. They told him that we collectively accepted the statement of Gedianyiin man Mohammed Ebeid. From that day onward, Mohammed Ebeid Dawuod el Hajj, of Gedianyiin clan, owned Tong. His other brother was Jageer Ebeid Dawuod El Hajj. Tong stayed under the care of Mohammed Ebeid looking after his cows and goats for three consecutive years.

The first place Mohammed took Tong to look after his animals was at Gasharik, a place where groundnuts were husked off covers and ground for oil, there he (Mohammed) attempted to sell me to a certain man who wished to cheat him in the buying, so he refused to be cheated and counseled the selling. Then again, we left to Kiir Abu Simsem. I stayed in his house by then looking after his calves. According to Mohammed Ebeid, I was his first-born boy, this he rapidly used to tell me. He loved me very much; he cared for me properly as one pampered his own blood seed. Sometimes I could face taunting and disrespectful treatment from Jageer, the brother of Mohammed in the times when he would go to take care of the goats in spring seasons because Jageer was the one in charge of the goats of his elderly brother Mohammed. In those four years. Jageer was the only one who mistreated me in the other side including buying for me unfitting shoes, those shoes, which could hurt my feet when I used to go looking after the goats.

2.2 Our First Visit to Dhein with Mohamed Ebeid

All those years, we had never stopped coming to the South, we used to come to as far as Aboodh village at Machar-Adut, Kiir-Kuo, Marial-Baai, Gok-machar—we penetrated any low lands and high lands across the place near to the Northern side of el Dhein South. Moreover, whenever we come to the South, I felt like escaping. Moreover, when he had realized in me that I was thinking of escape, for since we stayed for long time without rumors of civil wars, he realized that I had knew about the normalness of the situation in El Dhein and that I was planning to leave to go to my mother. It was on Tuesday, when my custodian Mohammed Ebeid decided to visit El Dhein with me. The pledge was that when we would be coming into el Dhein market that they could make us pass through the places where Dinka people were seriously working. He showed me also a certain woman who was carrying heavy items on her head and the police man following her. Then in order to intensify to me the seriousness of the bad situation of Dinka community living in el Dhein, he said, 'have you seen that woman my boy? He continued, they are forcing her to carry those heavy items and if she would refuse, the police man will kill her'. In addition, a poor and ignorant boy believed him quickly without reasoning. Moreover, from that time onward, I never thought of escaping—which gave my custodian good respite. It was common for Mohammed Ebeid migrating to the South Sudan in every dry season with me following the cattle. Moreover, it came to past, that I began to secretly question every Dinka people I could get in Kiir Adem residents. I used to introduce my names and clan telling them that I was from Gok-machar village.

2.3 I Escaped From Mohammed Ebeid

I first attempted to escape to where I was expecting to get any of my close relatives, but the situation was so vague because I did not know how to start. I grew desperate; nothing was able to make me happy, there was nothing that could engender pleasure in my sight, and this fact, even when I fibbed and masked it up in the of my custodian, yet he could vividly still see it in me. One day my grandma came to me in a dream, because we had good friendship with one another since my childhood. She loved me very much. So that night she appeared to me in a dream and re-buked me that I became so foolish and unthinkable as though I was not her intelligent little boy Tong she used to know. She told me in a dream that why shouldn't I escape or do something at least to get me away from these people who had enslaved me for quite a long time, she told me to go looking for her and my mother, because that they were still alive.

Moreover, one day, I got a good chance, because one of our black bulls was missing for the whole day, my custodian sent me in search after it. I was sleeping on the wooden bed around 12 o'clock midday when he woke me up and said, 'Mohammad, the black bull is missing, please go after it and find it'. Therefore, I quickly left. I thought of taking that chance to go to Kiir Adem where I used to hear that my close siblings used to come there.

To cross from where we were located to Kiir Adem was very far—it takes one and half days walk to cross it. People used to take water in jar-cans because people had to take rest three to four times before they could reach Kiir-kuo. There was also a very big forest that threatened people in crossing it, which peo-ple used to cross it when they amount to three, five or above. Nevertheless, with great zeal, I crossed it alone running. I ran as if I was just rushing to a nearby place, but I was realistically heading

to Kiir-dit Adem. On my way I found two old men also crossing to Kiir Adem—they asked me to stop and walk with them
if there was nobody accompanying me, but I lied to them saying, 'no, no fathers, I am not crossing to Kiir, but I am just going nearby here'. Therefore, they were convinced to let go of me,
they allowed me to leave, so I continued running. I ran for six
hours to reach Kiir Adem. I got my new friend Bol Angok Kuac-
dhuom. Bol told me exactly how I could get to the right Dinka
who would help me find my relatives. In the next day, Bol Angok
took me to a certain Chief called Akol Atheer. Akol told me that
he knew something about my uncles and the rest of my relatives. But to make it worse, I merely escaped from Mohammed
Ebeid in an intention get to my people only to be deceived by
the Chief who alleged to me that he knew my relatives and that
he could take me to them once he would hear the news of any
of my siblings coming across. However, he (the Chief) cunningly hired me again to look after the cattle of another Arab cattle keeper named Muhammad Derari from Mohammadon clan
for one more year. I had a new friend called Garang Tim Aluel
with whom we used to chatter as we looked after the cattle together all the months I spent in Mohammed Derari's camp. The
friend of mine, Garang Tim, encouraged me always to talk in my
Dinka tongue. That was good enough, and improved my mother tongue by that. I became Dinka dialect fluent after it took me
very long time to speak it.

Moreover, in the year that we returned to Kiir Adem, Garang
Tim encouraged me to talk to certain young Dinka men who

were passing by the main road that was heading to the North. I asked them whether they could know something about my relatives after I introduced myself to them. Moreover, good to say it, those young people knew something about my clan and the names of the people I mentioned, instantly they asked me how I got here, and for how long had I been working for a man whom I was taking care of his cows. In addition, after they finished talking to me, they told me that tomorrow some of my close relatives would come here, they continued, "please make sure that you come here tomorrow". Moreover, I quickly told them to hold on for few moments, I came back with full jar-can of milk for them to drink. In addition, the next day, its dawning to me was as if one full year had gone by. In the morning, I came to where I met those Dinka young men. They took me to the side where my Uncles' sons used to come to.

2.4 I Met With my Uncle's Sons

As I was approaching, one of my uncles 'son who was a deaf person, when seeing me began to roar seriously pointing at me with his hands, he was indicating that this boy was his brother without any doubt. Some of the Arabs who were in that same place said, "really this deaf man knew for sure that this boy is his blood brother" adding that the way the deaf roared indicated that this boy is his brother without any doubt. After we talked, I explained to them that the man with whom I lived now did not kidnapped me but I was just on hire to him by the Chief who pretended to know you. He deceived me, and then he later on handed me over to this man called Mohammed Derari. In addition, I told them to wait for me until I call him to them such that they could talk peacefully.

On the next day, I came with Mohammed Derari—I told him that these are my brothers and they want to take me with them. Nevertheless, Mohammed Derari in reply asked whether they wanted my wage right now or after I finished my full year pay agreement, but I retorted saying, "I don't need to spend the whole year now any longer, I just want to leave with them". When he saw that my brothers nodded their heads in affirmation, he said, "then not bad, I will give you only the half of your wage". I refused to wait for that half either—I told my brothers to let me be reunited with my mother whom we parted for four years without seeing her face again.

I also asked them whether they had ever been to Dhein, or did they hear something about the wellbeing of my mother, which they did confirm. I came to know that my mother had been pierced nine times in that perilous massacre day. She was filed up away with those dead bodies until in the evening when the grader that was ordered by the government to bury those casualties came to gather them. The police inspector realized that the woman who was amongst the dead was still alive though she was bloody. Moreover, he instantly called for the people to remove her from amongst the dead. She was taken to the hospital. Good enough, she survived the death toll. She became well, she lived with El Na'azir (great Chief) of el Dhein—she used to brew alcohol, which made her famous, prosperous and full of money. She used to hire everyone who alleged to know our whereabouts in order to go bring any one her missing children. After we talked, I came to learn that these Uncles' sons used even to come all the way from Machar-Akoon annually in search for me if they might get me amongst the camps of the Arabs migrants to the South for grazing in vicinity of Kiir Adem.

2.5 I Met With My Mother

Mohammed Derari left me with my uncles' sons. They made me rest with them until noon, when a certain man said that he knew where my mother lived in el Dhein, and that he could take me up to her. In addition, another person recommended me to an escort of two women who were passing by a few hours ago heading to el Dhein town. He added that these women also knew my mother's residence. However, the man insisted that I should not worry, that he knows where my Mom really was.

I accepted his ideas and we left together with him in that same afternoon from Kiir-kuo to el Dhein. We walked until when it was late in the night. We slept near a certain refugee camp, which was another full day's walk to reach Dhein area. Moreover, in the morning we took off until afternoon when I saw the two old women whom the man said they know mother's whereabouts. So I joined them, the man also introduced me to them that I was the lost son of Thiecjok whom she was desperately seeking. Moreover, when the man realized that I did not trust him to take me to where my mother was, but I remained glued to the old women, so he left. He reached where my mother was one hour before we could come with those old women. He just came and sat down quietly; he never made quick mention of me coming with him all the way from the South, but kept silent for almost half an hour.

My mother had just welcomed him hospitably as if any guests those who used to come to her house. Then gradually the man spoke up to her interrogatively saying, "Thiecjok, Thiecjok I had come with your little boy, I think you have not forgotten his open two teeth, and the small scar on his left lip Tong will be coming soon. But mother was bored from words as such. It became common and tedious, she had hired many people, who promised her that they will bring her children back, or they will come back with news of our whereabouts, but they failed to keep their promises to get her what she wants. Therefore, she gave in.

She could no longer trust anyone who may come with same song. However, the words of that man moved her, especially the way the man depict her son, with a humble and meek attitude, this made her at least to talk to the man. In reply to him she said, "please, my visitor, do not engender my heart for a fake jubilation, I had hired, inquired people everywhere but nothing was real". But the man insisted that this time, you will see your son Tong for sure. I left him with the two women who were coming from the South also to bring him to you because they said that they had good relationship with you, and that you know them very well'. Moreover, after not long time, she heard people screaming outside saying, "the son of Thiecjok Tong has come! Tong has come!" And she went outside in great curiosity to see what was going on, and when she saw that it was her son Tong, she couldn't bear the joy that filled her heart, she fell down, she tried to wake up the second time, but she fell down again and became unconscious.

A great mob thronged into our fence to see me. Everyone was congratulating my mysterious survival and the peaceful return. When my mother became conscious, she woke up and fell on me with tears, praising God and thanking the man who brought me from the South. She slaughtered a ram for the man. She ran quickly also to El Na'azir (Na'asir is a Paramount Chief) and told him that "Tong my son had come" the Na'azir with the rest of his relatives also rushed to see me. They were all happy for my coming and they wished me welcome. Moreover, in the morning, the Na'azir asked my mother to bring me to his court in order to sue a case against the man who kidnapped me. In addition, when I came and reportedly told him that I was taken by Mohammed Ebeid El Hajj, he (Na'azir) sent a tough summon to Mohammed Ebeid who had even sought for me until he gave up also. He came with trembling to El Na'azir and narrated the whole history to him. He explained to El Na'azir that he was just saving the life of this little boy, that he did never intend evil against the boy. Still El Na'azir harangued him saying, 'if you were really saving his life, why didn't you report him to me?' However, my mother said to El Na'azir, "please my lord, let

103

him go, I forgive him. Have you not seen that my son is well? Let him go." Therefore, the Na'azir released him after he had heavily paid bulk money to him.

2.6 Akoon and Abuk Were Found Earlier Before Me

My brother Akoon—who looked after the cows of a certain Arab man, when one day at the outskirts of el Dhein, it happened that the cattle Akoon was looking after broke into a certain garden of Sorghum. Moreover, for his surprise, an old woman came from her house in great rage. She came camouflaged, and holding her spears behind her. She swore that today she must kill the boy who let the cows entered her garden. In addition, when she came nearer to the boy, she recognized the boy. She knew that it was Akoon, her daughter's son. She abysmally screamed at him in a high voice, calling him with his name, "Akoon. Akoon my son, Is this you or somebody else?" She glued herself to him with tears on her cheeks! She started praising God for bringing this son to her. She took Akoon straight away to her master who ordered that the boy must be taken to his mother in el Dhein—because he had received orders from El Na'azir that if any kidnapped child is found, that that child must be brought to him immediately.

After two days' time, Akoon was escorted to Dhein town where my mother Thiecjok lived. When they came, both Akoon and my grandma were very excited when they saw me too. They did not believe that I was still alive. Moreover, good to say it, that after not very long time, that a certain Arab man came also, and reportedly told my mother that he had found her little child Abuk. Her kidnapper hid Abuk four hours away from Dhein town. Moreover, it came pass, that in the next day, El Na'azir ordered the police men to bring her—she was also brought safely. Nevertheless, my sisters Arek and Aduany were never found up to now. My mother lived at least with a happy heart when she found the three of us.

2.7 According to Dheiu Baak Dheiu Ngong

Dheiu Baak Dheiu Ngong, was just a rural man from Gok-Machar resident. He was born in 1969 from Majak-Amandit Aweil. He was exactly born in Mony village. He went to El Nyala in 1975. Dheiu Baak is a short and a funny person that can really make you smile, for nothing matters to him any longer after he had gone through all the turmoil. He used to speak everything in a humorous language, even things that could sullen the face. To be precise, Dheiu Baak Dheiu joined the Nyala police in the same year on 1975. He served under the province of Babanusa District where the Police Head Quarters was based. He happened to be in El Dhein 1987. He, Dheiu was an eyewitness and was one of the victims. When I met him, he explained to me the story of El Dhein massacre impeccably than the way I verbally used to hear it. He explained to me saying: "The fight actually started from the South, at the Kiir Adem, where civilian Arabs and Dinka cattle keepers who used to take their Cattles

105

both to Kiir-Adem's grazing lands grappled over the grazing fields". So the Arabs fought with Dinka people using spears and sticks where the Arabs were using rifles and other small guns which used to kill the people at distance. And that civil war ended in an unbalance of numbers, because many from Dinka people were killed. This provoked George Kuaac, who was leading a great host of the SPLA Army to intervene. In addition, on fourth March 1987 George Kuaac fired at them in Kang-abaar area where the Arabs were located. The men of Commander George Kuaac killed 14 in number and wounded six more in the camps of those cattle keepers Arabs who had no military training.

Therefore, in that civil war, it happened that a great tribe leader Omer Ga'adhim Al Na'azir of El Misseriyia community was killed in the tanker when he was also fighting seriously. His killing provoked a great friction in the hearts of the entire Arabs communities for a harsh revenge. Gradually those who were out for revenge started the killing of Dinka people who were in the Northern side. In addition, on Wednesday, two police officers from the avengers shot guns at the Dinka people whom I used to know, one died on the spot while Abuk Awan and Deng-kuei died after I took them from the station into the Nyala train house—because they were terribly wounded.

We should get ready—for the killing of Omer Ga'adhim will bring death to all of us Dinka people. On the same Thursday, the Arabs became so wild, they started killing even their Dinka slaves, and the real civil war broke out. Few from the Dinka people who tried to defend themselves on Friday and Saturday stood in resistance against them with spears and stones, which gave them little respite.

But the women of Misseriyia and Reziygat tribes came out, they started serious ululations and singing also songs of war in which they said that Arabs were the most powerful and courageous people in the entire world. The women sang their songs beating their drums saying, 'if you fear and run away from Dinka people, we will give them our vaginas for sexual intercourse, because we won't accept you after you had worn the feminine nature. Women used to do that as their cultural ways of fueling their men for war. In addition, Omkaltom, a Misseriyia woman began to pat onto her vagina continuously, and swore in a loud voice, quoting that she would give her vagina to Dinka men if the Misseriyia and Reziygat men won't kill these pests, so-called Dinka tribes.

People whom I know like Geram Garang Mathiang and his wife were killed. In addition, Spear Master (spiritual leader) Akot Anguek-dit from Patek clan, who used to live in a location called Hala-fook in Dhein was killed too. And on Friday and Saturday the situation grew really tenser. They came out from all around el Dhein areas with pangas, guns, swords and knives and they starting killing any Dinka beings they could see. They killed the Parish Catechist, called Benjamin and cut off his hands. He begun to wave at Dinka with his cut hands. A number of 2500-3000 of Dinka people were burned in the train houses on that Saturday, because those who preferred to sprint their children, wives, old men and women into the train houses did never again manage to save them from death.

I was confined in the station at 9 o'clock morning time; I was fully equipped with enough ammunition. Therefore, I locked myself up in the concrete station office and fired at them. I fought them for a half day, but no government intervention was granted me. I killed 75 men from those Arabs who were attempting to capture me alive. I was firing through the opening on the door lock because it was properly built all around. I tried to call all the numbers of cell phones and long ranges of our train police stations, asking for help but no station replied until noon when the Babanusa police station heard me and rushed to me in a train for my aid. I was taken to Babanusa the same day, and in the evening a certain European Journalist called Billson who flew from Europe all the way to Khartoum and reached Babanusa town, came and interviewed me on the incident where I reported to him what had really happened.

He asked me whether the government intervened or not. I explained to him that there was no governmental intervention in el Dhein. He also asked me the exact number of the people who died in the incident—I told him exactly also that 2500-3000 people were killed. After we finished, he left me and in the next day, I heard in the BBC News voiced out as "Dhein Massacre". Thiecjok Dut Anei, the mother of little Abuk, Akoon, Tong, Arek and Aduany who were kidnapped. She survived death with nine wounds of knives on her body and was interviewed also by a different person. And all that information was skyrocketing everywhere.

The Khartoum government begun to cover up those facts— the security officials were thoroughly searching out the people who gave out the source of the information. After three days, Khartoum Secret Services got my name in the Newspaper where I gave out the information about the incidents to European Journalist Billson. The Secret Service also detected out that the European Journalist Billson that he came the same day of the incident and retrieved the information. In addition, he, Billson left on that same day.

It was in 19th August 1987 when I was called in the office of Police Colonel Abdullatif who ordered my arms to be put down and my police uniforms stripped off. I nakedly remained standing orderly before him when he asked me, "had you given out the information about what happened in el Dhein yesterday?" Then before I could reply, he restricted me to answer him shortly, not to explain to him even how. So shortly, I told him yes, in reply. Good, good, very good! He exclaimed. He continued again, "had you also killed 75 civilians?" Yes, I replied. He grew wrathless and vigorously said, "you deceived death!" then he fired me from the police service without any pension forever. I was roughly ousted out of his office naked. From there I went to a certain friend of mine's house, who was shocked when he saw me naked. He quickly gave me clothes to wear.

Then I left to Dhein and after six days—from there I escaped with my children to the Republic of Chad for the safety of my life and the life of my family. When I was in Chad, I used to wash Chadian police officers' clothes throughout all the years of my stayed since 1987 until this 2008, until when I heard that South Sudan had adopted its Autonomous government.

In addition, Dr. Ushari Ahamad and his colleague in their well detailed book titled "The Dhein Massacre" gave clear information about this dilemma. They were a human rights activist who came to Dhein for their search on women and child's rights. These two human rights activists gave thorough information about all the unbecoming violations done in Sudan especially in Dhein. They collected the right data and gave the true figures of those who were killed in El Dhein massacre, which was exactly 3000 in number, concluded Dhieu Baak.

2.8 "The Differences" by Atak Anyuon Gop

Over many centuries, we stayed together in one territory as a nation—but totally different in cultures, beliefs, norms and mindset. For instance, Arabs use to give their daughters in marriage to their brothers' and sisters' sons, a culture that we cannot sustain—it is unacceptable to Southerners—it is considered as a great taboo and abominations.

Moreover, though we remained as one community, but Arabs strongly sustained preeminence of masters to slaves thoughts towards the southerners. They even encouraged this ideology to their children for centuries. And our hearts remained skeptical and suspicious, even our domestic animals. Our cattle or the animals we herded, they cannot mingle with theirs easily. So, we have gapes that can never be bridge no matter what.

Atak Anyuon Goop—who was born in the 1st of January 1975 at Pethatak village, from the clan of Parek—his story has identified the existed differences between these two tribes, Dinka and Arabs cattle keepers. According to Atak Nyuon Goop, he narrated that they were grazing normally in their surrounding grazing lands when it came pass, that on 13th of March 1986, that Murahiliin Arabs burned Warawaar market. Moreover, they fought with SPLA troops in Abodh village and in several other villages also, which led into hundreds of homes set on fire. But the SPLA soldiers could not manage to do anything about those serious hazards the Arab cattle keepers were inflicting.

The Arab killed Thiik Riiny Lual in that fierce conflict that day. The Sudan People Liberation Army (SPLA) soldiers were quickly defeated by civil attacks. The untrained civilian's fight, which the soldiers could not understand, confused them, and gave conducive ground for Arab's fighters. Those conflicts resulted into our complete unrest. We wandered from place to another with our cows in pursuit of safe places—which forced us to cross from Abodh to Panyuor, Warkuot up to the pool of Warcuei Ja'ama forests. We went to as far as Majok-Deng-dit at Raja village. I was with my father and my sister's husband Ngong KonAgoth including Atak Ngong Kon. Many other Dinka cattle keepers joined us from our residences. We met with Deng Ngok and his son Deng Deng Ngok and my aunt's son Makuei— plus Piol Deng Akot and late Thiep Akok Marum. In addition, Ngong the brother of Akok Mading joined us.

We stayed in the forest of Majok Deng-dit for eight consecutive days without food until it became hard for us even to swallow saliva. There was nothing edible and we suffered extremely, due to the days we spent without food. Finally, we came to realize that the war was still going on and it was not going to stop—so we decided to cross through Mony-Akol to Parajala and to Kang-Abaar at Kiir Adem side. There at Kiir Adem low land, we met with Arabs from the clan of Lueth-hanan, who had come with their cows also to graze at Southern sides, which they used to do annually in periods of summer. We joined Yusuf, Rashit and Mohammad Dada from same Arabs who we were familiar with Piol Deng Akot for years. They came with a great herd (cows) also to the grazing field. Some people from us did not like being together with Arabs—they saw it as senseless idea to joined the brothers of the same people from whom we fled from their brethren who were pursuing us seriously wishing kill us.

Now we could pretend to be friends to some of them on the other side—they condemned it and they took back their cows to as far as Majok-deng-dit. I was left with Thiep Akol, Mayen Akot, Makuei and Piol Deng Akot (the stepbrother of our current Aweil State Police Director, Akot Deng Akot). The rainy season arrived, finding us still hanging up there with these Arabs, undecided. Finally, the same Arabs were also leaving back to Dhein their residents, so Piol Deng Akot told us to come with them—saying that his other brother used to be one of these Arabs, from the same clan of Lueth-hanan.

Piol Deng Akot whose other stepbrother called Atak Deng Akot. He (Piol Deng) named himself after the clan of Ga'adhim Musa Karabat. Thus, he became a brother to Rashit Musa Karabat from the clan of Lueth-hanan. We accepted his pledge

112

willingly because we were tired of looking after cows in the South Sudanese areas where there was no proper security. We mingled our cows with theirs as we were leaving with them. It, became so obviously distinctive and difficult for us to keep our cows with theirs. Our cows refused to be mingled into the Arabs' cattle and used to shy away from the cows. We tried harder to make them remain as one, but completely our cows refused and stayed away. Finally we gave in, and made them walk a little bit away from those cows of Arabs.

This showed that there was no link between us and Arabs from the very beginning though we claimed that we could still live together. For one can see that their cows are wild, aggressive untamed, but ours were tamed, humble and normal that even a woman can milk them, unlike those of Arabs. So, I repeat, that this showed that we are different, our cows and theirs are different, our culture and theirs are different, our beliefs and theirs are different too!!! To conclude, we left from Kiir to Abu Matha'arik passing through Dhein up to Fashir. When we reached al Fashir where Ga'adhim lived, they welcomed us heartily as brothers to their brother, Ga'adhimMosa, from the sons of Mosa the great.

Our cows, as I said earlier, used to refuse to mingle with those of Arabs, we found out that it was not easy to keep them with us for more than this time and so we decided to sell them to the butcher for slaughter. We took ten sometime twenty to the market until they finished. After our cows had finished, the then Arabs stilled persuasively remained glued to us telling us that we could still live with them and be part of them. That was adoption, which is another cold kidnapping. I accepted it and stayed myself with them for another year, but I still felt disgust and rejection in my heart always especially when they spoke ill of John Garang or mentioned Southern Sudanese people in a teasing manner. These used to hurt my heart perpetually. In addition, it happened that on dry season, people use to go for marketing in some far markets.

We went to Omthuona province in the marketing day. Moreover, as we were still shopping around, as I was lingering about in the parking place, a certain lorry arrived full of commodities. The owner got out of it and asked for repairing some broken parts in his lorry. However, as he was still waiting for his lorry to be repaired, I saw looking sternly and pathetically at Dinka people. Moreover, suddenly without his notice, his lips broke out with words saying, "yesterday, such people were ugly terminated in all Dhein areas". His words were distinctively heard by every Dinka men and women—and all the Dinka people fled to different areas, some to South and others to isolated places. Nevertheless, I, being affected by it happening on the other side, I left to Khartoum with my sister's husband—who left me in Khartoum Schooling.

Chapter Three

1.1 Alek Atheer Dut Atheer

ALEK ATHEER DUT ATHEER was born in 1980 in Aweil town at Mathiang. Her father was from Duluit-Bol-Deng`s resident at Wun-Aruol village near Machar-Adut local market. Her mother is called Abang Malong. Alek was young girl from a well to do family, but who could fathom one`s fate? Rebecca is her Christian name as a name was allocated to every Christian` convert.

The Missionaries those who first came from the west or Italy, complained that our indigenous names were not easy for them to pronounce, thus they vocally ruled that every Christian member must have his or her Christian name. And to proceed, Alek`s father Atheer Dut was transferred to Wau in 1986, where Alek was escorted by her elderly brother to her grandma, at her father`s homeland, Duluit-Bol-Deng. And there she stayed for couple of months, until she got her teeth removed according to our cultural norms. Removal of the teeth is one of the important cultural norms that if a boy or a girl refuses to have his or her teeth removed, she or he could be teasingly called with many different rude words.

And after four days from the date of her teeth`s removal, her grandma sent her to Rumaker village in order to stay with her elderly Uncle's daughter who was married to a man from Rumaker. Alek was not warmly received. Yai, the husband of her step-sister remonstrated that her coming to stay within his house is unacceptable and that the place was also precarious to live in. Thus, after four days only, having no other alternative, her step-sister expelled her from home.

2.1 She Was Kidnapped – Alek's Story

As she started travelling back to her grandma at Duluit-Bol-Deng village, she was bushwhacked; she was kidnapped by cattle keeper Arabs who used to lurk behind bushes of Rumaker vicinity in wait to abduct the passing-by Dinka people. According to her, she said," I heard a voice shouting at me from a distance saying, stop! Hey you, stop!". They came running at us, because I was walking also with certain women, men and girls who were travelling on the same road. The kidnappers came and seized us, threating us with live guns. I suddenly found my left hand being caught and lifted up by one of their elderly men who was riding a horse. He put me right behind him at the back on his horse.

I was an amateur to ride on a horse, besides the horse's back was extremely big for me to spread my two legs upon it. And as he started geeing the horse to run faster, I began to slip off. Thus, he removed his towel and tied me at his back—then he began immediately again to gee his horse to run faster.

The journey started east-north into the bushy forest where we travelled for almost one and half days. The men and women they had kidnapped were acutely suffering from various issues, some were hungry, and others were complaining about injuries, because they were beaten and their situation was unpromising. Yet they were never shown pity at all. Then at midday exactly, we found ourselves in Rumaker—because they had some of their friends waiting for them there. Rumaker was full of them (cattle keeper Arabs) and their donkeys were ubiquitous, some were used to ride upon while others were for carrying goods and others movable items. My custodian prepared for me one donkey to carry me, which I hardly could manage to use, for I had never ridden upon a donkey. And so, whenever the donkey begun to move, I usually fell down, these happened several times thanks to my custodian, he never got tired of me. He used to pick me up again and put me back on my donkey.

Our journey through the forest took three days to Marem, due to the huge number of slave males and females which they had either raided or waylaid. When we reached southern outskirts of Marem, we found very large thorny fence into which a very great number of slaves were forced. Outside the fenced areas also were very, very bad picture. I was very young, a prude and weakling to withstand seeing many Arabs crassly raping young girls and women. Another vicious hazard I saw was the raping of Dinka girls who were even still underage which inspired more upset in me also. And so, you could see blood on the earth and on each young girl. Many girls were lying down halfway dead while others were already dead with their buttocks left naked after being ravished. You could smell very bad odour of their rotten buttocks at distance. You could easily get terrified from sorrowful noises of those who were still calling their parents and sighing of those who were still lying down and could not rise up, because they were disabled by reason of the assaults.

These ugly pictures completely refused to part from my eyes since 1987 up to now. And after not a very long time, we left, crossing through many small villages; El Jenina, Sanadiil, Touma, Jalhah, Amedhai at western side of Marem. We rested in Sanadiil for two days and then we could continue to their Camp at Udham. And so, when we arrived, I was warmly welcomed by Khademallah, the wife of Sulieman Shekel, my custodian. With Khademallah as my mother and Sulieman Shekel as my father I stayed for four years looking after cows, goats, sheep, fetching water and grinding millet. Khademallah, a barren woman was the housewife. I looked after cows in winter seasons because the cattle are brought in autumn, so all those months I was assigned to take care of very huge number of cows. And in the rest of the seasons which were summer and spring, I was instructed to look after goats and sheep. And in the afternoon until late hours after my retuning from shepherding, I was kept grinding millet all the time.

My hands became full of scars and my body dirty, my hair was very long but full with lice, you could see lice just walking over my entire head up to my neck and in all my clothes. But I didn't care. I was always busy, I didn't have time even to wash myself and to make it worse, I didn't have many clothes, only one skirt and blouse which I used to wash in the nights so that I could wear them in the dusk hours when the mornings were breaking. My father, Sulieman Shekel, loved me very much, and every time he used to go to Marem market or to any other markets, he usually bought me some clothes, those clothes I couldn't wear, because they were immediately taken away from me by my mother Khademallah, a woman who developed great hatred against me through and through.

I was gradually growing. I grew into very beautiful young girl, I looked cute and charming because my hair grew very long— with a brown skin, I surpassed many of their girls. My mother Khademallah, a woman whom I sincerely served from the bottom of my heart, she had never called my name twice to come, I made her compound clean and neat, her home became the abode of peace and happiness, because I cooked good food, and on time. Despite my wholehearted commitment, yet all the time, she held her eyes on me and kept me busy, she never allowed me to take rest at all. She severely chastened me with hard work. I got used to staying awake all nights. My body was used to hard work, even to stay idle, could give me no more joy at all because I got used to hard work and I become strong, skilled with all the hard work.

My mother, Khademallah, with her eyes full of hatred, thought that I would be taken for wife by her husband if she let me live in her house, because she was sick by the way she saw her husband solicitously treating me every time. And every time she used to hurl on me vicious insults, calling me with different names. I was taking cows to distant grazing places became another hard type of work, for I, as a mere girl, escaped many rape attempts from different bodies who desired to have me at the forest places. The only person I relied upon, was my father Suleiman Shekel, a man who loved me and cared for me as though I was his daughter. I loved him too. I stayed for four consecutive years. And in my fourth year, I experienced something strange in my body. I used to see small blood between my lap, I wondered whether these people might have cut my body under-parts while I was either sleeping or…or…? So, I went to a certain pool and washed all my clothes including my body, yet that small flow of blood re-fused to stop. It was in those days, when I was looking after cows.

3.1 The First Attempt to Escape

And not very long time, in Sanadiil village, as I was following our cows, the cows unfortunately sneaked into certain man's shrubs of water-melon. The cows crushed the water melons and ate food of the then water melons. It was a terrible mistake! And when I saw such a terrible mistake, I was scared and ran away. I rushed to as far as Marem market, where more Dinka people could be found. When I reached Marem, I found my father's step-sister, called Achuetwei Dut Atheer. I felt a bit secure and happy. But after not very much time, she told me that she could not afford to live with me in her house. She was wary by reasons which were completely vague to me. She only said, those from whom I escaped, might came at any time, and if I could be found in her house, that we would both be killed. She remonstrated my staying with her, because the place was precarious to live in, and that she could not manage to protect me, such were her worries.

Then without my consent, she sneakily colluded with certain men, and sold me to very terrible man from outside Marem. The new man knew me not and so he began to mistreat me severely. He made me to look after his sheep in remote areas, and sometimes I was slashed by farmers whom the sheep could sneak into their gardens without me seeing. I spent three months in that man's camp. And it happened that at the end of those three months, that one day, he decided to go to Marem market and so he took me with him in order help take the sheep he decided to sell. And at the vicinity of Marem market, a certain man reportedly told Osman Dawood, the in-law brother of Suleiman Shekel. The brothers of Khademallah were: Hamada, Osman and their sisters Amina and Khademallah, as their oldest sister. The then Osman took me to his motherhouse and for three days, he was aspiring to kill me.

One evening, he cunningly told me that we should go to the forest in order to get firewood. I thought his idea was for peace. But he was armed with a dagger and the rope was also in his pocket. And after we reached to a distant place, he smacked me terribly and begun to beat me for a long time till he got tired. I cried until I could no longer cry. My voice could no longer be heard at a distance. And finally, he started strangling me until I urinated and stools of defecation mingled in my clothes, yet he refused to release my throat. I begged him for mercy, but he went on still strangling me. Cascades of insults were flowing out of his mouth, "you uncircumcised (they used to circumcise girls), you tried to escape from our camp, now you will see, I will never leave you alive". Naturally, as a young girl, I was very energetic and fat. My soul refused to part away quickly from me. I prayed God to take my soul, because I suffered in the hands of this merciless man. And when I was almost to die, I said to him, "Osman, both you and I are human beings, I am not afraid of death, what you should also know, is that I am from a family of nobility and my father is a great man in the government" I continued, "you are only a mere cattle owner who does not even know Allah (God), though you don't know Allah, he is watching your evil deeds".

When he heard me say this, he quickly pulled out his hands from my throat and said, "could an uncircumcised Jengei (affront name for Dinka) know Allah?" then taking me by hands, he helped me up. I was very dirty when he led me back to the camp. His sister Amina and his brother Hamada were wondering as to where Alek had gone. And from far distant, I heard them calling me, "Alek! Alek! Alek! Where are you?". When I arrived home, with my dirty body, they felt terribly moved! And they began to question me, "who had done this? Speak! They demanded to know who and why he or she treated me like this for what reason. And when I tried to speak to them, I found myself crying and no word I could utter. Their brother Osman appeared as he was passing by, and he also looked dirty. Then with motion, I pointed at him. And all his brethren scolded him seriously. They began to ask him, "were you the one who brought Alek from Dar-Jengei (land of Dinka)? Who authorized you to discipline her and who are you even to mistreat her? They continued, "Suleiman Shekel himself, had never slashed her, why you?". The news spread everywhere until they reached my father Suleiman Shekel who came in a great rage. He harangued everybody including his wife Khademallah who though she was present, did not mind the deeds of her brother. So, Suleiman took me to Amina's house, although Amina was a sister to Khademallah, yet she was still different from her. But although Amina treated me courteously, yet my heart was already homesick. I could only think about Abang Malong, my mother, and about my father and all my brothers and sisters. I couldn't sleep all night.

4.1 The Second Attempt to Escape

And one night, I escaped again to Marem to the house of a woman I used to visit sometime back when I used to sell them milk from our camp. We normally come to Marem market. Kuenyom that was the name of the woman I settled in her house. She was the most cheerful woman I had ever known. She took proper care of me. She treated me even better than her own kids. She bought me clothes and instructed me to take baths and she said to me that I should eat only good food. She had two girls and one boy; Anok, Atong and Atak were their names. We became sisters and brother.

After not very long time, Suleiman Shekel, the then father, came to the house of Kuenyom. He knew that I had escaped to Marem. To my surprise, I didn't know how Suleiman knew that I would be in no other home except in Kuenyom house. Moreover, in his arrival, Kuenyom told him that Alek is my brother's daughter. She continued saying, "you can see now for yourself, Alek looked brownish exactly like me, because we are from one gene". In so much as he heard this, Suleiman became happier and said, "Kuenyom, you are a good woman, just within few days, you managed to change Alek's heart and body, but I and my wife, for years, we couldn't make her the way she looked now". He continued, 'now, don't worry, I am not going to take Alek away from you, she is my daughter, I brought her from Dar-Jengei but my wife mistreated her. So now, I am going to leave her here with you".

My father Suleiman Shekel went to the market and bought a lot of clothes for me. The clothes he bought were very, very fashionable and stylish. I became cuter and more attractive in the eyes of all men. Then same scenario happened to me at the end of the same month, I found blood again in my underwear. I felt ashamed and distanced myself from people as I used to fear that people might question me as what this was. But this time, I was not alone; Kuenyom was a very strict and sharp-eyed woman.

She knew that I was in my menstruation period. And so, without telling me, she went to the market and bought me a roll of something that looked white. And when she came from the market with 'something white' which I came to know its real name as "cotton" she then called me and politely questioned me saying, "my daughter, are you in menstruation period?". But I was still afraid and could not answer her straight away. She then explained to me that it was normal, and it must happen to every woman. Then with a big smile, she said, "you are becoming a woman my daughter!"

In not a very long time, the news of my presence in the house of Kuenyom reached my father's Uncle's Son, Chan Akol Dut Atheer. Chan's son was murdered in cold blood by then. The man who killed his boy allegedly complained that the boy had allowed the cows to enter into his farm. But thanks to Marem judge, he convicted him guilty and heavily fined and ordered him to compensate the dead boy to his father. After Chan's case was over, he came and took me to Babanossa where we met Arich Awan Anei, a sister to Malong Awan Anei. Arich was an Executive Officer, she quickly put me on a train herself and we left to Nyala where my parents were living by then. Both my mother and my father including all my brethren had long forgotten me. They believed that I was already non-existent.

But after we arrived home, at first, I was not recognized, because I looked so cute, grown-up and well built. Then Arich Awan said, "Why are you astonished, she told my mother, this is your daughter Alek!" But my mother in hearing this fell down

125

in great shock. We all cried. My sisters and brothers did not stop crying. And quickly somebody asked my father to return home from his workplace. When my father reached near our fence, he could hear shouting from the distance. And after he reached home, he asked, "What is going on here?" And he was reportedly also told that your daughter Alek is back. He couldn't believe it until when he saw me rushing to him. And as we were almost to hug ourselves, he too fell down in great shock. Both my mother and father were admitted in Nyala hospital for three days because they were unconscious and could not quickly recover.

3.1 The Arabs and Their Deeper Aims

3.1.1 I Worked For El Jazeera Arabs

We got freed in 1989, the same year in which the exsiting government was overthrown by a military coup which came to be known as "National Salvation Movement". The coup was organized by a stalwart Muslim Chiek Dr. Hassan el Turabi—expecting that the militarians would abdicate to Zibaer Mohammed Sa'ahli—but unfortunately the opportunist colonel Omar Hassan el Basher i.e. the current President, hijacked the power by the help from his colleagues.

In December of 1990-1991 the then new military government faced gigantic resistence from stuanch Muslim union, colluding with traders to skyrocket the prices of commodities. The prestigious politicians who expected the power to be lowered on to their hands, were also behind the dissidence. And that battle severely afflicted the Country, making the people of the entire Sudan starve .But thanks to the National Salvation Movement's behaviour, they had an undefeatable system, they addressed their problems. And in a very short while, the government cunningly decided to call all the traders included any one whom they suspect possessed bulk money to take his/her money to the National Bank.

The government stated that it wished to change the current currency, and those who would not co-operate to bring their money to the Central Bank for registration would regret it later. And so all of the high and the small scales brought their money for banking registration. Some brought ten millions, others brought eight millions and so on. And the government started giving out some loans to the traders to go and buy commodites, So that they sell them and get to prosper. And as I have said earlier, the battle betweent the government and the traders and some hidden enemies was still on. The prices in the markets were still skyrocketing. And the government, used the same money which was in his possession and bought its own commodities and between each shop of the traders a tent was put up there with commodities and were sold at cheap prices. And after just one to two months, the traders were losing their battle and they succumbed to the government's domination. They took their alleged complaints to the government, asking the government to reduce its prices.

We stated that they were not benefiting since 'we are buying the commodities at a very high price in foreign currencies' so, please do something, because we are paying taxes and zakahs to the Mosque. But in reply, the government said, 'the community are the ones who suffered from your high prices. The government had to intervene since you the traders had forgotten that these are your people and they needed your help, you refuse to help lower the prices and went on and on skyrocketing the prices of your commodities. As their govenrment it had no choice but to buy those commodities from my own money and sell them at low prices to these needy citizens. And so, the traders had no choice but submitted and begged the government to give them three months to sell their commodities at a flexible prices and that they were willing to sell their items at the prices that would be decided by the governmwent. And that was how the Nation Salvation Movement's government won its war with its camouflaged dissidents.

On the other hand, when all these economic wars were on— we were getting more vulnerable remaining in Babanusa where we attempted to stay.But my mum refused stating thatBabanusa was abit rural thus she chose to take us to another safer place which was El Jazeera State .Then we left from Babunusa by a train. We stayed in El Jazeera at a small town called Wadi el-Hadad. And in the three months of our stay, I and my elder brother decided to work for related families in small outskirts called Fa'aris. The Faaris people whom we worked for were in a halfway the same in spirit of those who took us captives. The first time we arrived in their houses, I thought they were enslaving us, because it was distinctively the same when dividing us like those pastoralists. And in every dawning of an early morning, they could order me to take the waste products of their young girls who were scared of going outside to the latrine at night. In my first mornings, I did not realize that these were urines until one day I took the basin to the corner and I began washing my face from the urines in the basin thinking that it was just clean water useful for washing. I washed my face from it and even rinsed my mouth, but I found it a bit salty. Despite the mother of the house watching me contaminating myself in such a dirty waste product, she did not inform me, Rather I heard her later on as she was speaking about it to her family with humor. I was even given the vests of the mature ladies to wash in the bath room.

One of the days as I was washing the girls' vests as I normally did, my eyes fell on one. And my heart got enticed when I saw the underwear of the beautiful girl I knew. The poor young Dinka boy began observing it curiously as if her thigh was wrapped in it. I begun to look at it with curiosity gasping it lavishly! When suddenly without my notice, the mother of the house saw me spotting the vest in a relaxing imagination as she was passing by! She did not harangue me but shyly and quietly sneaked away. And from that time onward she commanded those ladies to wash their respective vests alone. Though they accepted to wash their underwears on their own, there still were mockery done to me in one way or another.

3.2 Hajj Al Maugham: The Author's Story Continues

I said earlier that I worked for Arabs family of El Jazeera. The grandmother of that big family was called Hajj El Mugham. The important part of her story was how she and her whole house treated me. Hajj El Maugham was one of the toughest old women I had ever found—apart from her so selfish habits, she was also stern about every step I took in her family. She had never been at peace with me no matter how much I was praised by every one of her grandsons and granddaughters for my faithful conduct and hardworking habit—yet she could still find wrong with me anytime.

Whenever I happened to do something wrong, she could heinously recite at me cascade of her long-lasting insults as: *YaaMalong my son (that was how she used to call me) may you longo-longo-longo in the dust! Come here, may you come broken in pieces. Why have you done this? May you do it in hellfire where merciless demons are many, may your throat be spewed off and your legs left totally crippled—these eyes of yours I don't like them, may they get gushed off by reason of blindness—Allah ye Nal-salibak* (may Allah curse your cross) say amen. She could go on and on insulting me for a very long time without ceasing. Because she was gifted in insulting, all these humiliations always impelled to me retaliate. I used to avenge myself by beating her small children those born to her by her sons and daughters. But as bad as it was, she could always catch me beating the children red-handed, and as usual, she would attempt to slap me on my face which I normally dodged and so she could end up reciting on me humorously her long-lasting heinous insults.

I realized that even becoming their Muslim boy changed nothing about who really I was to them. Her old husband had another wife beside her, but sometime he used to come to his grand house (where I worked) on Thursdays and Friday evening. He had a big shop for wholesale. In addition, he used to call me always to take his filled-bag of money to the Ivory Bank for depositing. I faithfully used to do it without wavering, believing that I was doing good service to my father who loved and trusted me completely or who may not wish evil against me and my siblings. As usual as he used to wake me up for a morning prayer; he woke me up one of the mornings for prayer and we prayed together—after we finished the prayer, I went back to my bed leaving him still spending his time in a devotional prayer. To my greatest surprise, I heard him reciting some curses against the blacks in general and Dinka clans specifically–he forgotten that we had just prayed together, but he went on saying:

"Yaa Allah al Hai al ghayom (O, Allah the living and ruler) prosper the Nations of Arabs, let Islam be the dominating Religion against the infidel Nations, and make Dinka our slaves for life. Destroy Dinka utterly leaving no mark of their existence again in this Nation Yaa Allah! Because these thorns called Dinka, had troubled your chosen people, the Arabs—these tribe had completely became the bulwark for your holy Arm El Mujahedeen! May all those whom you let their skins remained dark be darkened even in life, show them no mercy Yaa Allah!

131

And glorify your Mohammadans in victory as you had glorified your messenger Mohammad!"

In addition, he could go on mentioning the names of some places where wars were going on between their government and Garang Mabior's rebels. He started repeating each place and hurled curses and defeats against the rebels but blessing and victories to his people and Islam. I was terribly awakened by his loud and assertive voice, completely marveled, astonished, confounded, afraid, disappointed, and rueful.

I was truly embittered not knowing what to do now! I wondered too whether this 'Allah' would be for my benefit or not. I ended up blaming myself for believing in a god of Arabs who called himself Allah—who did not love me and did create me with a cursed color. Whom the old man Tom called upon to finish his work of destroying me and my clans as he intended against us from the Creation when he darkened my skin as a stigma of slavery out of all human races!

I came to realize fully that we meant nothing to all the Arabs humanity—when my playmate Mutaz Abu Bakery, who was five years older than I, slapped me on my left cheek—when I wanted to reciprocate, he screamed, No! No! Do not do that, as if I was about to commit tragedy against an inviolable Being. Nevertheless, with an upset face I asked him, 'why not?' 'If you as black especially from the Dinka tribe as you are, slap me on my face, it won't work—because I am from Arabs the Nation of Mastery and True Religion, and you, are only have a heritage of slavery, the product of people who are worth nothing' he said.

To his surprise, I slapped him with all my might until he fell to the ground terribly. I was completely infuriated and disappointed. I wished to die if this superman's father would come and kill me instead of living in a world where I was already classified as bad and worth nothing! However, nothing happened of that sort. Their family knew already my aggression and strong headedness—and so this issue was counseled by calling it 'kids play' though they were not happy when they saw how badly the bond boy humiliated their precious boy.

3.3 According to El Ustaz Bashir A. Banegga

It was in the sameyear 1992 when I was still a devoted Muslim, I learned the little portion of the Sudan's History while I was still working for El Jazeera Arabs at Fa'aris. It was within that time I met with Ustaz Bashir Ahamed Banegga. He was a secondary school teacher whose lessons he taught best were history and kaueed (grammar) of the Arabic language. He was the most honest man I had ever encountered. After I finished my homework, washing the dishes and plates, making sure that the compound was also nicely swept, I loyally requested the mother of the house to allow me to go to the other nearby family where my elder brother worked. So she allowed me to. When I came running to see my elder brother, I found him on his way being sent to the market by that mother of the house.

As I remained waiting for him to come back, the mother of that house commanded me saying, 'Ahamed, instead for you waiting for your brother idly, please collect all those dirty plates and glasses and put them in basin(in our case, the slave had no right to remain idle, and he must not resist any instruction from anyone). Wash these materials, please, she continued, make sure that they are neatly clean—because I wanted them all very clean, she tuned each of her words with authority as if she was a prestigious judge passing his final verdict on the culprit. So, I took all the home utensils those dirty ones and collected them into a basin. After I made sure that everything was ready and nearby me to began washing; her brother came from outside agog and in a good mood.

He began to greet everyone including me, something unbelievable! I marveled at such great geniality! To my surprise, he asked me to get him a chair nearby me where I was washing the plates, so that we could both talk in a friendly way because he said, "you are very good-looking young boy" and that he wished to show me partiality, yes, not rudeness. Quickly I scurried to get him the chair. He sat. I brought a glass of water to him too. Then he asked me with a loving manner as he was holding the glass, sipping the water in the glass reluctantly saying, 'do you know Ahamed Malong how this Sudan came all about?; do you know which tribes of the Sudan aboriginally resided in Sudan before everybody else?'

His words struck me strongly in the heart, and something I did not know whispered to my heart saying, "this is something very important to you, because it had to do with all your slavery's fundamentalism". So I gently pushed myself backward as I

134

was lifting my face upward from my washing basin with a plate in my left hand and the washing-rubber in the other hand. Then I started asking him with searing questions but in a cunning and relaxed technique, 'was it not Arabs first then maybe, maybe......?' 'The first people who resided these places were Funj, Dinka, Shilluk, Nuba, Masalid and Nuer, these were the real aboriginal residents of the land' he said. Then he began to mention the names of the places, villages, mountains and rivers explaining them to me that they were called 'that' and not like 'this'. And he avowedly admitted that their fathers were known as Peninsula Arabs from El Jazeera lands of Sudia, Kuwait whilst as others came from tropical Deserts etcetra. Some came first as traders and some were just black raiders. But when they discovered that this land was beautiful with blessing of milk and honey, they changed their minds and eventually migrated into Sudan as traders.

Their trading was barter dealing whereby you give a leather of an animal or any buyable material for exchange of something. Peace followed and eventually they got intermingled and intermarried with the above mentioned tribes of Sudan. I abruptly retorted and asked him, 'did your grandpas come also, as I told you, "They came only as traders" he confessed. He continued, "but because Islam is a religion of all humanity, thus they preached Islam and the Funj Sultanate became Muslim and the little Christianity which exsisted was wiped off. Thus they penetrated". I looked down alarmed; then again I looked up straight at his face and asked him with another question, "what happened next?"

And with a big smile he said,"we lived together without any problem". But, but, but.... I said, "who became then the first Chief (President) who ruled Sudan from that time onwards?" But before he could answer this question now, he first asked me saying, 'do you want to know the whole history of grand Sudan Ahamed Malong? Yes. I responded without halting in great curiosity.

He laughed gaily and looked at me with contempt and little bit friendly—since he realized that I was valiantly keen waiting for the answer. Okay ya habibi (my beloved) he said as he sipped the water that I brought to him. He begun, "when the whole Sudan was under the white man's colonial rule", all the tribes of the Sudan joined hands together and fought against colonialism of the white men under the kingdom of Mahadiyia. They fought seriously against the white man but all their struggle did not terminate the white man's power over Sudan. And in 1950 up to 1954, Arabs' heroes started their uprooting mechanism in both political and militarily wars using different weapons. They struggled against the white man until they eventually drove them off. This dispute eventually resulted in the freedom that was attained in 1955-1956. Those great heroes were Aboud, Ismail el Azhari, Ali Abdallahtif and so many others from the real Sudanese Muslim fighters.

But, but, but.....how did the tribe of Arabs alone quickly rise up such that they could manage to expel the white men from the lands of Sudan? Do you mean that the freedom we had attained now came about as product of Arab's struggle alone?"I asked two same questions with little nuance. I was asking those questions because he first stated that the land was lived together with those black tribes of the Sudan—but according to the way he narrated the "historical heroes" he pointed out only Arab heroes omitting the black tribes' heroes.

As he was to respond to my questions he said, 'No, no, I forgot to say also that the black tribes were incorporated, they fought in same row with the Arabs. The agreement was made between Arabs and the black tribes that after they expelled the white men from the Sudanese lands, that they shall have . It was agreedthat the Arabs will rule five years followed by another five years for the Southern circle government. I nodded my head now in affirmation. But the mother of the house came out from inside her room agitated—she snapped at me in an interrogative language and hissing voice, "what is this you are doing, leaving my work and you started asking things which are not your right or even your standard?' please stop this nonsense of yours and wash my utensils!" Then she left instantly, leaving me with Bashir Banegga. But her brother went ahead saying, "Then the Flag of the Sudan was lifted'. Then….then…, then when the white men left, "who first took the lead based on the agreement that was made between those tribes and Arab heroes?"' I questioned. When he heard me say this now, his eyes turned rudely wild, red and sensitive, but still a little bit with weakness—realizing that I was probing him against his ancestors' tricks. I read in his face that he felt it as treason telling me the whole history of the grand Sudan. But, he still managed to finish the story saying, "the first turn was taken by Arabs, and"….but before he could finish saying the second turn, my throat ran dry, also my back begun to shake up to my thigh and my whole face turned pale. The heart speedily began to pump with high blood pressure. My whole body started shaking with a cold fever which I had never felt before!

"Finally", he concluded that "when the second turn came for the black tribes to take their opportunity, the government declined". His conclusion paralyzed my hands making them turned loose causing the plate I was holding in my other hand to fall and shattered two glasses in the basin. The mother of the house in hearing the rattling, she quickly rushed outside with cascade of insults mixed with curses demanding, "what did this dog do with my glasses? You will pay for these broken glasses you dirty black", and refused to draw her words back. But her brother intervened and nonchalantly said, "let him wash my clothes, and if he will not refuse, then forgive him". I did later. Then she went back without any responding to her brother's words but repeating, "dirty boy! Dirty boy!"

And so, alarmed and dumfounded by the story, I tried to restrain or calm myself down from the stress and pretended to look good, yet I found heartfelt tears rolling down on my cheeks. When Bashir was about to leave, he said, "Ahamed Malong, do you know that I know John Garang?'" He continued, "'Garang Mabior was my class mate when we were in the Secondary schools up to the University. He was a very sharp-minded man just like you. He pretended to be a loyal and simple man, but later he became a man who had really caused the whole Sudan's unrest. Please I warn you only once, beware that you are not collecting that information and later on you too will become another troublemaker. And he suddenly left seriously disappointed. Shy and afraid knowing not what to do, I finished washing the utensils with a jerk, and left back to the house where I worked.

Chapter Four

4.1 The Arabs' Ideology of Islamization and Arabization

Governances On Ideology, is the book title that decribed the Islamic governments which had been ruling Sudan since 1956 upto 9/11/ 2011. And, it is this ideology based on Islamization and Arabization, that had blinded one of Sudanese tribe Arabs to see and treat other tribes of Sudan like aliens in their own land. Which, resistence against this scornful bais, people of the same Country found themselves in endless civil wars.

Islamization in its real ideology is to force any non-Muslim into becoming and Islamist. You have to get to influence the infidels into becoming Muslim. You must retrain "Islamic conversion sayings" in order for an infidel to prove his/her worth in the eyes of every Muslim brothers across the globe. This religion commmands her believers to submit without questioning its beliefs and processes. After one becomes a Muslim, you are then entitled to support the Ideology of same Islamization also to pave way for Arabs' continuous encroachment over the world.

On Arabization ideology here, Arabs, in their ultimate vision, wished the entire world to become Arabs, examples are in Sudan of those tribes who had abandoned their original cultures and embraced Arabic cultures. Following are the examples of these tribe: El Mahas, Dandawa, Bedawiyiin, Nuba, Darfur, Shilluk and others. It did not matter what color you have got, once you believed in Islam, you are ultimately accepted in the families of Arabs though you might not be respected exactly like the orginal Arabs. Though the underlying mission is not really to make the world undestand or believe, but it is designed to promote interest of Arabs, for when you have already embraced Islam, then you are Mulism brother, and for sure you will not hinder your brother's affairs.

So, The Arabs came with these two dangerous daggers to our home land, yea, to our ignorant and unlearned communities of aboriginal tribes of Sudan's family of nations. According to Muslim Al Arabs, the Land of Sudan was theirs, an Allah given country that they have ruled. What remained thereafter was a mechanizim of how to eradicate these infidels, the black Communities from it, that was how Khartoum Arabs saw to the issue individually, including the entire Arab's world collectively. They looked at South Sudanese with haughty eyes due to their being neither Arabs nor Muslim like them. Thus living together with the infidels people, the Southerners which they primarily cheated in a cunning treaties, became difficult and un-wanted. Thus they started inventing myraid techniques of eliminating these infidels

141

as they termed them. And the issue of kidnapping Dinka tribes specifically, in the factual sense, was one of the Muslim politicians, it was their pledge for Jeing's (Dinka) annihilation.

It was proposed by the Khartoum government because they saw to it that Dinka tribes were the only threats to their Islamic-Arabia progression in Sudan. Thus the Islamist government properly equipped her militias which they termed Mujahidiin. It consisted of every tribe of Sudan starting from Darfur, Reziegat, Messiaryia, Islamised and spurned Dinka, Nuba and other gullible tribes. They made sure that each mercenary had to be spearheaded by stalwart and staunch Muslims. It had been given a name: jihad (holy war) for Islam in Sudan. Yes, to defending Islamic ideology. Those pastoralist nomadic Arabs known as baggara or Muraheliin were amongst those people who happened to have received the same secrecy regarding annihilating Mounyjieng (Dinka) from the South. The Khartoum government invented these facades in order to escape being suspected for the ugly taint of unfairness against Southerners in general and Dinka tribes specifically.

The baggara were told that if they could bring their slaves from Dinka people of the South, that none will interfere with that, and they were allowed to own guns legally by the Khartoum government. It is the old trick of the grand history of Sudan when Muslimiin Arabs entered the blacks' lands. The same story was spinning around rapidly in one way or the other, as they held the bait of Islam.

The Southerners on the other hand, are harmless creatures

142

engulfed with sincere simplicity in their hearts. It is naturally their traditional habit. As a custom, they usually welcome everyone hospitably and honor their guests by slaughtering he goats. Hospitality and accommodation are somethings they do widely boast of. They don't hold tenaciously to hatred or mischievous plans to hurt others, they are a forgving people. They don't have a global knowledge of how the world has gone so far. They don't know in advance the lures, briberies, flattering, and duping deceits of Muslim el Arabs. They were bewildered with their intellects through sugar and salt, profuse praises with smart ruses. The Arabs simply robbed them eventually.

Our enemy having known all our fathers' weaknesses in advance, easily came and nullified our cultures, took our power, and wealth. Instead they injected their ideology and bulldozed our cultures. It is detectable even if you can read Arabs' stories, poetries, songs, magazines, riddles, Administrative decrees and religion, they have precise and exceedingly long poems and quotations that say, "They will never and never give in for the non-Muslims to rule the Muslims community" They tactically coached their children to be likewise. They made their children to sing songs like, "it is our land and not for the slave blacks, because the blacks are cursed slaves." The Muslims are inseminating in the minds of some of the poor black tribes of Sudan like, Darfur, Masalid, and Shilluk, Dinka of Abyei, Funj and Nuba that the problem in Sudan is not the Islamic religion. Yet the actions were proofs, because those who had refused Islam were not allowed to hold high positions in government and society..

143

With profuse enthusiasm they shouted it out that "we are one" but inside their hearts they were real wolves alert to gnash us to pieces. That is the essence of cases of ours with Al Khartoum Arabs. They brought in very intricate rules and cofounded our Fathers' weakling knowledge. They had already hijacked our wealth, power, resources and suppressed our people into their cultures bulldozing our Fathers. The Arabs gave them their cultural names such as; Hammed Deng, Mohammad Kuku, Khadija Achol and so forth. They made men slaves to dig and weed their crops; build and wash their clothes in exchange for their lives. They made our women to wash plates and all home utensils and sweep compounds; wash children and clean all things in the families. All their aims were to see us only working hard for them— but without any dignity because they believed that we are nothing. It had never come to their minds that one day the black tribes of Sudan will 'rule' or 'dominate' in this Country. Simply they despised us and their hearts were laden with great daring to tell us that we don't deserve it. They coddled their children but our children, were considered dogs and toe-slippers. I wake up early in the morning to work hard and get to sleep late in the night. We were considered slaves, workers of no value. But solemnly the Arabs cannot grasp your things except when you accept their money and religion; to let the Quran be freely reiterated in your Communities. Surely that is dangling bait of Muslims and they will exploit you of everything eventually. For sure, they will work hard then to exterminate and dissipate all your cultures, secrets, power and take your wealth and all other means you may have.

My people struggled with Arabs using very poor weapons like; spears, fuel-bottles, axes and big sticks. My people fought reluctantly thinking that these Muslim Arabs will one day return back to their whereabouts', but to their surprise, it took them up to this C.P.A today. My people did not know the belief of Arabs which says, 'grasp the things of the Non-Muslims and they are your pure gifts from Allah all-providing'.One day, I deliberately talked to certain young Darfur men, I explained to them the goodness of Christians' aids and inclusively pointed out to them some of the women and men the Khartoum's Muslim government were sorely persecuting in Al Darfur areas.

We were sitting together with some traders. Fur men also and women who were present in that same place but remained silent. I said, "your people are killed every day by your Muslim brothers, and the Christians Organizations from America, Europe. All over the world are the ones supporting you with rations, tents, medicines and protection in your Camps. Compare this faith with your Arab-given faith Islam?' But they shouted at me angrily, "stop you khafir", meaning Infidel. They quelled our talk by giving me a serious warning to never repeat that again. Therefore, do not trust a Muslim even if he or she could be black, because they don't love truth. Since in the dark era of Sudan, the Khartoum Arabs had rampantly molested, tortured, murdered, dumped into pits and slaughtered our innocent and poor fathers in rather repulsively, humiliating manners. And any plans our fathers attempted to do against Arabs were indubitably impenetrable, because they were easily tricked by the Muslims' notorious security organisations with their focussed and strong leadership.

From time to time the Muslims met to pledge abhorrent and merciless plots against our fathers, with their tactful minds they molded our poor fathers into something else. Sadly, our fathers did not have the required knowledge for the making of their respective meetings or shrewd plans. Simply it was because they didn't agree with one another, victim I am. I believed one of the reasons to why they could not easily intermingle in unity against their foe was because they did not had faith in the Jehovah God. Yes, they didn't have Christ to unite and attract them to oneness. Had they united themselves earlier, their enemy would have been cleared off right in the morning of their entering. Faith is good, it harmonizes the hearts and brings about sound minds. In my opinion, I dare say that though we didn't know the politics of these Muslims, yet I am at the contrast, for there is no politics, but the Ideology, and there is no ideology, but the communal life shared together in common domain of all: such as dancing, singing, talking, walking, working, discussing marital issues, loans, trade, changing words, deals, representations and ways of how to administer one another.

These are the everyday livings that revolve around us for discussion and are shared deliberately. I say this for those who might not fathom the wheat from the weeds. In these, we automatically find ourselves sharing everything equally, so let's be wise always. To my personal surprise, I always ask, 'how did these Arabs come so recently in 164 AD, with little sugar, little salt and Islam and bewildered my people and took hold of everything. And as time went on, they blatantly asked for a treaty so that

146

they could intermarry from the blacks' daughters, and noone refused such fraudulent marriages. And for sure, the History stated that they married ladies from Funj, Nubians, Darfur, Masalid,
Shilluk and other tribes of Sudan. And after they became fully strong enough, then they started exhorting these tribes into
Islam. They colonized my people into Islam which is only but
traditions of Arabs. I am a victim. The very same trials which my
people passed through, I passed through it too. Therefore I perceived fully the 'why' and 'what' the Dr John Garang insurgency was for. I looked intensely at all the tribes of Sudan; they're in
same deteriorative situations. My people are victims as I was too.
I cried to God desperately about the conditions my people went
through until my eyes could not see properly in the next morning because they were swollen. My voice tuned:

*'I am black, I am an African Being; I am fine to be the way I am;
I am right to feel the way I do! I am a unique Being. I have a dignity and prerogative; I needed a savior not a religion! I need Freedom not
slavery; I want to walk alone! I need to decide on my own and fulfill
my own goals; I have my own languages and cultures! I need to sing my
own songs and express out who I am; solemnly if you perceive me, you
will truly leave me all alone!'* Look at me in the eyes and you will know
who I am. *'Yes, I have people to protect and cultures to defend; before
you could debate me on that, I wish to assure you that I will never be-
tray my own Nation nor would I defame my own Integrity. I have solely
believed and allowed ONE CULTURE to replace my bad parts, yes,
only ONE, and that is Jehovah God's words!*

You know what, I realized this, that there was something

amiss even from the Creation. In the Stone Age days, our people didn't know that there were people who have had the knowledge of flying in the skies by technology like Britain, Americans, Russia, French and so many other developed peoples. In addition, whenever they see something like a plane flying in the air, they assumed that those were the sons of gods flying in the air. They even go as far as telling their kids that, "those are the sons of God going for a party or maybe marriage". Moreover, they warned the kids not to look up for long time at them, because the sons of God might see you and they would come in the night and take you away. Moreover, in the first time when the airplane landed in the Dinka land, all the community emerged out singing songs of homage for their God, which came from the sky, the plane. I avowedly confess that the dark eras played so much with our grandpas' minds. They didn't had the knowledge to add up to the genuine faith, tactics and wise ideology. The important issue was that our grandfathers didn't acknowledge God, thus His quickening and cradling power was ineffective within them.

I believe that we have truly suffered and if there were other people who suffered intensely in this world also, still my people surpassed them all and we are the number one. If there was anybody who ate the wild trees' leaves still raw, my people will be the first of them all. If there were people who served other nations, still my people will be in the first position. Those who stayed without food or water, their sufferings were nothing to the gruesome story of ours. They really have gone through adventuresome lives in this world. The flames of their suffering could be seen even now visibly. Their agonies and sighing could be heard even now. Their wounds are not fully recovered still even now. Look at them and you will see them weak still. They are simple and illiterate still even now. If there were people who cried to other idols which could not avail, still my people surpassed them because they cried seriously to their idols which couldn't do anything for their welfare. If there is a census of peoples whose rights got lost and saw deprivations with their naked eyes, then count my people as their number one.

Our rights were not there even from the Creation. Even now we are naked and without clothes to cover our nakedness. We don't have enough food to satisfy us; advanced hospitals we did not know, thus a simplest illness could kill the elderly of the Community. Truly we are backward and not forward. My Communities are people whose mind is thoroughly cofounded and traumatized. They don't agree with one another because they don't fathom that they are but one people. The Arabs grasped their weakling understanding and influenced them. They were hijacked in so many agreements, for the Arabs used to cunningly and flatteringly promised our people that this great 'symposium' will be reliable. But all in vain; unmitigated liars. The Arabs coached their members to tell and do the same thing with forged verisimilitude unanimously on the black tribes of the Sudan.

Dear reader, it is noteworthy to know truly that the dark era proved to us the insincerity of Khartoum's muslim government . They destroyed both Fuj and Nubian Kingdoms and tore

149

off all the Christian symbols from the lands of Nubians who were staunch Christians. The Islamic government demolished the concrete churches and utterly held back Christianity's progress in the Sudan. They subdued the entire Fuj kingdoms and mastered everything and planted very strong Islamic belief in those lands. Such they could term this land as "the holy land of Muslims". And thus Sudan obtained an unrivaled credit in the entire African Nations, because through Sudan, Arabs entered into all African lands and converted them into Islam.

Sudan was and is still the cave of the great committed Muslim brothers. Arabs even some years ago agreed that they wanted this South Sudan emptied and terminated of any living black beings, such that they could freely utilize it for their Islamic idealism. They talked it over with an Egyptian President Jamal Adel Nasir who came to power through a military coup in 1957. And after Jamal equipped his men properly in order to execute the termination pledge of Southerners in the next morning, such that the land is cleared from her inhabitants, he was assissinated the same night, right in his bed. Wow. How dearly did God favour His creatures the Southerners. The same ideology came with his successor Anuor Sadad—who was murdered in 1981. He came up with the idea that all the Southerners should be brought to one place and there they could easily be burnt! Thousands of the poor Dinka in 1980 and 1981 again, they were put in fences with fuel poured around them all over and then they were set on fire! They died a merciless death. The Arabs did it in Babanusa, Fulla and Mujlad.

One day I heard a testimony of a survivor from Babanusa fire death in a local FM radio called weerbei 99.9 fm radio, a community radio in Wanyjok county, State Aweil. She stated that she was born inside the burning-fire those days. Her mother was in birth-pain while the people were burning in a bonfire inside the thatched house. Her grandma who was helping her mum did not die either. Something that shocked the Arabs in the morning when they saw such mysterious delivery of a new baby. The Arabs never fluctuated in wishing this land cleared from any so-called Southerners. This they believed would give Arabs good gardens and green land for grazing their animals, grow its fertile land and utilize it as zoos or entertainment arenas as well. And the Arabs craved the South Sudan oil for their Islamic strategies. All the "el Mujahidiin" believed that any death of their men in the South Sudan meant that this land had been sanctified by their holy bloods and thus this ground has become a holy Muslims' land rightfully.

It's unbelievable, since the time of UN and the United States of America launched a pursuit against terrorism in the presidential period of Bill Clinton.; This issue continued like that without anyone knowing how far the Muslims were mischievously guilty. The nation's President George W. Bush of the USA ordered to be bombed were the realistic Countries who were immensely targeting Southern Sudan wishing these poor people subdued and adopted into homeless and enslaved estates.

The Muslims' entire pledges prevailingly were executed therein. Yes, in the mean time when the United Nations and

151

US troops were desperately in pursuit of hunting for the ter-
rorist 'great Sheik' Osama Bin Laden everywhere, He was freely, peacefully and securely moving inside the "Muslim holy land
Sudan!". He was operating seriously and executing all his projects
in the western (Darfur), eastern (Damazin), northern (Shamalia
Dongola) Khartoum (Jebel Awilia) and southern Sudan (Juba).
He was conducting his serious meetings, reiterating that the
Muslim believer should fear nobody. Bin Laden built Islamic
schools, mosques and opened strong companies for supporting
the Islamic ideology everywhere in Sudan and beyond. He safely operated in Sudan for six good years under Sudanese staunch
Muslim security protection, he vehemently believed that his feet
were walking in the safe holy Muslim land. Another staunch
Muslim who happened to have done the same thing also was
Omer el Muktar of Libya. He was always safe whenever he fled
to el Sudan. He frequently left Libya and rushed to Sudanese
lands whenever he was wanted and hunted down by his enemy, the British. Gadhafi gets infuriated whenever he is not owed
homage from Sudanese Presidents, because he believes that he is
a Muslim father to this land.

El Sadam Hussain, Iraq's strongest men of war were taken
from Sudan—because the Khartoum government was and is
the heart of Islamic arms supporter to date. Philistines have a
special support cooperation from within Islamic government
of Khartoum. Thus whenever they are tortured by their Israeli
foes they sent fervent letters of militatry support to Sudanese
authorities. Egypt's life depends upon Sudanese waters—all the

Egyptians' hope falls upon the lands of Sudan. Egypt knows very well that what is between Sudan and Egypt is more than drinking and eating, because it is in Sudan where Egypt-Sudan Islamic vision is kept with her long history and strong relationship of Egypt-Sudan's antique oneness.

Libyian leader el Gadhafi knows very well that without Sudan in between, the surrounding African nations, there won't be success or progress in anything concerning Muslims' optimistic "go ahead": for the entire Arab's world. Iran can defend Khartoum from anything that could jeopardize her free flow of Islamic missions, those she is doing for the benefit of the entire Muslims to her last breath. Yeman received their Islamic faith's concrete fundamentalism from inside Sudan. All the Muslims' know properly that the strongest Islamic nation is Sudan because her converts are very strong and influential, full of Quranic scriptures. Saudi Arabia believed it strongly that the true and the only nations who are staunch Muslim brothers which did not lost their Islamic virgnity, and are still with Islamic vision and fluent Arabic language: are Iran, Libya, Iraq, Saudi, Turkey. But they count Sudan as the leading number one. Because Sudan remained as faithful and as a fortress for the entire Muslim world since in the long history of Islamization to date.

4.2 Exemplaries in Sudan of "El Mahadiyia"

The Sudanese tribes including both Muslims and non-muslims suffered so much under the tyrannical leadership of Mohammed

Ahamed El Mahadi. His intiative of declaring himself as'El Mahadiya' meaning the Saviour of Islamic Religion, was the core Islamic idealism.The zeal of saving the entire Muslim Al Arabs, to spread Islam and restore the Islamic virginity.That is the ideological meaning of El Mahadyia's kingdom. It was believed firmly by his Muslim kalifs such that they avowedly swore to establish El Mahadiya kingdom and make the whole world to embrace the Islam religion. They were optimistically prepared for only one thing "win the Islamic war or matyrdom". The Khalifa's statement was short and clear, "embrace Islam and Mahadyia or die". What the world does not sagely perceive is that Mohammed Ahmaed El Mahdi was not a bad person—rather he was just a stuanch Muslim who had inviolably enacted the Islamic ideology.

The way I am going to retrieve the familiar History of Sudan which is known to everyone, was and is still how the true Muslim should behave. We shall see in the best example of Sheik or Amir El Muslimiin Mohammed Ahamed el Mahdi who had the same vision of Mohammed in Sudan. He innovated the realistic belief of a true stuanch Muslim. Some of the things I will touch on here have not been put down in the history of Sudan, because the Muslim scientists have refused to put them down, those blemished parts of Sudan's dark era. And they have changed many things for instance, the Arabs entry in Sudan is now changed into 'the entry of the people in Sudan'. Moreover, the Amir in the term of social conduct, love for money and power, for instance, a father who wanted to give his daughter in marriage to someone else (if the girl for marriage looked pretty) her father was prompted first to take his daughter to El Amir El Mahdi for "first fruit test". El Amir must have sex with each lady first before her husband could do that. And if by any mistake that the lady happened to had been spoiled by somebody else before he does that first, the families of those girls would surely be punished and have their properties confiscated. So all the girls' fathers should come with their daughters and wait queued for her 'first fruit test' in the remote house where they were ordered by Amir el Mahdi to.

He declared that he was the Successor of Mohammed and commanded all the people of Sudan and beyond to submit to his leadership. He sent dispatches to every neighboring state in the top brass of African nations to embrace Islam. When his letter reached the King John of Ethiopia, he replied to it with aggression. He thought that this issue was a mere allegation, but a fierce battlewas launched against him by el Ansarjihadist till he was killed. And when the Amir became stronger, he sent the same dispatches to Asian nations and all sounding nations—asking them to embrace el Mahadyia! In Sudan people had gone as far as even taking oaths in the name of Amir El Mahadi saying, "in the name of el Mahdi". They drank the dirty water of El Mahdi through which he had washed his feet. His feet were handsomely kissed as a ritual of receiving blessings from Allah's favored Prophet. Muslims of Sudan firmly believed that he was the "Successor of Mohammad the Messenger of Allah".

But his Islamic colonization was abruptly eliminated by the

white men who came as a disaster to the whole land of Sudan. Nevertheless, all the tribes of Sudan without any other choices joined their hands together and struggled with the white man and they eventually ousted the British. El Zaeem Ismail Azahri took over the presidential power from the white men successfully with the tribal agreement of power sharing to both Mulims and Non-muslim Sudanese. But he abruptly changed and adopted his Islamic ideology which is the "vision of dominating everything by El Sharia Laws". After El Ismail, many Sudanese Presidents came with same attitudes of Islamization. Starting with Numeiri, he brought many other devoted Muslim' tribes into the Sudan from the neigboring Countries i.e. Zakawa from Chad, Libyans from Libya, Egyptians from Egypt, Iranians from Iran, Huwsah Muslims from Nigeria and Iraq.

They brought these peoples to stay with an intention to intermingle with the true aboriginal natives of Sudan such they could dissipate (do away with) the nativity of the true Sudanese., to eventually change these multifarious black tribes of Sudan into Muslims' Country. That won't have a tangible legacy. They didn't have any single doubt to do so, because they had influential fundamental means i.e. they brought expert traders from Zakawa, Libyans and Egyptians to win money from the hands of the black Communities so that they could fund their Islamic movement. And fight prevailingly with their wealth of which none of the black tribes could by any means surpass or resist .Since no black man or woman was civilized enough to know the secrect of how to prevail using the money's weapons.

They didn't know that even the hearts of their Chief leaders could be stolen and simply turned into gullible subjects with bribing money or donated materials. They had been supported with weapons to protect themselves with from Iran and Iraq, using Islamized men from Darfur, Nuba and Masalid as their fighters. In the era of Nimeiri, he first pretended to expose that he won't implement their Islamic ideology like those of Mahadiyia and others before him. Later on he went into executing many armed black recruits when he realized that their census was outnumbering others in the Sudan's army. He took the black high-ranking men into severe military training with jeopardy that if anyone escape from the training, that he would either be killed or lose his rank. He vehemently stated saying, "I am preparing you to be qualified officers". He was doing all those precautions as alternatives against Southerners such that they might not hold any ground to fight the Muslims. So he invented ways of executing and imposing on them mercilessly whenever one of them happened to reject some of their wrong and mischievous orders.

Millions of the blacks' recruits armed were intentionally sent away empty without their pensions—as long as they were not aligning loyally to the ultimate faith in Islamic observances. In the areas like Babanusa, Muglad and Meram millions from black innocent people worked for their Arabs in jobs like, laying bricks, buildings, tilling grounds and other hard jobs after the black Sudanese finished their jobs with expectations that they should receive their salaries. Unfortunately they could be murdered by

Arabs, so that they should not disturb them by asking or claiming their wages. And if it happened fortunately for the murdered ones to have relatives, the relatives would only be intimidated with questions, "are you unhappy for that?" "no. No. We are not angry, we are just 'requesting' for the dead bodies and the place where we could bury them so that their bad odor should not be smelt'" Those were the coward responses of any dead people's sensible relatives.

These were especially happening in the South Sudanese locations where Islamic soldiers had dominated. In the Hospitals, the midwives give a vital care to the Arabic mothers who were delivering in their pregnancies. But the blacks' mothers would easily die there with great agonies of the child deliverance. Because all the Doctors were from the Muslims' community, they were obligated only to take much care of their own women. The Khartoum government failed completely to make the unity of one Sudan conducive for the people.

All their Muslim leaders mismanaged these vast and inter-tribal lands—even when Mohammed Ahamed Thuor el Dhab came to power, he came with the same ideology but his military government abdicated quickly within one year's time when seeing the issue of the South tribes on going. Then he was followed by El Shiek Sadig el Mahdi. In his second rule, he repeated some Islamic ideology and as a result, many students from Khartoum and other strong Universities Candidates were murdered as long as they were blacks' potentials, just because they were not Muslims.

I was shocked when I heard the former president of Sudan Sir Sadig El Mahadi avowedly admitted that "in the dark era that the South Sudanese tribes were badly mistreated, they were not shown the true spirit of oneness, and that if there was true love and harmony amongst us then some of Sudanese tribes wouldn't have decided to split into a separate realm".Yet he declined to admit that it was through Islamic idealism that the rest of the tribes of Sudan were ugly, neglected and deprived of their legal rights. If their fathers didn't wrongly use Islamic creeds, the Sharia Laws as the liable law, which favored only Muslim brothers against the non-Muslims for the entire Country, there wouldn't be such great mistrust amongst one people'.

4.3 The Christians' Suffering in Sudan

The Islamic vision of Sadig El Mahadi was so severe that until it impelled an agitated Christian procession into protesting against it on 24th December 1976, the Muslims' notorious government security hindered that movement of believers.The Muslims sent their policemen. With pepper-guns and other explosives and livebullets and they radically did away with that protest. Those Christians yelled and utterly cried to God about Muslims' tyrannical treatment.A song was composed by the Christians with broken hearts from that ugly event which they had undergone.

The song goes as:

"O God,we wish the peace of God amongst us altogether, please God bring peace in our land, bring peace, bring peace amongst us all, and we will live with the Prince (Christ) of eternal life".

Many temples' buildings were broken into and had priests executed and detained for unmentionable time. In those days there were not many priests from the black tribes, but those priests were mostly from Italian Fathers and British Missionaries. As I mentioned earlier, that it was the same spirit, Salvation Partyof Omer El Bashir after he had overthrown the ruling system,launched also an Islamic gigantic influence. They worked harder to implement all the Islamic idealizm. He issued a proclamation that secret inscription was to be stamped between the buttocks with this title, "No other Allahs except Allah and Mohammad his Messenger".

The government did this to many black political leaders who wished to be in "the top part" of the Khartoum government. And those who happened to have beautiful young women or girls were in great troubles. The Muslims secretly forced those young ladies into relationships and they eventually coerced them to become Muslims. They lured the black ladies in to Islamic religion in order for them to be easily stirred up by the Islamic Laws, such that they should not reveal such ugly sexual abuses. They did it one way or the other. Omer el Bashir's government has been purely Islamic with distinctive tyranny. He set up a very strict and notorious security system in the South Sudanese areas that aggressively killed men who looked healthy. This was because they were flippantly suspectedof being from rebels whenever they visited their siblings, in the towns under the Khartoum's Islamic forces deployed in the south.

Some reckless black men and women were pointing out those whom they didn't know, falsely saying, "we were with him since in the rebellion Army. Eventually you will be tortured severely to death." We were never ever considered to sit on the chairs at parties. And it happened that whenever the black men or women sat on the bus seat, leaving the Arabs' man or woman standing, he or she could scornfully be teased. The Muslims' Judges were ordered to never execute justice to non-Muslim black tribes whenever the blacks' murdered relatives come to open any case in the courts, their cases were never considered. But the Muslims normally go to their Judges and had them talked down. They would give also warnings to their Muslim Judges so that the blacks' relatives received not much justice. The Muslims believed that the blacks' death means nothing to Allah, the Muslims' God. The Quran also quotes that the death of any infidels is not very noteworthy. I am very sure, any co-operation with Muslims are too risky.

The Islamic concept offensively hindered one of the world's preachers, from Germany who was called Reinhard Bonke when he had to come to Khartoum in 2001. He was first allowed to pass in with a pretend attitude from Khartoum's Islamic government to be welcomed highly by more than twenty five thousand black tribes people, including men and women from Arabs. All the sick came from every corner of Sudan. Many disabled and blind received their healing even from Muslim Arabs. A great number of the converts were increasing daily, something which annoyed the Khartoum government. The Islamic system set very

tyranical regulations immediately, such that on his second coming he could be thoroughly hindered. They hindered him seriously when he came the following year, which led to a great riot.
Because the government of Khartoum sent notorous Security
forces, they arrested many people and disappeared with many up
to this date.

The death of our late Father Dr. John Garang Maboir whose
absence has truly broken every black tribe of the Sudan's hearts.
His boldness, love for his own people, clear vision, political mind,
were so dear to us. But on the day when the black tribes of Sudan
were weeping bitterly to their incumbent President, the Muslims
broke into a great joy. They were enraptured over the death of
our dear true Son of Sudan. This caused great annoyance in the
hearts of the Blacks and a great riot took place on that day—
which led into killing of many Arabs by the hands of the black
tribes in the first day. On the second day, the Muslims discussed
this over inside their Mosques in agreement with their government. In the morning, blacks were killed by government forces.
On that day, it was vividly clear in the minds of every black tribe
of South Sudan, and on that day they found their hearts united
in one absorbed thing. They, united, found their mulish enemy.

We were in the room with certain sub-couples when the
BBC's News broke out "the assassination of Dr John Garang in
the plane crash". From that moment I and my colleagues broke
into great sighing and some of us were crying they remained
with their heads bowed low. I found myself deeply dazed, like a
man overcome by strong intoxicating drink. I found myself in a

great rage and my lips babbling words like, "they did it again" and my legs dawdled to the nearest wall-blackboard and wrote this title "land of ethnic and religious wars". This could be seen in the writings when all the Bishops of Sudan had written a number of letters to the Government. This included a letter which they wrote to the Sudanese Prime Minister with open frankness, stating to the President to either remove Catholic Church Mission's hinderances, and put an end to human rights violations, and bring immediately peace in the whole Sudan or resign from power.

4.4 Bishops of Sudan's Letter to Prime Minister

Your Excellency,

This Letter was found in an inspiring book titled "The Church in Sudan Journeying Toward Justice and Peace" by Bishop Caesar Mazzolari of Rumbek Diocese. The Letter went as follows:

We are addressing this document to you as an open letter because of the past failures to receive adequate responses to our previous communications. However, in view of the current crisis arising from the position the Sudanese Army has taken with respect to peace, and so that our position in this letter is understood as not taking advantage of the crisis, we send this letter to you personally, prior its publication.

The Sudanese Catholic Bishops' Conference is just concluding its 1988 Annual Conference in Khartoum. Among the many issues discussed at our Conference, were the spiritual and social problems besetting our Sudanese people at the moment: the issue of war and peace. untold suffering of innocent and defenseless members of our society; the difficulties placed in our way. The Church, to help these suffering people, the difficulties the Church currently encounters in the discharge of its spiritual functions and the difficult relations we have as a Catholic Church with your Government and your personally directed attacks on the Catholic Church and its leadership in the Sudan. These problems have occupied much time, deliberation and attention during our Conference. The Conference of the Catholic Bishops, therefore, resolves to address these concerns to you in this open letter. We wish the Sudanese people to be aware of our stand as a Church on these burning issues.

4.4.1 All Men Are Created in The Image of God (Gen. 1:27)

1. We protest the large-scale violation of basic human rights, both civil and religious perpetrated against individuals and groups, due to the disruption brought on by the extended civil war.

2. We have seen with our own eyes famine inflicted on large segments of our fellow citizens due to this power-struggle war. We hear with our own ears the many cries of the poor and displaced in all parts of our Country. In Greater Khartoum itself, with its over one million displaced, in Juba with over two hundred thousand, in Malakal with over one hundred thousand. The memories of those hundreds and thousands

who have died of famine in and around Wau, Abiyei, Aweil, Torit and other areas of the South continue to haunt us. The war that brings such famine and suffering must stop.

3. Tribal militias act out their ancient antagonisms armed with modern weapons that make their brutality more savage. In the face of the continued reports of killings, rapes and theft, we protest the continued toleration of such militias on the part of the Government.

4. Tribal militias of young women, such as the one formed amongst the Balanda tribe in the Nagero, Maringindo area (between Wau and Tombura), are particularly destructive of our traditional Sudanese culture and way of life, in addition to the continual conflict which they formed.

4.4.2 We Feel in Conscience Bound to State That

A. There is a breakdown of civil administration in large areas of our Country, where military action has taken place. In other areas, the presence of large groups of armed personnel who put themselves above the law, makes the ordinary administration of civil justice difficult, if not impossible. Such violations of basic justice against individuals and groups tear apart the very fabric of civil society. The massacre of civilians in August and September 1987, in Wau , are unfortunate instances of such injustices, nor is the suffering of the innocent confined to the war zones of Southern Sudan.

B. The present Government's push towards Islamization militias against harmony in our multi-religious and multi-cultural society, and contributes to the present state of civil unrest.

C. Seven villages in South Kordofan we burnt by the military during a search operation i.e. Endrafi, Karkar, in December 1988. A settlement of displaced people in Omdurman, and a settlement of displaced people near Shambat bridge were destroyed by bulldozers (January 1989).

D. There have been serious violations of our basic religious rights. We have pointed out to you many of them in detail on many occasions. Some continue to the present time. Amongst the most serious are:

a. The beatings, mistreatment and even on two occasions, murder of Catechists (Church personnel), and the burning, looting and desecration of Churches in South Kordofan.

b. Harassments of and vilification of Church:

i. You, Mr Prime Minister, have personally criticized Bishop Macram Max publicly in a televised session of the National Assembly, for speaking out against violations of human rights in our Country. What he said was said in the name of the Catholic Church Bishops. What he spoke about is common public knowledge both in Sudan and elsewhere.

ii. In a meeting in El Obeid on 8th December with the Governor of Kordofan Region, Bishop Macram was repeatedly asked to retract our public statement about human rights violation. This he refused to do. Later that same afternoon Radio Kordofan broadcasted incorrectly that Bishop Macram had stated in his interview with the Governor that the statement was the work of other Bishops and that he would correct these statements in a new version.

iii. In Kaduli, catholic personnel were prevented visiting the camps of the displaced and were told by the Government authorities that they were not supposed to distribute help to the displaced people.

4.4.3 Therefore We Feel in Conscience Bound

a. To point out: the lack of effective action by the present Government to work for peace, despite the initial promises made by you, the Prime Minister.

b. To remind you: Mr Prime Minister, of your promises to the Nation on taking office and note with regret the inaction of the present Government in fulfilling these promises.

c. To remind you: Mr Prime Minister, that on taking office you proposed as goals the remedying of evils brought on by the Sharia Law and the taking of effective steps to bring peace.

4.3.4 In Particular, We Point Out

a. The failure of your Government to endorse the Agreement of 16 November 1988; between the representatives of the DUP and SPLA;

b. The recent re-organization of the Government majority with the resulting promotion of Sharia Laws and Islamization in Government.

4.4.5 The Failure of Your Government

i.   Provide basic survival commodities for large segments of the population;

ii.   Ensure the protection of essential human rights

iii. Protect and defend the people from violence, corruption, and exploitations;

iv.   Take effective measures for unity in the face of tribalism and militias;

v.   Bring an end to the fratricidal and destructive war.

All the above show that your Government has gone from crisis to crisis and as a result has lost credibility amongst the family of nations. The recent cut backs in badly needed international aid clearly show this. Therefore, in the light of the above facts, we question the legitimacy of the present Government to speak for the people of the Sudan and recommend that either the Government should seek peace immediately or Resign!

4.4.6 And to Dear Brothers and Sisters in Christ

Why we write this Letter:
All of you are aware of the sad incidents involving our

Churches and faithful. You have heard of the attacks on the Church in El Nuhud (Kordofan). Similar attacks were launched against the Comboni School in Port Sudan—and again on April 21 in Hara 21 of Thaura in Omdurman Church, a group of Men rushed out of a Mosque after their Friday prayers and launched a vicious attack against the Sisters of Mother Teresa of Calcutta and the patients in their house of care.

The assailants evidently intended to kill the Mother Superior. For they hit her three times on her head with a club. The Sister fell, but managed miraculously to scramble off to safety. She could not receive treatment at Omdurman Hospital because the Doctor on duty wanted her to go into the theater all alone without (in order either to kill or rape her) any accompanying Sister, The Sister refused. So the Doctor dismissed her with a note that she had refused treatment. And on April 23rd, 1989 our prayer center in Kamlin was burned down. Again on April 30, 1989 our center in Gala'a (Thaura Omdurman) was set on fire. Our young men managed to put out the fire, but it was too late, for two of the halls, were burned down completely. This happened in spite of the promise by the Police to guard the Centrej. Strange enough twenty seven young men who put out the fire were arrested, when the police arrived on the scene.

You are aware of the mounting anti-Christian propaganda being launched from a number of mosques. The position of the Government continues to remain ambiguous. While it condemns the excesses being committed, it adds in the same breath that they are a legitimate "exercise of democracy". The two of us have reported all that is happening to the State Minister for Interior and the Governor of National Capital. Both Men assured us that the Government was taking appropriate measures to curb the growing wave of violence and instigation to violence. We hoped that the Government would not wait until more blood is shed. These Bishops went on, on and on explaining event those Christians working with the Islamized governemnt to stand out clearly for Christian rights.

Chapter Five

5.1 South Sudanese Community's Quest for Freedom

I AM HEREBY ENCOURAGED to speak about the quest that moved the hearts of South Sudanese to fight for their respective rights. The factors ushering tragedies which provoked civil wars were many, to be honest. Over many years, Sudanese people were never at peace. Conflicts about cattle robberies, rivalry, grazing land disputes between Cattle keepers nomadic Arabs, and amongst Southerners themselves, were teeming.

The entire problem was that there was no concerned government. The government that was governing the Country was biased to Islamization and Arabization interests. All the assets of the Country were used on consolidating that ideology. Many revolutionary's attempts for changes and peace talk were tried in order to bring about power sharing and economic equality which begun from 1940 up to 1956 which did not work. In addition, another civil war for freedom started again on 16th May in Bor, but the efforts made were not enough untill the agitated youths from different tribes from across the Sudan thronged together.

This freedom struggle stirred up comunities accordingly. Their collective initiative was cohesively fervent, it was for one reason, freedom. War for their defied dignity, had widely inspired them with a determined spirit. "The government of the people by the people and for the people"—that was the theme from Democratic Party of Americans, the same spirit. I do know there are many figures who knew the whole story better than I do. I just wish to touch little events of which I witnessed some, though it is a familiar history to everybody yet not clichéd. In a prerequisite, I am going to pave its correlations by retrieving succinct findings thereafter I get to explain its divine setting.

As I said earlier we passed through hard situations, the year of 1983, was the interval of the heroic revolt of the Southerners against the Khartoum government of Sudan. Freedom is a basic right of humanity; it is an inseparable possession of any people living under heaven that should be respected by all people. I do not know what evil persuades some to go on violating the very basic right of life, liberty and pursuits of peace and happiness of others. Whosoever causes it, or on whatsoever urge they cause it, shall undoubtedly receive penalties from God's hand on such inhumane deeds.

The child SPLA/M was born in that little area called Bor in Jongle. Nursed by Dr. John Garang De Mabior, Kerubino Kuenyin, William Nyoun Bany, from Aweil were Lual Diing and

Kawac Makuei who defected with many young compatriots. The 1983 was the date when the true agitated and stressed men and women 'South Sudanese' who were restless from Arabs' rampant humiliations thronged to Bilpam to get recruited into the movement. The system which is known now to be the third revolution. Its real name was not called 'Anya Nya' but SPLA/M. I called this Movement "God's Evangelized Movement and you will believe me as you will read her "simple and scurry starting actions."

I believe that this revolution was not organized by man but God Himself who inspired all the hearts of His people to begin from zero level. So, the military training center Bilpam's location fell at the Ethiopian's western boarder which was also very far from the provinces such as Aweil, Wau, Warrap, Lakes and Equatorians. Going to Bilpam in those days was not an easy job; countless problems met those comrades on their way to Bilpam such as hunger, thirst and the presence of some aggressive communities such as Nuer and Murlei. But still every person found him/herself compelled to go to Bilpam despite severe encounters. Despite the challenges of those aggressive communities' militias which were terminating the lives of many, bypassing young people on their way to join their colleagues, such that they could come back consolidated to face their enemy. Yet their hearts remained truly unfluctuating to accomplish their mission. Sincerely speaking, our comrades in the SPLA suffered immensely from different mischievous adventures from the Khartoum government, militias and Anya Nya, which were even the second mutineers after the Anya Nya one. Despite some of the SPLA/M's members coming from the same mutineers of both Any Nya II and Any Nya I insurgents, yet there was rigid maladjusted bickering over power, coupled by those hired by Arabs who fought against the movement vehemently for their own ulterior motives.

Rampant interceptions had faced them a lot, and lives were lost on the way from the other persons who refused to join in but invented their own battles. The Arabs supported the hands of those militias with food and ammunition in order to help fight her enemy the SPLA\M. The Khartoum government was helping these crooks in order to weakened the liberationists, for they knew very well that if all the black tribes of Sudan joined hands from the very beginning, that it would quickly result in their downfall. So going to Bilpam was all about enduring no rest, no fear of death—their journey was only aimed "to reach Bilpam" no matter how severe the consequences might be. They were determined to go and fight for their newborn South Sudan.

The movement was not prepared with the required ammunition and also was without proper military training. There were no ample rations for the men who were in frontlines. Sometimes whenever the hungers strike severely, the little maize bags those they would have could be distributed to the men though it could not be adequate go round for all men. A little container was used to constrain the utility of food distribution. Some tried to go hunting but since the bullets were few, there was also a constraint order issued to control the use of the bullets. Everything was almost edible to our comrades those days. They ate anything no matter even if it was raw; they just devoured. When thirst gets worse, they coerced one another's urine to drink! When the number of the recruits grew and there was no food, the late Dr. John gave them such cunning instructions that goes, "if you go to your communities' homes, do not rob them, rather ask them to give you food, but do not let them refuse to give you food".

Those years of 1983 up to 1992 were really perilous to our comrades. Many battalions were inaugurated but many of them died from thirst, hunger and surely through their huge enemy who had military genius. Despite all these challenges men and women mostly from Bhar el Ghazal and from other places within the South, they valiantly kept on going to Bilpam. All the movement's gearing mechanism was not discouraged instead they never minded any fatigue, since there was no any other choice, but to stay in the bush, as geurillas. Everybody was encouraging his or her friends to stay focused and determined to achieve one thing 'liberation of the entire Sudan'. Myriad numbers of people perished in the name of achieving their own realm with equal and maximum rights, with an ample democracy for all the Southerners! This was the vision in every heart of all those comrades who were martyred. Despite that there was no salary; it was not a case for everybody. The poor and weakling movement adopted perseverance, they even encouraged themselves by calling themselves 'geurilla'. They also perished from the enemy's unexpected attacks, as a result of the absence of their own colleagues who rampantly escaped from frontlines or deployment, leaving big gaps to the opportunists. Since the enemy they were fighting was not an easy one, the forces of that enemy could seize myriad numbers of SPLA soldiers and murder them—because the vacuum their colleagues left them in, cost lots of fatalities. Sometimes it would be a negligence from their commanders, who would randomly tarry, persuading the army saying 'wait for my way, it is not time yet to attack' until the army could be seized by their Islamic opportunists who procured a good ground and made them victims.

The soldiers were kept waiting with their hands on their triggers. Those slight redundancies their opportunists got, led to great loss of souls from the sides our dear brothers. It was an arbitrary, negligent death which occurred allowing their tactics several times to be overwhelmed and hijacked by their clever foes. Another arbitrary negligence or mistakethat was made were the assignments given to some commanders in the operations, who would not turn up quickly in giving men the required ammunition or ample equipment of warfare which could result into soldiers running short of bullets and their opportunists beat them.

Another worse habit was that the leadership assigned somebody who had just been captured from the enemy's side. And if the man in their custody happened to be a high-ranking officer, they leadership would just assign him into a high position such as "Training Centre's management or logistics administration." That currently captured enemy officer, would be detected later on that he had secretly smuggled all the system's secrects to his government. The enemy would also execute many new recruits by severe chastising which he could cunningly terminologize as "preparing men for higher capacity". It was a training through which the new recruits had to run the whole day without eating or drinking and when they ceased running, they could drink only a glass of water and boiled maize mixed with sands.

They also suffered from long distant issues, everything was very far and there were not enough lorries or transportation mechanisms. There were no heavy artilleries. Nothing was helping them except God's own care. Despite all those severe challenges I have not mentioned some in order to make it more detailed and deeper, the guerilla's valiant heart stood and remained firm, and never fluctuated nor alarmed. They stood their ground pushing forwards with great impelling zeal, gearing momentum.

5.2 The Spirit of Discipline and Orderliness

However, the movement consisted with radical men like Karbino Kuenyin, William Nyuon as top leaders and others, yet there was a still strong bonding order that was able to subjugate every soldier. Dr John Garang was not an easy human being; he had a stern concentration in whatsoever he wished to do always. He made sure that anything that blocked his way had to be cut down in the smartest ways possible. Though there were hostilities amongst his Commanders, yet his durability maintained the Board to continue on its long-term journey. There were jokeless security soldiers, which executed whatsoever pledge they received from their C-in-C (Commander In-Chief) Dr John Garang.

There was a concerned attitude in the hearts of every one of our comrades in the time of the movement. No one was ready to run after his respective needs or disobey the orders on any selfish motives in fact most of the comrades who died were killed by mistakes. A few were executed for their wrong deeds. Not much sabotage was permitted. Everyone was busy doing his job wholeheartedly without much compromising; for everyone was willing to record patriotic credits to his mission. Women were behind their husbands, no matter what was the situation; they were prepared to die with their husbands in any disaster. Any wrong deed done had got its accountability straight away. If there was no such durable orderliness in the guerilla group, it would have melted into nothing, in its process. Since there were aggressive and warlike tribes like Dinka, Nuer and others; their habits differed one from another. The Dinka had a habit of "decisive ways to ask" not "request", when they wanted something they didn't have. The Nuer tribe did the opposite; they aggressively stole and ran away. Unlike other tribes who say no somehow, seek, perhaps steal or work hard to get what they want. However, all these tribes were staying together in that hard life in camps, yet they were bound by one vision, orderliness and their discipline was unbelievable.

5.3 The Spirit of Diplomacy and Politics

The SPLA/M unlike other rebellions of those in 1940, had outperformed all those I Anya Nya and II Anya Nya. Those two insurgencies did not tackle their foes' tactics. They were defeated by their foes in both militarily and political arenas. The Arabs' idealism had cunningly outsmarted the Southerners' political members even in the parliamentary votes. When the votes were carried out, the Arabs attained 55% seats, and the colonial with 22% seats whilst the independent got 11% but our South Sudanese politicians merely got 9% seats. Thus it was simple for Arabs to outnumber them eventually in the parliament and in the top positions such as the Presidential position, Ministry of Defense, Ministry of Finance and Chairmanship of the House. Another thing that supported the Arabs was their collusion with the white men who seconded that the Arabs were the ones worthy and capable to lead. The white men sensed the vastness of the tribes in the south and that they could easily melt into segregation, and that it was difficult and challenging even for such people had no cohesive ideology to unify them.

But the Arabs were civilized and unified in Islamic Arabizational belief. You can also see when the Southern Sudanese people how they were politically outsmarted rapidly by their foes in all agreements such as those of Addis Ababa in Ethiopia and the one of Abuja in Nigeria. The whole diagnosis was that they were simply pampered with shallow and void words. They were fickle, signing by their foes' subtlest and ablest minded Arabs. Something which the President Numeiri blatantly conceded later on that those agreement documents which they both signed in Addis Ababa were not " Quran or Bible to be hallowed". He declared that he was just joking with his frail tribes of the southern Sudan.

For it is impossible for a Muslim to be led by the black Christians whom the Muslims termed as infidels. I happened to visit Juba University on 24th August 2010 when I found the Chief of Staff James Hoth who was invited by the University of Juba to come and present something about his book which he authored (I did not read the book). The book is all about the SPLA/M's movement. He stated in it how the SPLA/M traveled through the roads of hardship.

After he finished the lecture some events about the movement's fortunes and hazardous circumstances were discussed. I happened to ask him whether the movement was purely led militarily without any political wing. Hoth replied, "it was led in both militarily including political wing, but what happened was that those political leaders fought over power because each one of them was claiming he had a PhD, thus they split based on their vocational quest. Dr John Garang guaranteed the SPLA inclusive of SPLM's wings as a result. He (Garang Mabior) became both the Chairman and the Commander in-Chief, he used to maintain those positions to date".

I personally believed that everybody knows Dr John Garang's thinking and his outstanding intellect in politics. He perfectly explained to all the men and women the true core problem with its Islamic idealism. You can't outsmart Garang in term of politics with the vast vision that he had. He managed through God's cradling I believe, to sharpen everybody's intellect with the spirit of patriotism. Everybody had become aware of the real, basic problem. Diplomacy introduced, they went from nation to nation adjuring and persuading people to help provide them with either food rations or ammunitions for their military's welfare. They went explaining to the world the story of how these people (Arabs traders) came in and hijacked their land and they started exerting the entire black Southerners into Islam—adding that they neglected everybody from rightful rights those were supposed to be shared. Their opponents tried to oppose and denied that by sending letters against SPLA/M system to those Countries to convince them in order not to have any relationship with this insurgent.

The Khartoum government termed the SPLA\M as, "rebels with no tangible reason against their fair government". But the SPLA/M wiped out all those vehement propagandas and kept sending out men after them, spreading their propaganda of the subtlest lie of their deceit through which they smeared the "used bait" of cunning terminology. They had a void proverb that says, "we Arabs and black Southerners can share one piece of a nut", which was not realistically meant from the heart. The SPLA/M pressed her political way in methodical shrewdness, so they penetrated even against a hard wall of opposition.

Their vision was clear and understandable to the entire world even to the lay peasants. Their one problem was that Dr. John Garang. had a communist background, and most of the Countries who do not like communism could not made it to co-operate with them fully. The only nations which co-operated with SPLA/M were communist Countries such as China, Cuba, Ethiopia and some who sympathized with their weakling situation were persuaded without being given conditions. The movement struggled with so many things even for their unity; because for them to remain united was not something easy. Thus for them to succeed they had to be patient with any situation encouraging one another that though some sceptics were impatient, which led them to go back to the Khartoum government.

5.4 The Spirit of Negligence & Occults

Despite that zeal, political intelligence and durable determination, yet there was still a great negligence amongst the leaders towards their men. After every successful raiding or conquest, the commanders would adamantly demand the entire loot to be fully rendered to them. The leaders' tendency of self-centeredness was so high that they dared not appreciate their men who fought for something. The spoils or loot sometimes might be sugar, flour, instruments, money, goats, cows or anything of any kind. What these high ranking leaders would do, was to order the soldiers to show the items seen in their hands. Men were ordered to let go of it completely, but if the soldier wouldn't, he or she could be jeopardized to a humiliating arrest in the thorny fence for months. The victimized soldier would be minimized through the painful punishment, such that he must optimistically let go of the materials unwillingly, sighing from stress of negligence he felt inside his heart.

The late Dr Bol Akok advised in those same days that the Military part must be detached from Civil Affairs of the

Movement as soon as the SPLA/M was under its new preparation. Sadly,he was misunderstood and was assassinated as a result, but after a long time, his sage advice was understood that it
was right, after it was too late to honour it. My uncle Hon. Lual
Diing Wol said this humorously, in one of our conversations he
said, "when we understood that the SPLA leadership did not
perceive what Dr Akok said, they told him to leave and stay away
from SPLA's leading authority—and that they were doing that
to prevent him from being killed" Lual Diing avowedly admitted.
But Dr Bol Akok refused to stay away from the SPLA/M con-
ventions. Eventually he died because "of cancer" that was how
his death was described by Dr John Garang. He (Lual Diing) said
that it did not take them long to see the very thing which Dr Bol
Akok said became true.

Every commander accumulated for himself his own military
defense and it seemed that almost every leader was halfway hostile to Dr Garang Mabior—excerpt Kiir Mayar who did never
attempt to oppose his chairman Garang Maboir. Some from the
SPLA men and women fought patriotically with the expectation
that after, he or she could obtain promotion for his or her optimistically demonstrated commitment, but instead for the then
commanders to appreciate them, every Comander turned to his
siblings and in-laws by promoting them. Instead the commanders gave credits to those soliders who exerted their efforts, but
not for their respective kins, which is the true militarily action.
Sadly the commanders deliberately turned things all around and
selfishly considered promotions on tribal lines. They didn't easily

dare to show gratitude to the ones who deserved it.In fact, the promotions were solely rendered to the persons who would "do to them what they liked". They spent their energy helping partiality to their 'sister's sons, uncles, sons, plus in-laws i.e. they were the ones favored easily to attain promotions. They did not understand that it was same dilemma which eventually provoked them to rebel against the Khartoum government.

To came back to occultisms, in the movement of SPLA/M comrades, the occultic powers were used almost by everyone except a few. Myriad numbers of Army officers and privates, thronged to charm givers, wizards, spear masters and fortune-tellers those who were "well-spoken of" or "powerful magicians" as they were describing them. Everybody was looking for the 'best and powerful one whose powers were not yet known or could not be rivalled by any other powers. Such he could be the 'only one' with that unique power which can't be thwarted. All these were believed for protection as bulletproofed against the shootings. Their lives would frequently be in perilous conditions with their never ceasing foes. They preferred that it was vital for everybody to attain thorough protection, which would surely thwart every bullets' hurting such that one could still get back to the camp unscathed.

Without any other choice, the poor comrades ignorantly thronged into acquiring occult powers such as charms. For sure, every satanic or let me say occult protection entailed some observations and conditions, and requirements to be fulfilled and held dearly. Therefore, they were instructed by their charms' fortune-tellers, spears masters and other occults power givers—to give votives in forms of blood (goats, sheep, and bulls) and also offer them faith and trust! You could detect each and every one of them having been instructed vehemently by those magicians to observe his occult power in differently varying votives.

Therefore they gave countless votives to their fake protections in occult beliefs. And to make worse, in 1994 one of the prestigious and seductive magicians allegedly told the system that if he would be paid handsomely. He could ritually bury a dog alive, so that nothing would befallen the movement again. He continued saying, "such things like 'split or losing the warfare will never be heard once more in this system. Power for winning battles and getting wealth will be yours for the taking". And when he was believed and had the dog buried alive, thus the movement clumsily was almost to be dashed. But when the leaders sensed that the movement was splitting, they vehemently required the prayers from priests for its sustainibility and stability. Thus God's cradling power was somehow again seen fixing the movement back on its stride for one reason or another.

But still they could not adherently align to their vows those they made to the Jehovah God. Whenever the situations of the movement deteriorate, they often called for the Christian missionaries' helps, but once they could gain respite exhilarations, they quickly reverted to their occultism. Food items were brought or let me say donated by churches from Italy, America, England, Canada, UK, Norway through different humanitarian organizations. After the movement had received these rations from the Christians' churches, still they reverted back to their occult rituals. Sometimes the leaders would flippantly organize to appreciate the priests or let me say Christian's organizations for their kind humanitarian supports, and after they finished appreciating, they went right back to their occult beliefs.

Everybody was proud because they vehemently got a hint that his or her charm worked miracles. Everyone became aggressive and unruly because they have grasped and believed arrogantly that they were immune against any bullets' shooting. Their minds were obsessed with aimless pride and unbecoming misbehaviour slithered in seriously, such that mischievous murdering was rampantly occurring since those unruly ones did not dread the severe death of a firing squad! According to God's punishments because of such practices; he calls such things 'provocations' against him. angering him by their occult rites through those repetitive occult practices.

I believe those occult practices were one of the factors which had delayed the movement's instant progresses strides of success. If not, such millions of numbers of innocent souls would not all had died in order for us to attain freedom. But I believe God would have quickly intervened. What our people do not understand was that the most hated thing the Lord God does not compromise with is occult practices or let me say rituals, because by practicing them you ignore the saving POWER of God and refuse to acknowledge God the creator himself.

5.5 The Spirits of Roughness & Tribalism

Despite all the zeal and determination, still there used to be an existence of great roughness amidst those comrades towards one another. SPLA Forces, even in those days, for them to exist, used to rob foods brought to the malnourished children. The foods brought were in form of biscuits, flour. Nevertheless, SPLA troops, apart from grabbing and taking away Unimix and Unicef supports donations, their undisciplined characters included, looting to their own towns, raping their own girls and humiliating their young and old men. And every commander became a warlord with his own force. The aimless roughness was fueled by the spirit of tribalism. Boosted also by ego-centeredness in some commanders who embraced only their own kinsmen as their bodyguards.

Most of the SPLA Army were from major tribes like Dinka and Nuer, these thus were the ones who held big positions and influenced the movement, especially in promotions. Dr Riek departed from Ethiopia, the SPLA/M military site, and captured Ler, his home village. Slowly, he grew in antagonism against Garang whom he condemned saying, "Garang is steering the movement as if it is his own property". Culturally, both Dinka and Nuer practice different traditional religions with famous spiritual leaders who are well known among their communities. They are called spear-masters. Moreover, that in 1989-1991 when the Nuer men who were under Dr Riek Machar saw that their leaders were led by a spiritual leader whose name was

Wut Nyang. They considered that the prediction of Ngu–Deng (Nuer's grand Spear Master) almost getting to be fulfilled. The yound spiritual leader Wunt Nyang promised the Nuer community they were going to win their battle beweent them and coward Dinka people.

That new spiritual leader Wut Nyang prophesied that gods had given Dinka into their power to revenge their killed brothers Nuer. He vehemently proclaimed that those who will join this fight will return even if they are killed in battle. And he led young boys known as the White Army—who were eventually killed in great toll. That was first serious clash between Nuer-Dinka war which wrought great hatred between this two tribes up to date. This tribalism encited every tribe to align to the irrespective relatives, the consequences were sequenced by repetitive roughness. For when the spirit of tribalism mingled, the roughness grew. They seriously begun to devour the same Southerners. Once the soldiers would come from hot frontlines, whether they might happen to be escaping from over-staying in frontlines they got exhausted, homesick and impelled to visit their people. They started escaping back from the places where they were deployed. But they were never compromised on such mistakes by the system. To make it worse, once they would be encountered by any aggressive commanders on their way that they could be probed with searing questions and if any misdemeanors would be found, then they were mercilessly sentenced to a firing squad, no matter even if their number could amount to thirty or fifty, they were cut down in persecution.

The system suffered from such segregated minds - Commanders who had been mutinously aggressive and trigger-happy. The system also adopted the manifesto to govern the movement such that at least the system would admirably earn prestige or credit to satisfy the supposed international standard. But that Manifesto's lure massacred myriads of men in the hands of those who had gotten first the law's demand when it was executed. The manifesto stated that everybody should be under its mandate and no one could be above its power. In the first time when the manifesto was invented and legalized, everybody was mesmerized with its immaculate facts as they flippantly celebrated it, what it will give each person. Because they saw to it that there was something amiss, which they thought could only be the absence of 'a constitution to stop sabotages, decrease hostility, governs and orders everything rightly'.

Thus the manifesto gave powers even to sergeants and lieutenants to have legal mandate of executing sentences of the firing squads against their high officials, or anyone who were found guilty of any misdemeanors or happened to have escaped from the war, or maybe have stolen any property or committed sexual adultery with someone else' wife. Ravishing women become another great dilemma because most of the men did not come with their wives from their respective areas thus they had nowhere to get women to go to for sexual pleasures. That alone led to repetitive public death of firing squads because the manifesto legalized that so. The manifesto stated that if you commit any treason against the system such as speaking ill of it, you shall die.

Any sort of stealing of property, no matter even if it could be a tiny material i.e. an egg, a bag of wheat, you would die through the manifesto's power.

High ranking officials took this manifesto to their right hands with their misguided attitudes fueled by the lure of tribalism. They started pressing their command on triggers and executed thousands of their own comrade men. Critical to say that somebody knowing that he was the one who invented the manifesto with his friends, Martin Majiir with his other two colleagues perished from devouring the edge of the sharp manifesto of SPLA\M too. Because he was found guilty also of stealing the government's property, and was a suspect for speaking ill of the system. He stated that the system's leaders were not civilized and frankly disqualified them. So, tribalism empowered much meaningless roughnesses, which was one of the factors which delayed the movement's steps into quicker success than could be attained easily. They died in the meantime whereby even a death of one soldier was not necessarily vital. Due to their grasping self-centeredness, admiring and preferring oneself, vehemently wishing others to faithfully show respect to YOU. Those obessesd by "to me" were imperviously demanding everything and everybody to admire them. That was what fueled assassinations of your own stalwarts.

Tribal aspiration was very strong to begin with. Tribalism! Tribalism! Tribalism is what will afflict our success in our Country, even if we would attain our autonomous freedom! We all are black Southerners with the same color! Therefore I urge you brothers, sisters, fathers and mothers do not use some national identification, for it is like that of yours. I beseech all the Southerners in all the length and width of our land, with all your multicultural, multilinguals. All of you my people of whose dignity I am exceedingly proud, come down from tribal attitudes and be mingled with pure hearts of love towards one another in complete and cohesive union. Prevent your hearts from rigidness and selfish emotions towards your own God given clans, tribes and respective cultures. Be warned! Such a vast nation lived by these various clans cannot be run by tribalized vocational attitudes. Please allow God's word to wipe off such wrong hints and let's work toward developing our residences. Because if we allow our steering mechanism to be engulfed based on tribal attitudes, we will easily and awkwardly perish.

Tribalism has an inborn reeking putrid smell which incites people to speak ill of others whom the Creator loves madly. The Jehovah God said, "I created him or her after my Own Identity, likening unto my own image". Therefore any insults directed to any of the human creatures are not directed to that flesh, rather against God Himself. He is the author of all Creation. Someone said that tribalism is born within the blood of all human races, and that it cannot be easily erased, But for me I defy that. It can easily be conquered with sound mind, pure hearts and awareness that everybody else beside you is also important. The law of nature says so! Therefore when we wish to conquer tribalism, we must obligate ourselves to be active in nourishing perfect love toward all our homogeneous tribes. We should socially accept ourselves and psychologically be proud of this heterogenerosity deliberately. We should not nonchalantly sing unity while we exert no effort to support harmony even with a fingertip.

5.6 The Spirit of Enthusiasm & Patriotism

Despite all those challenges of meddlesome emotions, still fervent "brotherhood" towards one another existed amongst the comrades. They sent gifts to one another in forms of small items such as uniforms, shoes, casual clothes even small thing like caps! When they missed one another they could begin to write heartfelt letters to one another containing compliment greetings of "how are you over there?" They go visiting one another even though there were no good places. Their people were in the bushes and caves. Yet they toured their friends in their deployments. They shared little food and slept in a narrow plastic sheet upon rough places or muddy areas. They encouraged one another and comforted themselves to maintain that heart of love. Some even went far as promising themselves to stick to one another saying that they will never abandon their friendship. Some even when they heard that their colleagues felt into fiercest attacks, snuck there without orders issued by their commanders.

They go there and fought in rows together with their colleagues until they both died altogether. They were ready to die for one another's cause because of the fervent and strong chains of love toward one another. They sincerely adopted and demonstrated clear and distinctive sense of patriotic hearts of love to

the liberation movement. They could sing songs those that rein-
force and encourage their hearts to keep them standing valiantly, focused on the progress of the movement. They demonstrated
real feats and uncompromised standards. They carried out fiercest assaults against their foes with battalions whose hearts were
unflinching from a death fate. They just gnashed their teeth in
thorough boldness and rigor as their fingers-tips fell on triggers!

They began roaring with a true spirit of patriotism, asking
their leaders in composed songs for permission, in order to let
them go back for more assaults against their Islamic government
who alleged that the land belong to them. They began to adjure
one another in songs that they had to remain fearless and determined. Even if it was women, still they were ready to die! To
them death was not something to be feared or to be ran away
from, but they just welcomed death as simply as sitting in the
comfortable cold shadow of a huge tree! Their songs were from
patriotic hearts with a unique strength précising the liberation
of the entire Sudan. They challenged death and the entire Sudan
with threats of imperiling them all. And anyone found missing,
people didn't panic, but continued with the struggle. This remind me of France's great Military commander who said, *"soldiers don't die but they disappear"*. The used to state assuredly that
they were immune even to any fears of death since it was their
own land—because they said, 'the land knows her own', by this
they were meaning that the god of land will help them!

5.7 The Spirit of Illiteracy & Arbitrary Mutinies

To begin with, actually, the majority of the Southerners prevented their kids from going to schools in those days—so all those children in the colonial era were educated, deprived for generations. The children were held at the cattle camps in order to "look after cows" was the great job that boys must do. Moreover, girls also were only expected to remain at home, so that when they grow, they could bring more cows when they are married. Thus the children grew up unlearned and illiterate.

It was something that could not be denied at all. So it affected everything badly. There were no schools also by then—only catholic missions schools were there because the Khartoum government declined to academically develop the Southeners by opening schools for their chlidren to learn. In those days when the people were leaving to Bilpam, most people who left for recruitment in the army were not learned which meant 90% were illiterate. They were people driven only by agitations, who wasted no time to go first to schools for studies. The intellectual recruits were few but the majority were illiterate. So to them, being educated was meaningless and of no value, such that you could hear in their songs when addressing students, "our students, let's cease from so-called pen writing, but let's do it through gun fire" that was the only thing the majority knew.

Dr. John Garang kept narrating to them the importance of education—making examples through humorous words and even sending Red Army (young ones who went to Bilpam also)

194

to schools in the nearby Countries. Still nobody was easily convinced and some from the Red Army even escaped back to the frontlines! You can see from the time when they went and got recruited, in the first place, amongst these men and women were people who came as results of agitated hearts from their nearby tribes who were raiding their cattle. I came to know, that while we, especially black peolpe were still asleep, and lingering in illiteracy, the western world had already in their civilzation, jumped to its climax. For instance, the weapons, artileries, tankers, gunchiefs, pistols and many others guns we are using now.

According to Collier Encyclopedia (Volume S.) Biologists, for instance, in Europe, had invented many medicines for curing different diseases—example is Thomas Sydenham, (1620-1680) had already found quinine for fever and even explained gout—scarlet fever and influenza. Unlike other doctors, Thomas believed that medicine could only be learned at the bedside of patients—French scientist Michel Eugene Chevreul in 1800, discovered lye in another word. It is a detergent substance that could easily remove dirt, now days we called it soap. Alexander Fleming in 1940, he was the first to discover an antibiotic called Penicillin and Sulfa is attributed also to him. Jonas Salk in 1950 also, had discovered a polio vaccine and the strike of paralysis rate were minimized. Edward Jenner in 1795, discovered vaccine to be used against smallpox and things became more scientifically clearer when Louis Pasteur and Robert Koch discovered that germs could cause many diseases and infections and can perpetuate illness. Isaac Singer on the other hand, in 1851, had invented the sewing machine, thanks to Singer, now we could sew our clothes easily.

According to Collier Encyclopedia, William John Shakespeare, whose life ended in 1616, has his works remaining alive flowing to every generation, and had flooded the entire continent of Europe with his great dramatic gifts, through his writings, poems, and dramas. He wrought in Europe not only entertainments, but literature, peace and a noble legacy and the western world didn't remain the same. Wisdom had given birth earlier also even in Greece (469-399 BC) in fact, there were unrivaled writers and poets whose names are unforgettable in Greece up to now. For instance, Socrates, the Greek wise man who insisted on "know yourself, and stand truer for Truth's sake" was his greatest value. Then Oedipus, a great Greek writer, he could interpret riddles and expose knowledge, his wisdom was great and amazing. Then Sophocles, the Greek wise man who explained that man is naturally born with the ability to do great things especially when he lives in a way he is supposed to—then Aeschylus, the Greek wise man who described the divine punishment that can follow those who do evil things and deprive mankind of peace. Then Euripides was another great Greek Philosopher who wrote about different tragedies in great wisdom. He described tragedies in ways that could bring tears. The men I mentioned above were the wisest men in Greece, Aristotle, Plato and others were just their students.

To briefly explain the reasons of our problem on education and civilization. Some people were forced into the army; some got exhausted from day to day hiding in the bushes because they don't have guns to defend themselves. So, it seemed also that some came for different ulterior motives of attaining guns and defending themselves, retaliated against their enemies and achieve their quests. So the system teamed up with men and women who thronged into the system unprepared intellectually in a needy civilization. Those who were exiled to Australia, America, Egypt, Kenya, England, managed to attain their scholarship, but they did not assault the foe. So, the sole method Dr. John Garang De Mabior was able to prepare and downloaded into the SPLA/M idealism was through long meetings.

He used simple language, demonstrating it through visuals to explain them, since the presence of every tongue, culture and tribe hindered the talk. But though they were alerted properly by Dr John and by other thoughtful and visionary leaders also of 'why's, 'how's and 'what'. Yet there existed arbitrary mutinous deeds happening everywhere. Those random attacks were almost to call off our rightful and meaningful movement, which was initiated in a timely way. Some tribal-minded SPLA top brass began to persuade their men to do mutinous deeds for their self-vocations which led to myriads of souls dead. These deeds were geared by the love for power since everyone desired the Chairman's seat though without the required capacity, such as education, courage, vision given into the mind by God's and international interactions yet some were mad after their quest for power.

Overthrowing is not something that could be done while

the system would still be in a weak level and in the bush, but power hungry groups craved Power, saying no, "I wanted to be Bany right now" I thank God also for though He was silent, He was still present to intervene in so many issues relating to the Movement and though our beloved comrades did not perceive the Almighty God's avenues. You my people are called to understand the 'why', 'when', 'which' and 'what' caused all this.

5.8 The Spirit of Communism & Philosophy

Yes, the spirit of communism existed and has thoroughly engulfed the system. Communism, which started earlier years before Karl Marx and Vladimir Lenin, which aimed at leveling humanity in all life spheres. And wished to divide everything justly amongst people without any capitalization, was the zeal consuming our comrades. According to the political scientists they called it "enacted democracy". The uniqueness of communist ideology is a classless state where national assets are not privatized rather, they are shared equally. While we were still in the cage of deprivation and ignorance, the western world had already awakened spiritually, politically and biologically. According to the western scientists from different entities, civilization was wrought through various concepts: Biologically, academically, economically, spiritually and politically, and in my own view, to mentioned a few things on the political sphere.

Liberalism and socialism had paved the way for the western world to move with development. Some other writers limit

Socialism (democracy of communism) saying that it was started by Karl Marx and Vladimir Lenin. Socialism had already existed earlier in Britain and France in the late 1827 as an ideal,
by Francis Marie, Charles Fourier, Comt de Saint-Simon and
Owen Louis Blanc in (1811-1882) worked to have French adopt
many socialist principles during the late 1840s.

According to Collier encyclopedia -The Socialist Party has
advanced many proposals for political reforms. Most of these
were designed to make the national government more flexible and more responsive to the will of the people. it states that
Socialist platforms have commonly included: (a) the socializa-
tion and democratic control of the national resources, money,
banking and credit and monopolies and semi-monopolies (b)
better protection for workers and their families, such like higher wages and shorter hours of work, health and accidents insur-
ance and old-age and mothers' pensions (c) the extensive spread
of free education and (d) various political changes including the
direct election of the President and Vice President, plus some
devices by which, in case of deadlock between congress and the
President, an appeal can be taken to the voters.

To come back, socialism or communist fraction is an ideology
which the capitalists thoroughly hate but in fact, it had enlight-
ened both Europe and Africa so much. Most of the nations who
had already adopted this ideology are Russian Vladimir Lenin,
Republic of the People of China, North Korea and South Korea,
Soviet Union, Germany and other half part of Europe, Ethiopia,
Libya and many others. In fact, most of the leaders who liberated

African Nations were Communists Candidates like Mwalimo Julius Nyerere of Tanganyika the current Tanzania, Gomo Kenyatta of Republic of Kenya, Fidel Castro of Cuba, Gadhafi of Libya,Ali Selassie Mariam of Ethiopia which did not go colonialism. But Jonas Savimbi of Angola, Mahatma Gandhi of India, Ghana and many others including Nelson Mandela of South Africa all faced wars to attain freedom.

Their aims were to liberate their people from colonialists' regimes and provide their people with very good governments. The philosophy of Communism was that we should not first ask for God to move things, but that we must handle our own human affairs or belongings. A negative part of Communism is profanity. Communists hate any initiatives of religions, no matter how much you can titivate it with accurate proof, this ideology will never believe your proofs. No matter how much you could debate with communist minded, you will still end up later disturbed. Of course the communist candidates will never agree with you to admit the theology of God behind everything. Many Missionaries suffered badly when they were taking the Gospel of Christ to these Communist Countries. Notwithstanding, this ideology,its driving force from the back of the liberation of entire lands of Sudan—meaning in its philosophy that no religion is important because faith has no relation with hegemony, it belongs respectively to human's free will, yes, not religion or God.

They do not know that the Almighty God is behind everything which He has created with absolute autocratic dominion overall. So when you say the whole thing is all about man, God would absolutely be at the ignored and neglected side. To make it even worse, some from commanding top brass did not even want the Christians' songs to be sung in the frontlines where fierce attacks were rampantly occurring. They said these Christians songs do not encourage the hearts rather they melt. They believed that it was not good. I believe it was also one of the factors that provoked God to prolonged the system's pace for quicker pentration and proved the prophsy of Isaiah the Prophet (Isaiah18) about these people. God turned those unbeliever's profaneity into more prolonged years of agony and failures. The more they hardened their hearts in idolatry; God resolved it into fulfilling His ordained prophecies against profane punishment.

Until 1994 the Movement began to listen to Missionaries who came and persistently preached the Gospel of Christ. Asking to trust not themeslves rather ask God for help. There began the people to move away from communism, ceasing from its lure and the quest thereby. Thus God started by giving them favors in the eyes of many Supreme nations. It went for them by winning the hearts of the Congress, the United Nations including the enemy of the United Soviet, the Americans. Their appeal for support was then accommodated because Dr John Garang was now aligned by Kofi Henan of Ghana who became optimally vital. He told Father Dr. John to let go of his communistic ideology and change all his profiles. Moreover, Mr. Henan did not stop there alone but he introduced our father to all UN organizations appealing to them for support. Finally, I am ending that all the above mentioned behavourial spirit, could be seen as something of a greater value. But in the next topic, you will see how the same people got their independence and what will be happening eventually. We will see in this next topic, the anticipated future worries which eventually occurred. The need for change and continuty, without which if it is not responsively adherent to cohesiveness, then the entire Nation will suffer ugly social and economic corruptions!

Chapter Six

6.1 Return Homeland and This Land Belongs to Me!

After we stayed for a very long time and we became mature enough then, Mum realized that it was time to take us back to our Dad who had been in the rebels' Army SPL/M. My father's life was spent in revolutions. My elderly brother Madut was likewise. Day after another they were sending us messengers with the messages in order for us to return home. When we quit, I was not willing to go back home with my people since I loved staying in Khartoum. But my Dad was badly troubled intensely all days and nights long—he was blaming himself. He was stating in his messages those he sent us that let none of his sons remain to come. My elder brother who was in the Red Army beside was persuading us that his young brothers and sister be brought as soon as possible. So we went back to our home land. And in 1996, the year that I will never forget, because by that time we came from Khartoum to Meram: We arrived in Meram in March of that same year.

When we arrived there, some of our relatives told my Mum that she should not take us to the South because the starvation was striking severely therein. So mum therefore decided to make us stay in Meram for that whole year. We accepted our mother's decision and we inquired from those Muonyjieng how to find work and they told us that the only work in Meram was cultivation. We accepted. We worked in the garden of a certain baggara-man (nick-name for cattle keeper) in his very large field. To make my point brief and précise, we were told that Meram had a drought also which annually began from September up to the month of June every year. All the people who wanted to survive must dig their wells earlier before those thirst months come. We dug four drinking wells for ourselves.

And one day, my elder sister with some of the women whose husbands were also working for Arabs went fetching water in the very earlier hour at 9:00 PM; so that they could come back in the morning early. Unfortunately they spent the whole night there; in fact, they stayed there until the late hours of the day. We all got disappointed and the husbands of those women started going to see what might have overtaken the ladies at the wells which caused such delay for a long time. But later on every one of them came back walking slowly, frustrated and discouraged. I questioned what has happened that would make them discouraged and frustrated without the ladies nor the water? One from those relatives answered saying, "They are delayed by a certain

baggara man". He continued, "the man wanted to get his camels drink first and fill his jar cans before those women", he said.
Being agitated and choked by the answer, I sneaked away slowly
pretending to be normal and not annoyed and frustrated or discouraged as they were.

The distance of that area was one and half hours walk, but I
crossed the place within thirty five minutes' time. As I arrived
at the wells' I observed everywhere with stern eyes around all
the wells' area. I looked inside the wells and I saw them full of
water but the ladies were made to stay far away by that man. I
looked here and there but there was nobody nearby to inquire
from about the man who made my women delayed. With a loud
voice I called those ladies to come to where I was standing by
the well side. But they refused to come and gestured to me from
afar telling me in cowardice that there is disaster there. I snapped
at them toning my words with authority, since I was a boy, they
feared a bit because women have to submit. So they came with
their jar cans. I commanded them to fetch water into their jar
cans since the wells were their own not of somebody else. But
they refused and said, "that young man was about to kill us last
night, if not so, we would have filled our jar cans right at the day
break". My heart got kindled radically with fierceness! The ladies' answers agitated me seriously till I could see as if trees were
running about me! I became drunk with anger; I tried to cool
myself down again and told them to begin fetching their wells'
water without fearing. Never mind the threats of that baggara
man. So they began to fetch the water looking here and there

fearing still of what would happen if that fierce man comes and retaliate by killing us all as they were filling their jar cans.

Instantly I saw one of the youngest girl suddenly throwing her jar can away and screamed, "he is coming" and all the ladies got to their feet fearfully and begun to pull themselves away from the wells. I roared and snapped them, 'why are you stopping and beginning to walk away?'. And one of the ladies answered saying, 'that baggara man is coming to us over there'. I adamantly scolded them and said, 'did I not tell you never mind his threats? You should keep yourselves busy fetching your water''. And as they began taking their well water again, the young and vigorous man came carrying his gun on the back but holding a spear and big stick in his hands shouting furiously. He angrily and arrogantly begun to snap at the women, "Stop! Stop! Who told you to draw the water from wells which I warned you not to do last night?''.

But before he could add another sentence I retorted to him valiantly with a firing voice saying, "who are you to stop my women from fetching their own well water?''. He responded back, "these are not yours, but they are mine!" My heart teeming with flames of anger, I vehemently harangued him with true death threats stating that he should stop pointing at either the wells or my women, else I will kill you! All the crowd from Dinka people at the wells stood together on their feet, alarmed of the consequences. Then they began to escape away, men first and followed by women. They thought we will all be executed. My heart was fearless and was not even moved by fatal deaths that would follow. The man resorted to solve the issue in benevolence and he began to tell me that he would forgive me if I can only stop my insulting language and get away from the wells. He vehemently began to give me threatening advice saying,"this is our land" and he could kill me simply and no one would stop him from doing so.

But I severely snapped at him saying,"go away from my rightful wells!" I harangued him saying that we were the ones who dug these wells and they belonged to us. Despite that I had no deadly weapon, but one small spear with arm knife in its sheath, but I stood against him adamantly. So he changed his mind, and he begun to dawdle backwards insulting me abusively,"dirty black boy!" he continued,"aren't you and your people our slaves? And all this land belonged to us? And we the Arabs are the black tribes' masters, and this land belonged to us the Baggara. And that we the black were born without land". But I valiantly responded back disgruntled in a hissing motion saying, 'I am from a Royal Family, I am the Amir of the land your feet are standing upon, for all this land belonged to Me, all! I promise you stranger,"you will see with your own eyes one day what am telling you today! You won't arrogantly bewilder me any longer due to my docile attitude—mark me well, I am well familiar with all your ruses!" Then with repetitive insults, we both ended our argument as he was leaving our place. The Arabs on the other hand, were marveled at such unequaled courage, asking themselves as from which side did such radical and hot-tempered young man from Dinka, who feared nobody emerge? In addition, fear swept into their hearts, such that when they saw their young man gave in, that they didn't wish to encourage him to fight but they saw it as wise to do it that way. There was a great tension as we ceased. Nobody dared to add a single word to our argument. We returned back to the camp and my Mom was reportedly told about what took place at the well. She swore that she must beat me. But good enough some women who were from the Dinka women told her, "our sister, what your son did today was unbelievably shocking but to us in our opinion, he has really lifted our faces up in front of Arabs. They had realized now that the wormbs of Dinka women could also bear such a typical barbarian ". And while others were still condemning it calling it a blind act without proper thinking, my Mom was alrady won over by those statements the women had already made, and she did not scold but warned me to do it no more and silently prepared us for leaving for the South.

6.2 Meeting our Elder Brother Madut

Then on the 8th March 1997, we made our way home. As we were returning from the North we had to use a time of eight hours walk from Meiram to the South towards the locality of Malith village. To precisely put the point, we were going to meet with our elder brother Madut Baak Malong whom we had never met for twelve years. After we reached Malith in the evening, we were told that our elder Brother Madut had left to another small village which was forty minute walk. So we slept that night in the Malith market with a few police men, but our eyes remained blinking the whole night wishing the day break such we could see our elder Bro. And in the morning early Mom asked her daughter Nyigut who had been two years earlier to home before us, and she had come to welcome us with the Madut, saying where is your brother Madut? Whereas her elder son Madut had now came already.

Then teasingly both my sister and Tong Ngong (uncle's son) told her that she should ask this young man who was sitting right by her side whether he knows something about her son Madut or not. Mom turned to the young man who sat beside her moment ago and asked, "Please, have you seen my son Madut, I have been waiting for him since morning, I was told that he will come to see me earlier?" And when that young man tried to answer his Mom jokingly as his sister did, he found tears rolling down on his cheek! My Mom asked him with twinkles on her face as what would be wrong with the lad that he cried, but before she could finish that sentence she recognized that it was her son, Madut! "You had grown enough into a mature man! She screamed out "Wow! Wow! This is you my kid? You have grown. You have grown. I did not realize that it is you my kid!" She melted upon her long missed son with tears. But with us, it was little bit different, we greeted him yet not with much heartfelt hugging because we needed to spend sometime, since we became mature enough also without being together. None of us recognized each other until after some couple of hours as we went into deeper conversation; he began to narrate to us some of the things we could still remember, and then beyond doubt, we came to our sense that he was Madut, our elder brother. We looked at one another with curiosity, each one of us wished to know something about where the other came from.

Our brother Madut was interested in the things of the Northern Sudan while we also want to know about his. We were keenly requesting him to tell us about the SPLA/M and how they are progressing in the South. He could arrogantly answer but with few words while he was keenly asking about Arabs of Khartoum wishing to hear the goodness of Khartoum Town. His face shone whenever we began to talk to him about the Northern Sudan's betterment. But he could abruptly retort us with a tone of "though Khartoum is better than our forest, still Khartoum is for Arabs and Arabs are our enemies. We should not yoke up with our enemies, for an enemy can kill you intentionally any time". Thereafter in the same day of our stay, we proceeded to our village Cibiliek. While we were walking for couple of hours, each one of us was tired and we were divided two by two. My uncle's son Tong Ngong used to call him 'Cornelius' (a name of certain Christian Soldier in a rank of Captain who was converted into the Apostles' teachings) a name that I perpetually disliked to mention with my mouth because I hate Christians' names. I was walking ahead with my uncle's son Tong Ngong as we suddenly heard a cascade of rebuking and warnings of "don`t move! Don`t move!" from certain men who were armed. My brother Madut was left behind at not very far distance. At first, I did not know who were these men in worn black clothes with guns. The men ordered us that we should put down the bags and step aside. Tong murmured to me that I should stop because these are SPLA Soldiers—but I asked with aggression, "then why should we stop if they are our Army?" At first I did not know that this so-called SPLA army do also rob the civilians, those coming from the North. I was still walking as I was talking back to my uncle's son Dominic Tong telling him that he should not dare to stop but should keep walking.

But as the two men arrived they were seriously still scolding and rebuking us for not stopping, calling me Jihadist, saying that I know where I left my colleague the mujahidiin. Instantly I could not control my temper as normally was my habit and I roared at them with a hissing voice! They were surprised by what could this barehanded little boy have to do in order to help him out of their jokeless clutch. And we were responding to each other with repetitive questions by questions, my elder brother arrived with my mother. Madut retortingly asked them what the problem could be, but they replied, "We asked this jihadist to stop but instead he insulted us that we are fools and naked soldiers who do not know their mission. He stated that we are only but gangs of robbers ".

My mum knowing her son's taunting aggression, quickly tried to help alleviate the issue in benevolence, but Madut stopped her. As one of them was still threating us, Madut retorted him teasingly and said, "I did not see anything provoking to anger in the lad's reply to your questions, seeing that what he said was suiting your conduct". He continued, "besides he is not a jihadist as you used to ill call him; he is just a little boy from here." Agitatedly, one of them said, "Are you also mocking us?" But Madut asked them, "From which brigade do you belong?" But the aggressive one retorted by asking him, "are you a soldier or student or a civilian?" None of those you mentioned, I missed one, replied my elder brother aggressively. But seeing that my brother was young, the aggressive one said, "if you are from the red army, I don't admire the Red Army because we the Black Army consider you as little boys, yes, not qualified soldiers".

But my elder brother replied to him with a greater wisdom than he could imagine, by saying, "there is nothing called little soldier in the military terminology, except I noticed this from your silly understanding of the thing". Then he haranguingly ordered them into military displinary attention in order that they should salute him. But they declined and ran away.

At four o'clock that evening we arrived to our uncle Ngong Matuong's house where we were welcomed with tears. He asked us to stop at the edge of the compound before we could greet everybody in their hands, then he starting pouring water on our feet—sprinkling us with water saying his words of thanks to our ancestors. Then eventually after he finished, we were ritually welcomed. A he goat was slaughtered that same night for us to feast on.

After three days we started again going to Warapath to Uncle Deng Malong's house for seeing our of father's side. But before we could arrive, my Mom begun to suffer severely from rampant and arbitrary fallings! She became weak and skinny; I could see her picture exactly vivid in mind as she looked exactly like the time when we were taken away from her! And unfortunately on that 13th of March of same 1997 finally we came home expecting to see our father, but we did not. We got the news that he died three days before we arrived. He was in a Mission at Nyamlel the same date of our arrival. It was agreed traditionally that was why my Mom was in such rampant fallings and sicknesses. Sad. From that moment my mother recovered from her risky and random sickness which proved the biblical factual quotations to me, "and the two shall become one flesh".Despite my dad having other wives, but still he specifically loved my Mom.

6.3 The Journey to Maridi, Western Equatoria Region

After a funeral, my uncle Daniel Deng Malong told my Elder brother to take me with him to Western Equatoria at Maridi County for my schooling. But at first my mum declined saying, "uncle, you don't know this lad yet, this boy is totally hot-tempered, I fear that he might be murdered away if he goes far from my reach." She continued, the lad is still new here also, how dare you take him away just quickly as that?" But my brother Madut titivated the Equatoria region as a peaceful place full of mango trees, banana, oranges and so many edible raw foods! He dramatically stretched out his hands and enthusaistically spread his fingers in the air as if he was picking fruits from banana or mango trees humorously, as he described it! And so eventually my mum was convinced. But before I could be taken by my elder brother to Maridi, mom called me aside and said, "My Son, now that

213

you are leaving to a foreign land called Maridi with your elder brother, I want you to let go of your warlike habit". She continued, "do not tamper either with your big brother Madut or with his wife, be harmless as a weaned child."

"If you are not near your Mum, I beech you my son to accept any way you will be treated either by your big brother or his wife". Then she gently rubbed my shoulders with her right hand as she quoted this parable, "*he who heeds the instruction of his mum and despise not the rebuke of a father will eventually become both the instructor, leader and the esteemed of all men*". So, we started off on our journey. Commander Deng Alor was the governor of Greater Bhar el Ghazal by then. And when we were leaving from Wanyjok to Maridi, we had first to pass through the concerned office that gave pass permits

It was my first time to see Commander Paul Malong Awan Anei in Pariak Military Barrack. I and my elder brother Madut came to him to sign for us our departure order. In addition, I saw another handsome man called Abuk Abuk whose real name was Dut Dut. Moreover, my elder brother told me that Abuk is the head Military Intelligence Officer. Malong Awan, was a man of few words, patriotic and warlike, and as my brother gave him our document, he looked at him with contempt and sharply asked, 'where are you and that gentle man going—leaving the Bhar el Ghazal land under harassment of Arabs while you are going to take rest somewhere?'. But my brother in reply said, 'there is nowhere said to be clear of Arabs soldiers even Equatoria region, and this young boy, as you can see, he is a school boy and I am

214

taking him back to school'. Aggressively they parted each other, for that was their famous characters, because if you look weak, then you will surely suffer.

The way to Maridi was tragically full of risking militia of rebelled Commander Kerubino Kuenyin Bol who defected from SPLA leadership, accusing the system of unfairness, stating that the Movement was biased by the fears of one man against the wills of others. He asserted that Dr John Garang declines any attributes from his counterparts. Let me come back to the point precisely to say that by God's grace we managed to penetrate through those notorious militias. After we left Pariak, we spent two days walking until we reached another Commander at the outskirts of Wau, a man who looked so peaceful, peasant-faced being. He spoke slowly but with naked command of words. He was so masked in simple attire, but believe me that guy was a real death commander, his name was Bol Madut. In the same day's afternoon we reached where a very young handsome, full of laughter and good-hearted Commander, he was the one who commanded the Division that was under Wau patrol he was called Commander Dau Atorjong Nyiuol. Dau happily welcomed us to his thatched hut, and we ate together with him, such hospitality always annoyed his chief guard Deng through and through. However, according to Dau, "this land belonged to these small students. They are the ones we whom are fighting for their cause." He always stated that.

After my one year's stay in Maridi, I left to Jambo where I met with a short, brown and young-faced man. That guy was full of military tactics and discipline. He spoke precisely in few words, He loved everyone and talked to anyone. He was commanding the Division of Jambo, which was the head-quarters for the Sudan People Liberation Army in patrol of the entire Juba. He was called Commander Santino Deng Wol. His deputy was Major Mayiik Ngor. In Maridi, I met with all Liberation Commanders, for the safest area by then was Maridi County, in the Western Equatoria Region. It was in the celebration of sixteen May of 1998 when I saw face to face Commander Samuel Abu John who was the governor of the Western Equatoria Region by then. Commander Lual Diing Wol. I met Giir Chuang Aluong, the Commander of the Army Division in Maridi County, his deputy was Nubian, called Commander Telephon Kuku. The short and funny person I saw in Maridi was called Commander James Wani Igga who was nicknamed Adel Imam by the Commander–in–Chief.

Maridi County was the first safest SPLA area, which the movement captured from the Khartoum Armies in 1991. In addition, Maridi County was where most of their Commanders resided. I met Commander Ali Guatalla, a man who really hated Arabs whole-heartedly. I also got Commander Daniel Awet Akot, Garang Mabil. Santo Ayang, James Hoth Mayia, Oyai Deng Ajak, Ager Gum and so many others. It was after the generosity of Commander Santino Deng Wol who used to support students with food and transportation, that I found no ration in his camp, He preferred to transport me in his greenish Jeep to Yei.

When I reached Yei, I fully managed to encounter Commander Silva Kiir Mayar and the Late Commander in-Chief Dr John

Garang De Mabior the second time with so many others. I was studying in Affa at the outskirts of Maridi, in Bhar el Nham under Mambe Payam. I came to know the difficult to explain person I left in Maridi county seated under mango tree in uniform that his name was Commander Kuol Manyang Juuk. He looked so focused and struggle minded. I was already familiar with Martin Mawein Anyuon whose well-known name was 'Agokrial' who was the Commander in charge of SPLA Military Training Center in Bongo the border to Ethiopia. He lived in Affa before he quit to Maridi. I was schooling in Affa. Affa was resided also by many different tribes i.e. Nubians, Dinka Pana-Aruol, Atuot of Yirol, Dinka Aweil and the surrounding natives tribes—who were put there by the movement.

It was in Maridi County, where I came to learn that South Sudan is not just a small village, but that it is a real realm, with great Chiefdoms and Kingdoms, possessed by myriad numbers of tribes, languages, cultures and values, with very large territories. In our school, I was a good student trusted in all things, because they said that I was humble and willing young boy. I possessed all the Smart Character, Humbly Obeying Orders Loyally, which is the abbreviation of SCHOOL. All teachers loved me wholeheartedly, no one tempted to speak ill of me .No good qualifications rivalled mine in our school ground. Nevertheless, I peacefully waited upon them to realize that we're here to be taught, until the day came when I was checked in my discipline. The teachers who used to teach us had unbecomingly neglected us in teaching. They used to take us for digging their gardens and when we came back from one of their gardens we were just then asked to go home to take rest but no lessons to be taught. Such deeds disturbed me perpetually. I was desperate for knowledge; I wanted to learn, because I wished to fill up my academic gap.

I started my education in class four and jumped to class six— omitting primary one, two, three and five. In addition, when I saw that our head teacher Wilson Mogga was redundant, and our school Administrator Mogga Tom sat back, I took my pen and wrote a complaint. A letter that became historically "the first stubbornness of a pupil." I wrote the letter on Friday morning and in the afternoon, I submitted it to our School Admin Mogga Tom. I started the letter by appreciating the facades of our school building with its good environmental aspects, then ended up my letter by asking very sharp questions which shoked the school administration so terribly. I was suspected of 'a hidden agenda'. Moreover, quickly the school administration called for an emergency meeting, all parents association, Payam Administrator and chiefs were requested to come. Our Payam Administrator's bodyguards were vehemently and aggressively deployed in the school compound. The issue was discussed over for two days, from Saturday and again on Sunday after prayer. In addition, on Monday morning our entire school parade was called in front of the school office. The investigation started from primary one. One by one, class by class until it reached me, I was the last person to be called in. In addition, mockingly the Headmaster asked, "which language do you speak well Malong, Arabic or English?" In reply, I shortly said, "any one of them". Then deliberately he questioned me as to whether I know something about the letter that was written to the School Administration, I quickly said, "I wrote it myself".

The room was full of all teachers, Chiefs, Parents, churches' Pastors, Muslims soldiers from Jebel Nuba and our Mambe Payam Administrator. Moreover, in hearing such a bold reply to this big offensive case, everybody hushed up: Silence swept in the room. A paper and pen were thrown on the table to me by our school Headmaster who sharply said, "write exactly the same letter like what we have now, if you really were the one who wrote the first one". I took the paper and started it in the same way. Before I could finish write the date, the Headmaster roughly pulled out the paper, pen from my hands, and terribly began to harangue me. Our Payam Administrator was a soldier with the rank of Major. He was infuriated by this disloyal instigation and started to request the school Headmaster saying, "'if this case is not going to be solved here, please then, hand this aggressive boy over to me, for I will militarily get it done quickly".

Our school Headmaster was a strong Christian who loved justice. He realized from the very beginning that the mistake was not mine, but theirs. But what disturbed him was the way I boldly wrote the letter. He didn't wish any bad fate to overtake me also, and deliberately declined saying, "I will ask him my way, if he fails to comply, then I will hand him over to you". Moreover, after I was investigated, I was sent outside for two minutes then I was called again to hear my punishments for those offences. Such penalties were suggested to me, that I must dig a latrine of three meters by one, to cut down the grasses of our school garden. In addition, I must be beaten with ten slashes and finally I should write an apology letter. Before I could finish the punishments that I was allowed not to attend any lesson. I willingly accepted those punishments without hesitation and showed no any sign of being alarmed.

After I was called to stand before the school parade, I was commanded to lie down before my classmates, then our school Administration Mogga Tom slashed me ten times so terribly that my school uniform shorts were torn by his energetic slashing. From that day thereafter, I perpetually hated school for humiliating me but I still liked education. In addition, within short moments all our school working tools were lowered under my feet by Mogga Tom. The place to dig for a school latrine was marked for me. Moreover, after not least than thirty minutes my hands were scratched by the rough mattock and badly hurt, for it was a rocky ground. My schoolmates looked at me at a distance with sullen faces of cowardice, for such terrible punishments were hated by each one of them wholeheartedly. They punished me for their own failure.

I dug until noon time when my class one pupils stood it no longer and wildly ousted me out of the pit and broke into helping me dig it. In the next day all the classes rebelled and started to dig, ignoring all the warnings and threats of same punishments against anyone who would attempt to help the "stubborn boy", as I was titled. Moreover, on the third day all my schoolmates came with their slashes and refused even to line up in parade, but deliberately started cutting down the grass in our school garden. The Headmaster with his staff stood at a distance with disgraced faces, helpless and unable to say nothing of a good or bad moral. I stood in the middle of my schoolmates like a king observing all the young and the mature ones, saying in my heart to our school Headmaster and the Payam Administrator:

"And now, you have seen with your naked eyes, whether the need for teaching was my own hint or it is a collective demand. Yesterday but one you checked my discipline, but today you will never bear the disgrace that will surly cover your faces!"

Some of my mates brought poles, timbers, thatching grass and the robes. Those experts in making rural huts were seriously putting it up. Zaruffa Zechariah was a fat, pretty but hard-working and good-hearted girl, started collecting little money from her school friends and bought small sandwiches for the fainting children. And Margret Jakudu Ahamad—a young girl that you can quickly admire her cheerful heart, but that day changed her completely. Her smiling face doggedly stayed sullen, a habit that she never attempted to have. No one cared about the sun heat or the school bell that ran to make us go home, but we worked until three forty (3:40 PM) in the afternoon. Hoes begun to hurt those who became tired but determined to finish the work. We left our school compound with smeared bodies, exhausted but with smiling faces. After I finished doing all my punishments, I wrote a very sincere and humble apology, which shoked the school Administration again and which engendered the Administration to valuably identified me as "the future leader". Moreover, thereafter our school Headmaster set very strong school regulations, teaching timetable, school attendance chart and school discipline! I was elected as the school Head Boy. I used to give speeches in the marking of every graduation occasions. I performed my speech excellently, which engendered our Payam Administrator with perpetual great joy.

Chapter Seven

7.1 The 9th 11, 2011 Independence day
My independence day song!

In the first time when I saw the New Sudan's Flag raised, my heart was seriously moved—tears rolled down on my cheeks! I was severely cut deeply in the heart! I found myself exalted!

The heats of destitution and wounds of deprivation, together with regrets of colonialism begun to roll away! While the Flag was shaking in the air, my mind flashed back in the death of our Martyrs;

I reflected in retrospect my thoughts to the wailing mothers and the screaming children! I considered the death toll of old men and women with all the catastrophes, which we have undergone as the birth-pain into a New coming South Sudan as a Nation!

As the Flag was up waving, when I was still staring at it, with my eyes reading its symbols, I found my heart saying words like, 'I am exalted! I am established! Then I truly found my heart swollen with pride and dignity without measure that I am a Nation!

As the Flag was waving in the blue air, with my face lifted high towards heaven at the blue sky watching it, with my eyes still blinking at its symbols; I find myself deeply moved with a great zeal and vigor I have never felt before!

My mouth babbled and broke out with murmuring words those I can't express or even translate. I thanked the Almighty God deeply with all my heart for the right He bestowed upon me!

When I pondered all these, I realized that the hand of God for discipline to this land is over, and behold a new covenant of peace and prosperity has begun!

O Lord God! Hear the simple prayer of your young and simple Servant! Let me understand your purposes and wills towards this up-coming nation.

I plead with you to give me wisdom and knowledge, favors your lad and bless his people—A men!

7.2 The Anticipated Future's Worries

When any people stand up for their Country, their first challenges include the immediate realization about ways for which the people must get to survive. I mean that the executive of that Country must quickly draw the ways for her Citizens to get enhanced such that they retain skills on how to use their hands. This must be the major concern for the government. Those who lacked professionalism must get supported, such that one should manage to run his or her own firms. Most importantly,

the governing body should help everybody on finding compen-
sations and loans including capacity building.

Jobs must be availed for jobs seekers; this helps in stopping
dependency and paves ways for personal improvement, without which the entire Country will never get out from wails of
aggressions fueled by poverty. Mozee Jomo Kenyatta reiterated after the independence of Kenya that Kenyans suffered three
things, namely poverty, disease, ignorance, and that Kenyans
should learn to be self-reliant in the spirit of concerted effort
which he called, Harambee. Moreover, in order for him help re-
awaken his people to supplement government efforts in development. President Moi seconded the same ideology in what is
known as Nyayoism, which means following the footsteps of the
founder, Harambeeism of Kenyatta. Our South Sudanese friend
Rev. Claudio Zaninotto of Italy talked about it willingly in his
well-spirited book titled, "When two elephants are fighting, it is
the grass that suffers". He says that what South Sudanese leaders
do not really know after their independence are the dilemmas on
how they will govern this gigantic Country, after it will be fully
lowered upon their own hands.

This book is here as an attempt intended to always keep re-
minding us on the humiliations we underwent in the hands of
our camouflaged enemies. Those who in their first entry asked
us for the peaceful co-existence. Thereafter they turned down
our Southern Communities in subtle fraud in all life's aspects. To
speak but the truth, it is the Arabs' ideology and politics hidden in
their religion for centuries; from Islamic origin, which according

to my terminology I call it, "Arabs' ruse on hijacking other people's belongings". I came to myself also, that I should add a few tales on my South Sudanese, because they're not heard, thus I saw to it as of greater meanings to be added herein. Yes, in the July 9th 2011, the very important Day in our lives as South Sudanese people all, I haven't celebrated it. It happened that when I heard microphones shouting: SPLA Oyeeee! New Sudan Oyeeee! South Sudan Oyeeee! Salva Kiir Mayar-dit Oyeeee! Paul Malong Awan Oyeeee! SPLM Oyeeee! SPLA Oyeeee! SPLM Oyeeee! Come out all of you the people of Aweil come...come...all...all..... all! Come all! Come all! Come to Aweil Freedom Square—today it is your very, very, very important Day! It's a very important Day! Today! Today! The microphones repeated that over and over, repeatedly.

All the politicians in collaboration with other parties were urging the Community to come out to celebration their very eventful and the awaited Day of their Independence. Therefore, the influx in to the Aweil Freedom Square of men, women, girls and boys, both civilians and the army were great.

All my colleagues from different sectors disturbed me by their phone calls, encouraging me to come out and meet them, such we could go together for a celebration venue. My colleagues from teachers, Pastors and others were persuasively urging me to come out well dressed for celebration, but unfortunately, I could not. I wished to make them happy by joining them in such a historical Day of my Country's Independence, yet my heart was blunt about that. I could not tolerate this: *that in any society whose*

226

people used to praise the rich and eulogize their top ones, will always
have swollen prideful and neglectful hearts. The pride that will even-
tually distort all the nobility of man. I stayed home until mid-day
whereas everyone including my own wife was already at celebration's arena. Then at mid-day I finally made up my mind go
to the Freedom Square where there was a great mob seriously
chanting. Though I did come to the place, yet I was still rigid to
come closer, rather I seated myself at a distance under a certain
mahogany tree where a woman was making her tea, and ordered
one cup of my favorite. Then I gazed at them from faraway, fran-
tically exasperated at the jubilating crowd with a wrinkled face.
I looked at them ruefully every now and then, not sensing that
someone might be watching my unbecoming reactions even.

   In addition, as I was still looking at the jubilating crowd—observing how a certain young man from Lou tribe was energetically brandishing his buttocks repeatedly, as he danced. Moreover,
other young Dinka women who were enthusiastically singing
songs with countless ululation, and some old men and women
were jumping dances, jubilating abysmally and ceaselessly and it
repeatedly jarred me!

   I, as I was just exasperated from such irresponsible dances—
not realizing that I was still in the tea place, rashly said: "'These
people are really chicken minded and ignorant types, why are
they dancing now?" I continued, "They're dull enough to fore-
see what it means to get Independence at the other side!"

   I recklessly repeated such words with loud voice until Abuk
Akech Deng, a tea-maker woman retorted me with her searing

questions, and she said, "Malong! Malong, you know I used to respect you so much, because I have known you to be a knowledgeable and noble person and without haughtiness. Today you proved the opposite. What happened to you today? You're not even happy and are asking such questions that what are these enchanting dances and jubilations for?" She continued, "I have seen your face wrinkled and displeased even, why?" She went on to explain to me saying, "Have you forgotten that these people are celebrating their Independence Day? If I were to be free from tea work, I would have joined them, but because my kids will eat nothing eventually at the end of the day if I do not make tea. That is why I am here now, you see". Then she finally concluded saying, "We are now a free people" as she was collecting her empty glasses.

I quickly rebuffed and questioned her back, "freed from what?" She said, "Free from Arabs of course", she hastily replied confidently. Nevertheless, as I leaned back on my chair, I said, "you do not know yet these people how craving and neglectful their ways are". I continued, have not these same reckless leaders governed us? I pointed at them with my three fingers. I continued, "were they not the same people who are egging these poor Communities and falsely addressing them that they'll render good services to them?", I continued, "are they not the same ones governing us since 2005 up to this very July 9th of 2011?

"Yes, she replied to my questions, in a rather weak voice. Then I said, "Then what changes have they made, these unruly, and 'twenty one years-minded groups'. They vaguely think about

228

some neediest people who are sincerely looking forward with expectation to have their needs met. This, is something that is unbelievably contrary to these militias who took this Day for granted as their privileged day. A one party merit for Credited Day" this day which they allegedly claimed as One party efforts exerted achievement and we are going to make these peasants "share with them in its harvest".

These blunt hearted politicians never thought it even that the battle is fought collectively. Even, to mention but few, there were both rural and urban people, including the intellectuals inside the Sudan and those in Diasporas, nationalists who did not know or hear about anything called Party. Nevertheless, they fought for freedom heartily to death!

However, I explained all these to Abuk Akech Deng, that the achieved Independence day was an outcome of a collective struggle by all the South Sudanese in and outside this Country cohesively. In addition, that it was regardless of any party, religion or tribe yet she was still passive and keenly urged me to specifically give SPLM/A, the privileged, more time. She said, "They will indulge for such times, but later on they might realize that what they were doing is wrong, and sure, they will improve into becoming good leaders."

I was very depressed by her senseless answers and from her recklessness and ignorance about all that I said. I sobbingly walked away in bad stress. Though in an attempt, she tried to apologise to me saying, "Please, Malong, come back, see you have not even finished your tea". I never looked even back again.

My heart became so rigidly unhappy, I loathed seeing any South Sudanese human beings. My heart went further asking me questions like, "Your Creator has assigned you with the fatigues of suffering, hasn't he? You are from failed Beings, aren't you? You are destined for everlasting misfortunes, aren't you? I went even further noting down every time whenever I could take steps to any place or in any conversation for the two days of the Jubilee."

These are the fears which remain to pump my heart until today, my greatest worries and question is not whether south Sudanese community love our country or not. But my greatest fears a question on the years we spent under the influence of iron rule of that extremist government: the leadership which had indoctrinated the thoughts and hearts of all our ways of life and actions. The influences we got used to, to the extent that we can easily revert to them either knowingly or unknowingly. We sustained low self-esteemed i.e. we doubt ourselves, disrespect ourselves and fear even to make erected decisions in our own ways—it seemed we don't even have one way to, because the voices of the masters haranguing their bonds for many years yonder still exist in us; screaming deeply down in our hearts.

Under iron leadership as one people, we had lost integrity and our thoughts crippled, though our feet still kick for autonomous realm, but from the day we accepted to be led by those extremist governments for centuries, tightened us behind. Because step by step, we love it that way, we feel happier with them more than with ourselves, for the extremist government engraved into our minds that our cultures and norms are not very much important,

and today we are influenced by their Arabic cultures. For instance, our women love to attend Islamic occasions and are comfortable to wear the Islamic attires, talk like Arab women, behave
like them and worse of all, thinking like them! So from outside
we are independent, but inside, we are a dependent realm.

7.3 What Do The Laws of Curses and Blessings Dictate?

In his book titled "Back to Work" the former American President
Bill Clinton inspired his people on the importance of work; not
begging. We get used to rations and donations given to us by
USAID Agencies and other Countries whose aims are to get us
working in order for us to outgrow those starvations and stand on
our own feet, and be relying on our own resources. But shameful
to mention this continuous phenomenon, we are not willing to
get independent, we refused to improve and fend for ourselves,
we are not using our domestic resources, instead we turned into
beggars and depending on others. Is it not a great chagrin? Is it
not a curse for the whole Country to beg as if God has not created us with our own hands to work with? On the other hand,
don't we have abundant resources like other Countries living
under the heavens which if we can accountably, responsibly and
sensibly use them; we can be rich even more than they are?
If I am to ask, whoever becomes rich from among those sons
and daughters of open street beggars? Tell me if you know one!
Therefore, if the answer is that none of them from those who
used to beg became rich, so shall the story of ours be the same.

Don't you know that it is better to be poor because certain situations forced you to be so, then to be a cursed rich? What evil incited you to remain an ignorant and un-awaking society seeing even the executive hand of the Nation relies on outside supports, why? Because she has wasted her assets in corruptible tasks of buying weapons and ammunitions—against whom? Against her own citizens! Then how does the law of curse strike us? The law of curse strikes when Traders go on borrowing from foreigner investors, government goes on begging for international hands of support, National Organizations write proposals for funding and donations from the western world, bishops go on requesting help from their sister churches in the western world. Can we call luckiest, those who use the name of God's Saints to get rich? I am shocked at such ignorance! Nowadays, it has become habits for many Africans bishops going to the western Countries for supports and they eventually end up using those donations and funds for themselves not for the purposes upon which they wrote their requests. That is why becoming a bishop here in the South is getting another serious meaning!

However, what is supposed for us to do as South Sudanese Citizens? We are supposed to be open-mined and to be honest with ourselves and work hard like other Nations of the world responsibly. Mark this; God, the Author and Creator of the creations, has foremost-blessed seeds and ordained hardworking hands for richness. Once you plant any seed, it will yield to you and me very great yields. He (God) rewards any responsible and honest human beings those who toil with their efforts. He respects our laboring! In an honest sense, would God allow such attitudes of robbing and thefts to get rich? Would He bless you for something if you did not toil for it with your own hands?

Are you and your subordinates not cursed for cunningly stealing from others? Who is clean in this Country? We all have become beggars, robbers, cheaters and above all, we turned into dependency on easy and ready foods put in our hands by foreign hands in different forms. You should know this perfectly, that the Author of Creation has only ordained the blind, disabled, and vulnerable, orphans, and widows to beg or receive gifts, but apart from those I mentioned, they are dammed. We decided to curse ourselves by our own doings; we refused the ordained way of blessings and loved to follow redlines of curses, because we refused to adhere to the law of God who laid ordained blessings! We were wrong when we said, "The Khartoum government had deprived us of our political, economic, and social freedom". Because when someone says something of those sorts and then forgets to live, true up to the demands of your statements that definitely prove you to be liars!

Our SPLM/A politicians were persuasively encouraging our Community that let all South Sudanese efforts be joined together against the Khartoum government. Their reasoning was that we had been deprived, and neglected on service deliveries.

The (SPLM/A) vehemently stated that once we liberate this Country, this issue of inequity, inequality, negligence, deprivations, unfair distributions of national assets plus dictatorships in all their forms will end. Now the students of truth and reasoning will be disillusioned seeing the real colors of our alleged leadership. Because we are so cunning, speaking like angels of light but acting trickily like the devil. This shows blatantly that we are too weak to keep our own promises and as a result, the same politicians defect now and start going wherever. To go to the Khartoum government and bow their heads for it, requesting its help on solving the South Sudanese problems. Therefore, this proves that the problem was not the Khartoum government alone, which was erroneous, but the problem was co-shared. If you can see now, who among the governments of the world still incite its tribes against one another like our South Sudanese government herein? We are still destroying our next generations by our stupid attitudes!

7.4 Who Voted for Wars in South Sudanese Newborn Country?

You know what, when you do something, it will inevitably be followed with consequences. For instance, when you light a fire, smoke appears and too much sneezing causes the blood to flow from the nose. Therefore, this April 2010 riggings, intimidation and detentions will follow irresponsible deeds, because it has invited in the lawless, real doubts and mistrust. To come back to answer the question laid above as who voted for war? For this question, I would like to take a live example on the holy priests of God, the Pharisees—who had been, for a long time teaching and admonishing the Israelites. The hire of the Kingdom of God must positively respond for the prophetic coming of Messiah, the Prince of Peace.

Unfortunately, what happened when the expected Prince of Peace came? The Community went out welcoming their Messiah with ululation and shouts of welcome, welcome son of David! Exactly as the Prophets predicted it. Even they, (Priests) had been teaching about His coming a couple of days before; they were teaching that the Messiah of God would be welcomed with such and such great joy. This same is true on SPLM/A leaders, when they were enthusiastically saying, "peace will bless us once again!" Dr. John Gerang's favored speech in Nyayo stadium in Kenya. Unfortunately, like the holy priests, they were not prepared to welcome the Messiah with humble attitudes, which was how He (The Messiah) was supposed to be welcomed.

Therefore, what happened when the Messiah did come, finding the priests of God unprepared to welcome him wholeheartedly? The answer is, "they were offended by His coming!" Nevertheless, being offended so much on His great symposium arrival, they voted for war against the Messiah! One day, as he was coming into the Holy City Jerusalem, a great crowd met him at the city outskirts, welcoming him with shouts singing, "Hosanna to the Son of David! However, offended, agitated and disturbed by such blatant joy, they shouted at Him, "Heeey! Heeeyyou! Tell these people to stop their noises! What is this melee all for? Nevertheless, Jesus knowing their ill attitudes and self- pride, boldly said, "If these people stop to shout for joy, the stones will not be quieted!" In addition, as he came near the gates of the holy city Jerusalem—knowing that there will be Great War between Him and these power-hungry Pharisees, he wept at Jerusalem's main gate on the unfaithfulness in their hearts and said, "Jerusalem! Jerusalem! Killer of prophets and Messengers of God. How I wished that you would have known the coming day of your LORD (Prince of Peace), but you did not. He continued, "So you and your children will one day be seized and crushed, no stone will be left over another because you have not realized the day of the coming of your LORD!"

That story eventually ended with the very holy priests killing the Messiah whom they toiled for many, many, many years on His role, teaching the people about his blissful coming! The same is true on the SPLM/A who rallied the people against the Khartoum government a couple of years ago, preaching that when we will attain our own autonomous right, everybody will be very, very happy. Dr. John Garang quoted that there will be many opportunities for the opportunity seekers.

He used the scriptures from the Bible book of John 14 that says, *"There are many opportunities in my father's house, if not so I would not have told you"*. Unfortunately, their compatriots those who were not fortunate to get into executive part of the government, are left out severely suffering even from acute poverty. They got no reward over the same Country which they all fought to attain. Not many rooms whatsoever, because when Jesus said that quotation, he was very sure about his own attitude and mission. Therefore, in my own Opinion, I realize that the only man that had the vision on how such great nation could get along peacefully and blissfully among his SPLM/A colleagues was Dr. John Garang. I can see that he was the only man who understands the demands and the languages the "nation-mak-ing" speaks.

7.5 Therefore, Will These Conflicts Have a Sooner End?

My first answer is: these power-affiliated conflicts will never have an end soon. Who told you that empty stomachs are ever con-strained to be kept silent? War will continue to wreck this new-born Country as far as truth is concerned. Another question is; then what will be the consequences, if this bad phenomenon re-mains to wreck this newborn nation? To answer that; it will force some to vote also. Others will vote on footing (walking away from the Country, displacement); others will vote by their hands (fight continually) while others will vote emotionally (run mad as you can see many people walking naked in our towns) and others will vote for lawlessness (raping, robbing, killing by un-known gunmen and dictatorship) and so on.

No matter what attempts could this current government do to bring order or nourish prosperity, it will never avail since she has already voted for war against peace and its blessings. For the law of peace's blessings says, "If you bless your neighbors, thus you've blessed yourself too". The same is quite true with the law of Nation-making. For if this current system would not stop detaining, intimidating, killing, using malice, censoring Media houses, use of military dictates and above all, the phrase "we have liberated this Country, hate speech" individualizing the entire Nation as a property or belonging of certain group or figures, then we will not and cannot attain the lasting peace.

7.6 However, What Will be The Effects of These Parties?

To answer this, my first answer is that those groups who are struggling against this system will not be able to get this government toppled—because she has many potential grounds. First, this community has been laden with fear, this society does not know her rights, because they have never been exposed to a better life before. They know nothing about the child's rights, women's rights, right not to be detained arbitrarily, citizenship rights, and rights to speak up for one's own rights without intimidation from anybody and above all, right even to strike against bad governance! Therefore, within such stone minds plus ignorance, it helps so much to give any opportunists a great opportunity for such a system to carry on dictating the situation all along. Even against a mere effort for good governance from the one percent of those who know their rights, they will be forced into silence.

However, be very careful still, for when it comes for Power; be very careful about it, for it is very deadly like a dangerous beast! This Power is harmful like a dangerous snake. Its calls with two very dangerous languages. The first is, "please, leave me alone peacefully". However, another language is too venomous! It is very cruel language. It bites you suddenly using its tail (the people you trusted, especially your sublimates) and it flips up and down her body roughly. That body is called the change of nationalism. It had been experienced by very many empires, which

238

led to their total destruction when those kingdoms did not answer to its poisonous bites

Very many emperors, in those stone ages even up to date, the only king that survived its bites, was King David from the Hebrews sons. He committed adultery with one of his sublimates, called Uriah, with his wife Beersheba from the children of Hittites. Nathan, the prophet, came to him and spoke to the King, *"Thus said the LORD, you have rebelled against the command of the LORD by taking Beersheba, the wife of your servant Uriah who served you faithfully, to your wife and you have killed him"*. He (the prophet) continued, *"You have done it secretly but I the LORD, will do it (expose David's wives for public sex) openly, the sword shall never leave your house, but concerning your life, none of your hair shall fall to the ground"*. That biblical story ended with King David ousted out from power by his own son, Absalom. Had he not repented in tears before the Living God, his life would have bitten by the beast—the snake called Power!

Very many great military men like Adolf Hitler, M. Gadhafi, and presidents I do not want to waste my ink mentioning them. Just know they were crushed by the same Power! When this SPLM/A movement generals were in the bush, it seemed that they had not satisfactorily enjoyed sexual pleasures. Which when they arrived in towns, they turned against any women no matter whose wife a woman could be, they just devoured! Thanks to one of my cousins, who used to say, "I love every beautiful woman, I don't care to whom she belongs, I just got to get her for myself". Mark this well in your mind dear reader: Any

239

wrongdoings committed in the presidential palaces are punishable by God through His Divine law of maintaining power.

7.7 Who is The Government, in The Logical Sense?

People (Nations) are likely to fall into an imbroglio phenomenon when they fail to realize the true set of rights and obligations (that include loyalty) and the conditions those realize as the true memorandum of understanding between the chosen (government) and the chooser (people). What qualifications anchoring the role of nominee in a form that must be satisfactory (responsibility). People must in the foremost, realize what they want, and how they wish it and when they want it. Moreover, in this context, they (people) must get to harmonize their Opinions, and strongly stand for their common rights and have a critical language (boldness and sound mind).

However, that can never happen except with an informed society. People with an open mind, they can clearly see things with a reasoning mind. Such people don't beat the elephant's shadow, rather they hit at the perpetrators' heads! Therefore, the only people who could quickly survive such imbroglios more easily are those who question the liability, with thorough follow ups on their set rules. Those governing them in absolute courage with clauses why?, when? How? Which? Moreover, who? One of the wise men once said, *"The best ways to hide a lie is between two truths"*. To continue with that lesson of who is the government, I have tried all my best level to present you my points on who really is the true source of the government with legality censure and to compel.

7.7.1 Definition of the Government

"The government is a small organ of a nominee chosen by the people to represent them on service deliveries. It serves to render order and execute the regulations governing that particular society or community. These can be changed from time to another as merit its mandated ends or when it is seen incompetent or unresponsive or unsuitable and ineligible on reasons stipulated by law."

7.7.2 Definition of People

People are the majority of the Citizens that flocked or resided in one certain large area of land known as cities, towns, counties, Payam and villages. Who resided in those locations with total right and freedom to conduct their daily lives. Who, when the need for order and law arise, can resort to choose capable men and women in small-scale groups to represent them in order to solve cases that arise among them from time to time? They usher in order and obligations, fines, and reprove the culprits without impartiality. That is what is called in another language indirect democratic rule of people.

7.7.3 The Memorandum of Understanding
Between People/Government

The People: A law of loyalty within the boundary of content-ment binds People, or when that organ is able enough to qualify the positions, they have occupied. That is the anchoring condi-tion. The people remain obedient to its nominee (government) as far as the law of cooperation and loyalty is concerned. That is what we called Obligation.

The government: The government on the other hand, must work with great stamina to ensure that all the necessarily securi-ty, shrewd maintenance of public assets, services deliveries, pro-tection of the rights of everybody equally and open vacancies for job seekers. That is what we called Responsibilities.

Government is answerable to the People: the law of loyalty and responsibility binds the people when the government real-izes their needs. It is only when that small organ (government) can be able enough to realize the anticipated needs which de-velop from time to time or which vary from time to another. Failure to do so, that organ must abdicate that position immedi-ately. However, if that organ qualifies its position, the then organ can merit remaining in its position as a steering system, govern-ing its people. The government has not many powers amounting from its own, but is operating within the consented regulations. She must from time to time verify herself before the people she is governing. That is what we called accountability. Therefore, the government is answerable to her people. Moreover, in this context, people are the ones to tick good or wrong on any system that represents them, because there is a possibility for people to live without government but there isn't possibility for government to exist without people. In that content, government goes away, but people don't.

Coming to my siblings (South Sudanese citizens): What has happened to us (conflicts) is not something new or a strange thing. Simply, it is a call for Nationalism. It is a core test of our capacity and ability to come together and solidly unite as One Family of Nations regardless of our clans or traditions. Those elements are what prove that we are able to govern ourselves by ourselves, without which we are lying if we allege that we can establish One Nation like such a great Country. South Sudan whose tribes, cultures, customs and languages differ absolutely from the others. The test is, if we, as peoples in the same Country can lower our own self-centered and aimless pride and cohesively stand for our common right as people of the same interest. Then we can make it to one. Some of us used to say that certain tribes cause these dilemmas. In addition, others say there are certain tribes which are the ones disrespecting others that led to provocation of these conflicts. My opinions are different completely; I just call such Opinions "senseless Opinions". For if I am to ask that: who among our tribes escaped displacement, starvation, poor health, destruction of livelihoods and lives, what can be your answer? The right answer is that these bad happenings have victimized us all. I meant that we all have suffered its consequences—our Country has been pushed into it ignorantly and it has already fallen on all fours.

Here in this context, the students of truth can ask himself or herself, that what is then the real problem? So to answer that, allow me first to narrate to you this little story. It goes; certain people were caught in a bad happening. That situation set them in total imbroglio, and they were desperately looking for solutions. The problem was that one of the bus fore-wheels got punctured when they were driving on the road to their long, long destination. And when the fore-wheel got punctured, some began to say that the bus must be downloaded of some of the items, people and everything else, which some quickly rebuffed saying that the heavy vehicle should be pushed. But another group who seemed to be more conservative advised that they should wait, even if it could take them long time, they must endure to stay where they were stuck in. These different Opinions resulted into a heated argument. It got tenser against each one of them escalated into another conflict. However, by a good luck, a madman happened to be passing by, who, in hearing what such caused negative brawling, got shocked! He (mad-man) interrupted them saying, *"instead of you disputing over the same bus with different Opinions, why not just replace this punctured fore-wheel with the good one from those hind-wheels?*

"He continued, *"You can use that until you reach your destination, then you can buy another new fore-wheel and put it in the place where you have removed one—so don't waste your time and energy"*. But one from the group defiantly said, *"But you are a madman, you are not supposed to be one to tell us what is right to do?"* But the madman in a reply said, *"Yes, I am a madman, but I am not a fool"*. That small and simple story covers our situation exactly!

7.8 Therefore, in This Content, Immediate Change For Good Governance is Vital

Are we not now stuck in blaming our identities minus seeing the real problems from the right perspectives?

Are we really identifying what we need? I mean: haven't we allowed ourselves to be exploited. No equity, no services delivery, no transparency, no financial stability, no health, no education, no security, no good roads, no freedom of speech (Media houses censured) no fair elections in order for us to have a chance to elect our capable men and women?

For us to achieve that: we need to have strong mental capacity, open mindedness is vitally needed, because it is the informed mind that can analyze what can avail to us, common interests, as One Family of Nations.

Note this: we South Sudanese Citizens are the ones robbed, exploited, fooled, raped, destroyed, killed, ridiculed, neglected and deprived by these profligates who are wise enough to cheat us by Former Detainees (FDs), South Sudan Opposition Alliance (SSOA), Sudan Peoples Liberation Army & Movement In-opposition (SPLA/M-IO), and South Sudan Liberation Army and Movement In-government (SPLA/M In-G), and other reps in "a divide and rule methodology".

For if I can ask you this question: that who among our tribes

245

of this Country are still flourishing in their own bliss, then what could your right answer be? The true and right answer is that we, all South Sudanese are: cheated, misused and above all, we are forced to be silent about it, through the use of military dictates and intimidations by this current government.

In this content: It calls for us to not dwell on the fabricated lies, this privileged clique is just pursuing its own interests or let me say its own projects. Its bigger aim is to maintain the power by any cause even if it can take them to provoke racial conflicts. They believed that it would be fine as long as it will keep them rooted in power longer. The SPLM compatriot even the current SPLM Chairman before he came to power, was a very humble man. He could abdicate the chair at one glance of disdainful look. He was ready to let go of power at any glimpse of aggression, but now, things have changed, and they are no longer the freedom fighters we used to know. Now they have become power hungry representatives that can shed any Citizen's blood because of remaining in power, for they have found out that being in power is sweet!

Mark the above statement well, it is the central truth. So you should know this fact, that you will find it hard to attain stability, prosperity and peace no matter what. This leadership cannot do anything that would avail prosperity, equity, peace because it is incompetent to do so. For peace is an enemy of any leadership that wants to stay in power, because peace opens possibilities for democratic governments, and as result, it can change the positions of the current system. Nothing profitable is in this leadership. Our struggles are conflicts based on individuals' interests not for the public interests. Therefore, we are in a captured State i.e. a small number of individuals are the ones dictating the nation for personal interests.

With those few facts I have just mentioned above, of which you (South Sudanese Citizens) my people know some better than I do; I wish to frankly tell you to be wise and stand true to your common rights. For days are passing by, clocks are ticking, months and years missing. If you don't cut down the tree before it is too late, you will be too late to cut it down when it gets more roots and change to become a habit that will never be rooted out. Know this for sure, that our struggle is not against colors or tribes, we the South Sudanese citizens because we have no problems on staying as one people.

Our supposed target is a privileged group who neglect and deprive us at all sectors i.e. Army section, civil section including the community. This regime has taken it for granted that this Country belonged to them minus us, the people who will always be here. Therefore, having understood that concept, we don't again need to bite ourselves or one another, but we must logically and collectively join our efforts and demand a real path for democratic governance!

a. But, where will we really be heading our destination right now, as we have fully possessed an Independent State? I am afraid, from where will we export shrewd leaders who will govern our Country with transparency and selflessly exert their commitment in building this Country?

b. Will not these fervent politicians with their tribal minds, which had already engulfed our Nations, cut us to pieces and feed us to vultures?

c. Now that we have a sworn in president, from Dinka clans, will he perceive that a leader must be above his own tribe? Or will he be partial to his 21 year colleagues and let go of our public assets? His reckless colleagues extravagantly waste them? Surely, they won't be economically sage, rather they'll squander the State finances on irresponsible aliens and native women, they will be lured into bankruptcy and this Country will be poor very soon!

d. I am quite sure, they will not hurry up equipping their Country with the best educational system, yes, I know, they will redundantly malinger about in fantasies and chase after endless pleasures. Moreover, whenever the sense of educating their children is imminent, I am sure; they will solely send their kids out of their Country in order to learn in foreign schools. Hence, not realizing that it is wastage. Eventually, they'll spoil their kids' wits through other bad cultures. These infants will wrongly get molded into different human beings. They will not realize that their kids will come back disoriented and thoroughly different people from them by reason of the education they get from different continents. Those children taken abroad will definitely be strange to their Country. Because education is not merely meant for reading, speaking and writing, rather it is more than that. You must teach the child his/her values, intimate love for his/her Country—adherence to the truth, responsibility to initiate and govern his/her affairs shrewdly, respect for his/her dignity and dearly uphold the cause of his/her integrity. To eschew evil deeds of all kind. To teach the child solely to know writing and reading, won't make such kids far from those bandit members of failed parliamentarians who vaguely say Yes, when it's worthy saying No, and say no, when it's time for Yes!

e. Our Country is full of robbers who threaten the community at nights. Who can believe that they are our very soldiers' survivors? They're not properly reintegrated into Units for a good management system. They have deployed themselves into robbery. They aren't ashamed from such acts, why not be ashamed since they were merely doing this as a habit even in a Guerilla time.

f. I don't see any reason to not panic from unexpected perils, for who can convince me that there is security in this State. If the security personnel sit with their pistols exposed out in a show under temporary platforms for sweet tea maker ladies! Who will take shrewd care of us? There is no one!

g. I repeatedly question myself saying, 'will these peasants who had been rurally using under tree roots for medication get helped?" Will these reckless politicians really know that it's time to erect good health care and put-up good hospitals for these communities? I know, these blind politicians. The best thing they'll do is only waste, they'll squander our Country money to India, Jordan and Egyptians' hospitals abroad. Yet they will come back never recuperated and will still take more money for the reasons of their unpromising health.

h. I know they will resort to their heretical communistic ideology defying the existence of Almighty God and doggedly resorting to so-called witchcraft: Ignorantly eventually provoking strikes of God's Autocratic curses and punishments upon their Country. Because this must be clear to every South Sudanese citizen that we didn't liberate ourselves by our own strength, but God snatched us out from mulish hands of Khartoum government's strong clutches.

i. In the next evening, my Mum came from Aweil East, our County filled with excitement and jubilation. She made a visit to see me with my family. She reportedly told me every single joy-making fact of how they'd celebrated yesterday their SPLA/M given freedom as they termed it as a "happy new year gift" after Dr. John Garang. She explained to me saying, "Today, our Chief Government's Official reminded us to pay true homage for our heroes and heroines who fell in the war time and we stood up for five minutes in silence to their remembrance". I replied to her in a rather taunting way, "in a true homage?" I continued, "Mum, your words are contradicting, for you first said that the martyrs were remembered in a "true homage" but last for "five minutes". "What do you mean?" she replied. I said, "The true part of your words were 'for five minutes' only, because these politicians don't have in their minds any tangible mfechanism for serving these vulnerable families of our martyrs. They have just mocked our true heroes and heroines who laid down their souls for this Country. Had they not died, we won't have this Country which we boast about today. Therefore, both I and my Mum recalling the death our fathers, Uncles and Aunts. Thus we ruefully asked the same question, "will these profligates realistically remember them by easing living for their families?"

j. Any Nation that gets its Independence through struggle, if those liberationists maintain the power in their complete grasp; and don't let it go, such that their communities fairly elect their own leaders, which is the true democratic procedure. If they do the opposite, that Country will never get to be Democratic again at all. Now, our reckless politicians called themselves democratically elected leaders, saying this Country as a "Democratic State". I used to wonder how? When could revolts that fought their government (I said this regardless of color, tribe and religion) still be democratic? They are not even equipped with true knowledge of Democratic values.

k. When we do not care to work hard, our ways of generating incomes will turn to be by "begging and gossiping" with one another, in order to get bulk amount of money. This style is not hard, it doesn't need much effort. It is subtly taken into hearts by these poor peasants. They have realized that the easiest way to get money is just to go to the top brass and utter lies, and you will be rewarded hugely. Thus, I wondered, will education really have any value or effect since the academic qualifications have no credit? For when the shortest cut to get to become a millionaire is just to "gossip and lie" you will earn bulk money? I really wondered; will this Country prosper under such slack bodies' hands, when men and women who don't bother to cultivate their grounds for food, rather resorting into beggary. How will they come out from famine? When have ever beggars or thieves happened to become rich?

1) Polygamy, marrying of many wives is our inseparable culture, so we have become extremely proud about it that we have even crossed all boundaries of responsibilities. For instance, one of my friends, who happened to be an Honorable raped a certain student of fourteen years old. This act amazed me and when I questioned him that he has violated the rights of the school girl, he cunning replied both to me and the poor parents of the girl saying, "don't worry, I will adjust this marriage through our cultural ways of marrying". In addition, the parents of that girl so quickly believed him. Before I could explain more about its badness or goodness, I was ousted out of the entire agenda! So I wondered where we will find responsible leaders who would perceive that such irresponsible acts devastate the entire future of the Country. The Laws of the Country should be observed by all, with no one to tamper or fly above them, but these profligate politicians declined to adhere to the Country's Laws. Moreover, every one of them is predisposed into holding three or even more positions or titles like, "Hon MP, rank of Lt. General, H.E Minister and Business man" at the same time. They are

holding the laws, public assets and business in their hands. I wondered which Country, could ever survive in the hands of such gourmand and profligates' care?

7.9 Letter Directed to Mr. President Salva Kiir

When it comes to governing the nation, my lord, one should mostly adhere to the public views on whatsoever you say or do; it must be in the consent to their opinions. A nation, my lord, is not a private vein that one could glue himself to its cup, which has been obtained by the will of its community. Power is given, it's not grabbed. You have done several coups in this office. You committed great treason even to those who picked (of course you are handpicked by comrades) you for this office.

If you don't know, you think that this society is a fool, and use the language of divide and control occupying your mind. If you concealed that in your heart that you will always intimidate the society by your soldiers, or those security men whom you molded into your bodyguards. You must know for sure that the time for change has fully ripped, any mulish attempt to remain in power will cost you your very life; not your life alone, but many of your close siblings and friends will pay their lives for this.

Our economy has subsided and people are in a dire situation, everyone is suffering varyingly and daily dying inside and outside their homeland whilst you and your siblings, plus those you loved, are living luxuriously, and pride has become your garments.

The societal fabric is no more, your leadership has turned women into harlots, both the young men and women are vile, consumed by the habit of begging for victuals daily.

Mr. President, to introduce myself, I am a man who is wrought by honesty. I have mounted upon the wing of truth in order to tell you these words. Because you have not understood the call, the language of humanity. People died. They continue to die, for your leadership, my lord, lacked coverage on life protection, the first obligation of man.

Yes, those who poisoned your heart should be accursed, for they've damaged the good substance in you that impelled God to favor you amongst your brethren. You were chosen to lead His people. For when it comes to leading humans, my lord, it needs a vision, it's the compass and the tying knot, which if one lacked its morals; people will perish no matter what you can suggest. For you ignorantly worked for separation, not independence. This is the very question on our civil wars upon which men, women and children willingly laid down their lives as martyrs.

The Author of Creation in whose eyes the life of everyone is important, suffered on me his will—we are impelled to assert our NO, on this blind system, the blood of my fallen Martyrs cry to me out of their graves, 'shout out our voices' I said, what to shout?, "quit! Quit! Quit! Let these blind leaders leave, let them never continue in Power, because they have made fools out of our deaths. They cheated on us. They didn't raise the right scepter, the scepter of good judgment; they've neglected to build the Kingdom of Equity and Prosperity for all. They've not allowed Justice to reign. They've broken Prosperity by her legs, so that she became handicaped to dance for all. They became cruel to Peace, by tossing her down under boots of Violence. Their umbilical cord of wickedness has not been cut. They're blind leaders whose hearts are pits of theft and lewdness, They love to shed innocent blood. Truth is unknown to them from birth. Their hearts boasted on mediums, their fingers are wide spread before their gods, their feet rash to sorceries, on fortunetellers, they lavished their coins. But the fear of LORD God is not in their hearts, their ears are deaf, their eyes are blind to heed the Law of The Almighty One, thus their Souls have become detestable in the Eyes Of The Most High".

Therefore, I am here to let you know that you've crossed the red line. You've became a tragedy, a tragedy to old men and women who found themselves compromised and exposed to death. Death of huger and diseases. You've became a tragedy! Tragic to disabled and those with special needs, who found themselves mercilessly pushed into a hard life, where they cannot afford to pay. They believed it as cruel negligence and deprivation of their inalienable, citizen's rights, because they deserved to be taken care of. You have crossed the boundary, and have become a tragedy to these peasants who know nowhere to go for survival. Now they're direly hunger stricken victims. You've became a tragedy to these poor soldiers, who depend totally on their salary, who found not the wages and their families are starving to death!

- We would have considered you my hero, if you had stepped down in 2013 or even in 2015—leaving the true mark of democracy to prevail in our Country.

- We would have considered you our hero, if you had detached the National Army from being used by the same ill-motivated SPLA/M elites who liked the flow of the things for their personalized accounts. In addition, they irresponsibly declined the supposed change of things into the hands of the public, that can enable the withdrawing (access) of the collectivity to prevail in the Country.

- We would have considered you our hero, if you had in the prerequisite promoted the primacy of the people's voices and opinions to be

255

upheld. Not imposing on them at first your military dictate which threatened the National cornerstone and made the community who were supposed to be respected and adhered to, neglected.

- *We would have considered you our hero, if you would have promoted Justice to thrive, but not mesmerizing with your money hungry elites who have eventually brought the Nation's economy down hastily without the public voices saying "No!"*

- *We would have considered you our hero, if you would have stopped playing with minds of others with your Machiavellians at both National and International attempts for truth-making peace progress.*

- *Up to now, I would have considered you my true hero, if you have not grabbed the power by our National Army's strength. Nevertheless, humbly and willingly lower down our power and accept justice to prevail by surrendering yourself, with your privileged elites, to the Supreme Court for the genocides committed in Wau, Juba, Yambio, Malakal and in Bentiu—leaving the power to its people.*

- *I would have considered you my good historical leader who has signed for us our referendum unto independence, not this truest enemy of my South Sudanese society!*

Therefore, in the light of the above facts, we question the legitimacy of the present Government to speak for the people of South Sudan. This you must know my Lord, as soon as this message get to you, that the mission is ripped, next will come the Great Judge, The LORD, is his Name; The Commander of the Heavenly Hosts, in whose innocent blood those who perished under your leadership lay, accusing you day and night for their slain souls! Remember this, your arrogance has reached His ears, and your sins, have you multiplied. He will surely send His messengers, the messengers of His wrath, and on that day, you will seek the good days, but you shall find none, You've refused to hearken to His people's voices on you to resign!

7.10 A Letter to South Sudanese People Across The Globe

I wish in my letter to you South Sudanese, to sincerely apologize, I am sorry, sorry, sorry and sorry again!!! I know, this was not the type of a Country you were longing for. You did not expect the Country to take this direction. I know, you are shocked, for you did not also expect to live in such an acute situation or outside your country either. Owing to these misdeeds that erupted which has left the Nation desolated and unwanted to live in, due to the upheaval ruse of racism? Our sincere advice is that; do not admire this regime any longer, for it has already brought into disrepair and disrepute her governmental office! Do not fear its machismo also, for it has no more legitimacy over you. In addition, the date of the ballots you voted for its supposed term have already expired.

Truth restores a nation to strength ...When we need truly a healthy nation; we must accept to act truthfully and willingly upholding the habit of doing the rights things for all people and Country at large. It is only the Truth that can heal and this nation and could also restore its lost dignity and glory. South Sudan's wound is very deep and it needs special concentrated work that can reach her four corners to remedy this wound.

A war torn and underdeveloped Country like our nation (South Sudan) for it to thrive, and put her feet down on peace and prosperity, we must be honest and trustworthy in all things that we can put our hands upon. There is not any Country which has ever succeeded without honest leadership that earns dignity, reliability. It is only upon men and women of integrity, can a nation be built. Therefore, we the National Restoration Party strongly aimed to work towards establishing a healthy nation that must be founded upon truthful values.

Americans struggle for a better nation that serves all American people did stop to continue to fight for their full rights after their revolutionary struggle for freedom. Those who fought the civil war for freedom against British colonialism, had put down clear tips which stated that "all are free, all deserve the right do anything deemed possible to enjoy life, all have the right to become what you desire to be".

This shows that these people were not ignorant about what they were fighting for. We have tangible examples of those who continue to fight for their full freedom like Abraham Lincoln, who spoke up for the right of the blacks and John F. Kennedy admonished white Americans that they should not enslave others; and that all must be free. The same with Dr. Martin Luther King , but all these great men died for a segment of freedom that the white did not wish to continue, unfolding it for American natives.

i. **No Justice or Accountability...** *Under Kiir's leadership, his seventy five (75) who stole the Public money were not brought to book. He knew very well that they had taken bulk amounts of money in USD to the outside into foreign Countries' banks.*

ii. **Soldiers are neglected...** *His leadership did not meet the needs of our South Sudanese Army whose families' lives are completely deteriorating every day. They lack proper medical care because there is no money; including the lack of food to their children, which escalated the breaking away of soldiers' children from homes.*

Because their salaries are either delayed or traded by Salva Kiir's Commanders who know very well that their leader is a man of no-accountability-at-all!

iii. **Education Is Neglected...** *Under Kiir's leadership, academic qualifications do not matter so much, so educating the children is not so important—thus people with true academic qualifications who are seeking jobs are helplessly wandering outside SPLA/M offices.*

iv. **Corruption And Exploitation...** *Under this leadership, the National Petroleum, Borders collections' and Donations from well-wishing Countries, fell not into the Country-building processes, rather into their respective hands. We normally hear these names as, 'Oil, Taxations and Donations' in the national and International Medias and disappeared into Salva Kiir and his elites' pockets—leaving its supposed people languishing in destitution and deprivation.*

v. **National Demonization...** *The President, these privileged elites, right Counsels are not taken from educated figures, wise men, or from the people's voices, rather their best Counsels are obtained from Mediums, Charmers and Soothsayers, for the governing of the State. Upon that faith they have lavished replete national wealth i.e. money, ammunitions guns, good buildings and expensive cars, so that they are thoroughly protected. The President and his privileged elites used demonic powers which thirst for human blood. That is why I am saying: our war is against a demons used system! Most intellectual and close South Sudanese people know this fact but they are afraid to eschew that out of fear for their lives.*

vi. **Continuum Neglecting Generations...** *Under This leadership, the Country is sinking down deeper without development—the* *death toll is skyrocketing and we are losing generations under such meaningless devastating conflicts by these power-hungry profligates.*

vii.It is acceptable worldwide to fight for one's rights... *We should not be of two opinions when we see violations, a lifeline— we should not conceal in pretense or compromise our stand against this dehumanization. There are acceptable ways to claim your right i.e. these are common ways of taking your rights: a) It is acceptable worldwide to fight for one's rights—henceforth please, directly go and claim them from someone who has deprived you of your rights... b) It is acceptable worldwide to fight for one's rights—henceforth please, if you can sue him/her, then you must go and sue him/her before the court of law. c) It is acceptable worldwide to fight for one's rights—henceforth please, if he/she drags you down for bad ramifications, fight him/her until you get your stolen rights. d) It is acceptable worldwide to fight for one's rights—henceforth please, if it can be dialogued—you can go for dialogue, if he or she is an honest and compromisingly gives you your right... e) It is acceptable worldwide to fight for one's rights—please, a peace talk is appropriate when the talk is fair and reliable enough to give you your rights...Those are some conflict resolution ways acceptable worldwide both at the lower and higher level, every problem has its way of solving it accordingly—apart from those techniques, accept no other ways.*

viii. *Our problem is that we South Sudanese have a problem, due to lack of understanding—we don't know how to sincerely claim our rights. To make matters worst even, we don't know which is our right and which is not ours. We don't know duties and responsibilities. That is why those who are exposed robbed us of our rights and*

*go free untouched. We must claim our rights to a better life, i.e. so-
cial rights, economic rights to good jobs that pay enough, right to run
for public positions, right to speak up and express oneself without
any threat from anyone, and many more. Therefore, there is no need
to wait—remember, to get the spiritual, social and economic liberty of accessing your rights and the rights of the coming generations
is a very hard process—it is continuous process that must be fought
throughout the ages. The western world knows this very well—they
are reaping the fruit of what they collectively fought for. Many races
across the globe are thronging to western countries just to get a better
life. Not knowing that what they are going to enjoy has cost these
people their lives. These western people strove harder and tenaciously
refused to neither give up nor give into subsistence. They know very
well what it means to live under someone else' mercy.*

ix. **Note To Youths...** *Firstly, my word is to Youth across the Country
and those in the Diasporas: this program is yours, it is by you, for
you and up to you. In order to help you possess an entity where you
can access your potential life better! You know what, no matter what
has befallen your current life i.e. whether you are privileged or destitute, still you can join the battle for a better South Sudan. Do not
live in the cave of fear of death, in this world if you don't venture to
do something that will liberate you, you will remain a failure in life
throughout your life time. Let's not be fooled by this shallow minded
regime that the youths cannot be national leaders that is a lie, a bad
lie! You must do something to save your sinking Country.*

x. **To The Intellectuals...** *I wonder as to why the university students of South Sudan don't see their expropriated privileges. Why*

have the intellectual eyes become so dull on such serious matters? Why did you accept yourselves to be buried before you die? Why have you accepted to be enslaved in your own motherland by individuals who used to fool you with empty promises? Don't you know that they're merely convincing you to be silent in order not to struggle for your academic privileges and the rights of your people? Why do you chain yourselves by consoling yourselves and comforting that nothing last forever, but you should mark this; such a habit is going to wreck this generation and the still- to- come generations. Why have you chosen slavery rights in your own country? If you are only assigned as private secretaries by these illiterate opportunists who refuse to let go of academic positions, which are supposed to be occupied by intellectuals. Why wish to live subserviced life for how long? We must change this country by the continuous spirit of nationalism I realize, that rogue African heads of state, have found very conducive ground by wielding sharp edges of the power we entrusted to them. To make matters worse, we who trust on the other hand, have forgotten that we are the very people who gave them this power, and we can take it away from them if we come together and say no, refusing to be threatened by our own power. If we take such courage and refuse to live like slaves in our country and oust anyone who forgets that the presidential office is not for profligates—believe me, South Sudan plus Africa will sooner be "heaven on earth". Africa, the land which the dog's teeth were not supposed to eat bones, because of the replete of meat to fill its jaws; Africa, the safest land on earth even the hen could walk with its chickens leaping freely. Heartless African leaders whose main issues are their stomachs, have turned Africa into jungle where everyone survived at one's own risk. Therefore, why continue fearing death—death is not the end—but one dies and goes into history with dignity—and another dies but goes into a grave and forgotten. Therefore, fear nothing, for torturing and jailing are downfalls of such governments. It is the sign that predicts that our enemies are weak and lack sound morals and dignity. They're fading away from our sight, they came to power honored, but they be ousted from the power dishonored.

xxiv) **To All Our People In Diasporas...** *Prove to be a strong Society: Let's not be weakling societies who are tossed here and there by any opinions. Let's not be a society with the habit of giving up or give in quickly even in such a great and noblest struggle. We should not loosely permit our rights and the national progress to be thwarted and have our Country's potential future cracked down upon. This we should all hold in mind, that to have a great NATION like any other sophisticatedly developed Countries in the world, we must have strong will, stamina, mind, heart, faith in ourselves and in God, identity, vision and the capacity of translating down that vision tangibly. Other societies of the world should see the quality of who we truly are. We must work it out for all to see which realm we are!*

xi) **Unleash Yourselves from Double Mindedness...** *There is no nation under the heaven which grew so strong without great men and women of justice—who could strongly wield daggers of JUSTICE. So rise up and fight for justice and accountability. No matter might become, look not at menacing sides, and consider no one, especially those who oppose the power of justice to prevail.*

xi. **Let Public Opinion Be The Primacy...** *For weakling*

societies breed dependent nations. Whilst strongly willed society those who aren't easily bent down by any duping, or gullibly believe any fabricated hints, be it small or big—such societies had already won their path into prosperity, safety and pursuit of their collective and individual happiness! To get a greatly blessed Country leaned unto the reach of your hands, is like getting heavy jet leaning down on something with its never changing law, "strongly cemented ground first". That is price through which we can attain our abundant life.

xii. Defining What Inspire Feeble Minded People... *Out of tribal mind: when people follow someone who is defecting because that he is from my tribe or clan, it is a very wrong idea, you shouldn't be motivated by tribal spirit and make a fool out of your own. Rather firstly you should understand the man's motive and intents before you could scarify your life to ill-noble struggle.*

xiii.   Motivated By Money... *Some societies can be easily bend down because of money inspiration, once they see money nothing again is of a value in their eyes, even their very lives! Such money motivated societies always never win any noble struggle. They die for today's gain, but not for a noble cause knowing that tomorrow will reward them good things!*

xiv. Out Of Cowardice... *Some of the societies can be pulled by their ears—and they can even eulogize you for not killing them rather, greeting them by the ears! Such societies are easily inspired by fear of those who could kill their human body. They don't know that the death of a human body is normal but the worse is the death of your dignity and the cutting down of your integrity! Such a quickly inspired by fear society can follow anyone who out of fear had*

264

motivated them. These types of societies don't follow any one who is struggling for a collective and noble struggle.

xv. Impressed Into Pessimism... *Don't be impressed and fall into pessimism, don't stay unfolded and allow the things to "go like that in your homeland" or be only motivated by your tribal hints alone. Why not die as one Family of Nations? It is in fact the noblest war! Accept not to be divided—easy to divide people who never ever acquire something of moral element; any divided realm remained as the abode of acute poverty and death resident, until they should learn to maintain a mutual belief and understanding, rebuffing any regime that wishes to build its nest in the path of JUSTICE—of promoting crooked and deceitful ways: NO is its answer!*

xvi. Let's Not Be Fooled Around... *When it comes to the Sudanese struggles, I wish to remind you that do not hastily forget who really fought the 1956-2011 civil wars for our freedom. Those Anyanya II and Anyanya I including SPLA/M were just myths, the true heroes who fought those civil wars were peoples. I meant you! In fact, also some Arabs Sudanese, Africans, Egyptians, Asians, Europeans, Americans, these peoples should not be ignored, for without their supportive hands and prayers we won't had have our freedom. They supported us to the point of death or let me say killed in struggle for our freedom! For how long, will we remain undecided—for how long will this heart with mixtures in cowardice coupled with unbecomingly unreasonable thoughts mulishly remain to divide our collective No's and Yes'? I know "You might not perceive what we're doing or why we are doing it, whilst in another corner, rather you can see it better when you are at mine". Please stand up and support this* *noble struggle, the drastic National Reformation initiative, for the sake of our dear Country S. Sudan which has been cracked down to dust by failed Kiir's government. In addition, what you still see now is a myth of traitors with three aims:*

(1) Of strongly grabbed desire to continue indulging in your national positions and wealth.

(2) They've made our power as their hideout from facing Justice.

(3) They're there to impose on us total submission, such that we could either give in or up to their will. Therefore, it is up to us all to do something noble. Know assuredly that it's due to our redundancy and lack of enough collective will to openly shake them off, or crash them against the cliffs of punishment. That is why they are still there controlling us with biased rulings. Moreover, for this very reason I emerge to tell you that always step out against any dehumanization to oust them!

7.11 A Letter to Friends of The Reformation

Furthermore, I would wish to appreciate my beloved friend Deng Athuai Mawiir Rehan, the first Civil Society Alliance Chairman to South Sudan. His heart thirsted for a Country with replete prosperity, democracy and fair governance—which he stringently strove for a long time but which he didn't attain. Secondly, I wish to appreciate my Western Equatoria Governor, Gen. Joseph Benghazi Bakosoro of Yambio for his patriotic heart.

You know what; it is not too late to tell you that I am sorry even when we parted from the Nile Bitch Hotel sorely offended over our initiative of reforming the Nation, in which I sternly rebuked you over what I called "cowardice and mesmerizing with this regime", without even regarding your virtue as my Governor. But it was because my heart was in the state of burnout, seeing that our people are acutely weighed down under the heaviest fatigue of suffering. The suffering those provoked arbitrarily by this so-called SPLM/A government.

I pray that God should put the same seed of consuming zeal into your heart which I suffered in my heart for so long, knowing that we are but one people with same identity. That our problem should not be tackled from tribal perspectives but must be seen from the horizons of collectiveness. Owing to our belief, it is clear and reasonable: if the untold plights occurred to the South Sudanese, people are to be solved; they must be tackled by wider perspectives in order to reach its holistic remediation.

Truth must be said: for the South Sudanese people are the most marginalized, they were marginalized first under the Khartoum's leadership, when the ideology of Islamization and Arabization mulishly refused to bend down for harmony to thrive in one Nation. In addition, South Sudanese tribes were tauntingly conditioned to embrace Islam to depict their spiritual note worthiness, and to become Arabs. To portray their ultimate loyalty, those were the two sharp daggers wielded on their faces as the laws for peaceful co-existence. Now, we again found ourselves disillusioned by the failed and racial regime of Salva Kiir that cheated on us, to trust and vote for its SPLA/M: that in return we will own a Country that would be happily enjoying its fair and good governance. Nevertheless, who can really believe now, that today we are languishing in hell again! We suffer acute poverty; gunshot death, illiteracy, poor health facilities, tribal catastrophes and so many other problems. To speak, but the truth, we were tempted twice to mention all the names of those who have ruined our Country, but we saw to it as a taboo even to use my pen to write their collective names all—so I kept "Under Salva Kiir" for the prudence to the truth.

In addition, we decided to describe their collective names as, 'them, they and their' but used 'we, I, us and our' to make our drastic motive towards the same Society clear and different towards same lands. Woe we are! Who will help such people under this heavy fatigue and indescribable suffering! We call upon God, The Author of Creation, to help, and to all the Countries who ushered into our Independence, including the International Community, yea, to rise up!

The Country that was supposed to bless and sustain all her Citizens inclusive of its sisters Countries, is now faltering on the despotic arm of Salva Kiir's military dictatorship. And who may not get disillusioned by this despotism, one may ask himself or herself, "is this was what our late fathers were martyred for?" Because the land has fallen on all fours into the hands of blind and carefree—Salva Kiir and his privileged elites! Yes, "The rain of TRUTH must rain no matter what ails". They are working in dangerous collusions, escalating their entrenchment under the SPLA/M name.

We are shocked by such upheaval, disillusionment! It has reached to the extent that we are imposed by this situation to flee, because the Country is no longer accommodating us for a peaceful life. The SPLM Chairmanship's military dictatorship demands only to destroy those who are only wishing to have a Country of transparency, equality, equity and prosperity for all. These are the most neglected and impossible things to happen. If we insist, we could simply be ordered to come down on our knees in servile submission or else our sure hope for survival will be only in Diasporas' accommodations, in exile, because we won't find security for our lives again.

All our peoples now are fully languishing in the corners of foreign societies, to find themselves fugitives. Aliens in nomadic life; eating the morsels of shame and drinking water from the cups of humiliations. Under the privileged feigned foreign permissions who are allowing them to share their food ssometimes, expecting their sooner return to where they truly belong.

We dare say that these 'trying to govern' people, "their fathers did not provide them with toys to repair when they were young, so they turned the Country and the lives of these poor societies into toys for recreation!" I must fight for our societal legacy of diversity, the legacy of my Country is more valuable to me than little systematic organization (government) or polity of whatsoever—that instigates conflicts and mulishly negates our beautiful diversity, which could be fantastically enjoyable. We are ready to repudiate SPLM with its privileged elites; I am very ready to defy Salva Kiir's regime: we are asserting our NO in the loudest voice! Woe is me if I will be silent again! Yes, true to say that, "I was a human being all along—until I reached South Sudan where I became a dying castaway".

I will never be silent: "though the waves of the Indian Ocean are stilled, I shall never be calmed but will roar." For The Author of Creation in whose eyes the life of everyone is better, suffered on me his will, we are impelled to add our NO, against this racial system—the blood of my fallen Martyrs cry to me out of their graves, "shout out our voices" I said, what to shout?, "quit! Quit! Quit! Let racist's Regime leave, let them *never continue in the power, because they have made fools out of our death, they cheated on us. They didn't raise the right scepter, the scepter of good judgment; they've neglected to build the Kingdom of Equity and Equality for all.*

They've not allowed Justice to reign. They've broken prosperity by her legs, so that she became handicapped to dance for all. They've become cruel to peace, leaving her trodden down under "boots of violence". From therein, my heart remains to condemn me through and through over my numbness in the cave of silence, for keeping the roof of my lips locked up as if I don't see what is occurring in my Country.

If we need peace, we must value Truth: "For it is from out of the man of truth, that truth is meant to be real, and it's in the hearts of the family of Truth that the Truth is sincerely valued and recognized above the purest diamond". I never find peace within my Soul; tears never cease flowing down on my cheeks. Happiness I wished it back, but it deserted me for good. I sleep almost when it is already time for the people to wake up, because my eyes have rebelled against me, they doggedly refuse to get locked, though I press them together with my two hands, they still open. I am a man of heavy heart, although I try to laugh, it is all feigned laughter. Because all the sounds of my laughter, who can believe that it is feigned and fibbed ones. They are not from my real heart!

Why be happy, when my peoples are expelled out of their Country every day, all my birds have flown away from their nests. They left their residues, because they are peoples with no strong-handed government to truly care for what they want. It takes one's courage to reveal his truest inside out, I said this for truth's sake. My Soul needs to see the change, the true one that should make all of us to get settled happily in the pastures of transparency, with Justice allowed to gaily distribute us its fruits, hugged by her sister Prosperity in ultimate harmony for all. True to say it, If I still have an aggressive enemy left, I should be the man that disdainfully wields the dagger of injustice on anyone anywhere

7.12 I Appreciate My People!

I appreciate these people, they are a people whom their Creator showed them no mercy. The way of peace declined them, They are a people punished beyond repair. Their hearts are blunt, dull and forgetful!

They are a people smashed by their Creator in discipline. The Lord their Husband brought them down into destitution, and caused them to beg like widows. He did not make them go through an easy road, else they would quickly forget his slashing on their backs. He followed them to wherever they turn to go, and with his notorous jealousy he stripped them naked and rebuked them. He pursued them seriously from behind. He cut off all the fragments of the arrogance that was in them, and made them simple.

I appreciate them, for they are my people. I appreciate the way they are and what they are or who they are. I appreciate how my people endured all these exceeding sufferings; they are a people whom the Lord God allowed them to be smashed, slain by famine and ebbed because of many sins. They still endured the Lord's sword's wrath. They still bore those sufferings and even adopted it as something to be accepted willingly and without complaints. They walked distances from the South and to the North bare-footed;

They go distances in order to fetch water and carry it on their heads,

271

and pound their Dura with their local mortals. They traded riding on bi-cycles all from the South to as far the North carrying heavy goods; they rode on bicycles to Uganda, Kenya and Congo and to as far as Central Africa. Facing immense obstacles and threats of death, yet they managed to save lives. They ate all tasteless wild-fruits; they risked their lives by being almost killed by Arabs, and even by the hands of their own sons from SPLA's wrong conduct

They have undergone lots of rapes and robbing, yet they withstood it all and survived through them all. I appreciate them who they are, what they are. I appreciate the life they lived as nomads travelling from place to another, facing lots of threats and adventures. They were eaten by the wild animals and bitten by the poisonous snakes, Yet despite all those catastrophes they endure it all. Their own beloved members of the families died as they watched them dying, yet they still took courage and bore that.

The woman could give all her last morsel which remained to her children and husband and willingly die of hunger. I appreciate that heart I admire those lovely women who endured with their husbands all those exceeding sufferings. When will my enemies of this world stop pointing their hands at me with contempt, trivialising my dark skin. When will they learn that I am one of God's Creations. I am part of His mankind. When will these people believe that I can do it as they believed for themselves? Do you love yourselves? So do I too.

Peoples called me 'poor and needy' all nations nicknamed me 'the vulnerable' I had received lots of relief and support from peoples and nations; I am fed by the hands of many strangers, yes, from Diasporas' aid. I am full of many loans those I cannot even attain to return; all languages are waiting to tell me 'what did you do with our aid? Expecting from

272

me the good answers!

But believe me, when the Lord will rise me up; I promise you Nations, when the Almighty God settles me; I will "Be a Faithful Father to all the fatherless" I will "Be The Defender of the weak" I will liberally give to all those in need, recalling it no more; I will open my arms to the widows and the orphans. They shall be my own sisters and brothers. All day long they will be reclining at my own royal table and share my bread. My heart shall overflow with love towards them ceaselessly—for I would be the FATHER to all. For the Almighty God has disciplined me well!

Chapter Eight

8.1 Inclusivity, Sage Vision and Stamina for Erecting a Nation

TO BEGIN MY TALK on this topic, I would like to start it with my own legend of the four great birds, which happened to have met one day upon a big almond tree, as each one of them was coming from a very far away valley. The first one sat on in the branch of that tree with its long and widely spread wings. It looked with its stern eyes observing all round as it was settling down in the tree. And next then came another bird with a strong gust of wind blown as it was settling in the tree, and followed by the third and the fourth. Each one of them was about to fight the other, but one of them shouted saying, "No! No! Let's not fight just before we knew ourselves! What is your name? Said one of them. I am called Faith, he replied as he was still looking at things here and there in a simplifying and trivializing manner, which disturbed everyone".

Then one of them retorted, "Where did you come from? 'I came from where truth is reality, where the impossible things are turned into tangible substances", he continued, "I am durable and optimistic, I am never moved, afraid or alarmed of anything". He went on explaining himself to the rest such that they got agitated from such exaggerated introduction. In addition, turning to the nearby one and he said, "What are you called". "I am called Value; I came from an aristocratic family. They used to call me 'The Important One of All or First Born". In explaining himself to the rest he said, 'I am born with an inborn important nature, I used to keep the records of every Nation that wishes to live longer with dignity, thus everybody is supposed to kneel for me but I kneel back not in return. I am not to be ignored or profaned but kept inviolable.

In hearing this, every one of them saw it as a bane. Such an arrogant introduction. Pointing with its beak, asked Faith the nearby bird who was still silent. In replying to it said, 'I am called Vision. I came from a very far place. No one had ever been to where I used to belong. Everybody there used to keenly hearken to my counsel because I speak of what I have vividly seen and perceived. I can see things from hundreds of kilometers, ten to thousands of years afar. Before they can take place and set a relevant answer to life's challenges". All his audience looked at him with goggled mouths as he was still speaking. His words were considered debilitating, wizardry and exaggerated. Each one of them looked at one another with enquiring eyes of "who can see something at the distance of one kilometer's end, let alone ten thousand kilometers"

They hated him through and through—he was told to keep silent because they said he took it so much on himself. In addition, who are you, are you Mr. so great, great…great…as these figures required Mr. Faith his still silent bird. But in reply, he said, 'I am called Work"; spoke the silent bird as he showed them his swollen muscles with confidence. Everyone was quickly annoyed from how he exposed his swollen muscles. They turned on him with cascades of inquiries saying: "tell us who do you think you are"? "Or why do you think you are better than us? Open your mouth, speak," shouted the bird Value. Opening his mouth to speak, Mr. Work as he was still flapping its long feathers and wide wings, said, "do not be surprised to know that without me nothing could be done. I am the only being born with an incredible strength. In addition, with this power and hard work of mine, I am nick-named Mr. Prosperity because anything I put my hands on, would surely get done. Thus, I am loved, respected by both youth and the aged". Nevertheless, they all roared at him saying, "Stop it! Stop it! You are lying. 'I can see things that a normal person cannot see them yet I did not exaggerate it when I was introducing myself!" said Mr. Vision. "Hold on please; hold on," said Mr. Bird Faith. He continued, instead for us to harangue ourselves in irresponsible debate, why not come together in harmony and choose for ourselves one to lead us". All accepted it.

Moreover, as they went on seeking the right qualifications, they elected Mr Vision. They told him, "Please, you will be seeing things for us from afar off and tell us how to deal with those challenges so that we could get rid of them in advance". The bird

Work was chosen to be the secretary, such that he could write everything down. In addition, the Bird Faith was made their keeper, while Mr.Value was appointed as their adviser. Moreover, after ten years of their harmonious and hard work, they built a very gigantic and splendid Kingdom, which the birds from all over four corners of the world come to see, such a very great and significant realm.

Everybody wished to do like them, because they had set a very good example. Though the bird Value, Faith and Work died later, yet the bird Vision adopted on himself the double virtues of his colleagues and worked harder and harder. He called their Nation 'Kingdom *of Four Wise Men*'.

Throughout the history, when it comes to the founding of a Country, be it spoken or written on dehumanization, Nationalism is the spirit that has the charm: it is the key for restoring what is expropriated by rogue persons, from betrayal and corruption of enemies of truth of all types. Nothing promises true change or yields the nice fruit of change besides nationalism.

When a nation fails, it doesn't mean that failure has just emerged from nowhere or no one, but that failure is a result which indicates that the power in place (people in power) lacked genuine nationalistic values in their hearts. Therefore, if one wishes to adjust or bring life back to its normal equity, we must summon the heart of nationalism for true change for the betterment of all.

Those great history makers did not have odd human organs, or special information more than us, but what set them apart was their love for their peoples and Soils—that keenness were bestowed into their hearts by Creator for the benefit of all. Dear if you love your child, then why don't love the rest of the children of your neighbors dearly also? If you love your woman or man and would wish to offer him or her all good things, why then don't you think that the same elements are important to your neighbors?

The people are groaning: when people begin to loathe and quit their own Country and prefer to leave their motherland and go seeking for better life in places which are not their own— that is the evidence for which we should do something notable to better the living for someone who is leaving her/his soil. And to give meaning to the love which the leadership has toward its people or Country—that love must galvanize someone not to damage the image of one's own Country selfishly or ignorantly.

Therefore, this is why nationalist reformation must start within this beloved Country to rise up with greater efforts to hasten change into this beloved Country. For this soil suffered negligence for so long. But we kept silent and distanced ourselves from declaring our airtight stand.

The land is robbed out of the hands of its rightful Citizens; and you, the community, are merely used as tools of perpetuating the pledge of remaining in the power longer. Good ideas are considered threats, to demand something that could empower all the community is considered a menacing threat and one can be murdered for wishing that noble thing.

The SPLA/M as a Revolutionary Movement, has not failed,

but those who currently took over the leadership after the death of Dr. John Garang de Mabior are the ones who failed. They did not take to heart those sage elements Garang perpetually spoke about—because the elements which Dr. John Garang mentioned several times, were the core values upon which the SPLA/M stood. And they were the elements which attracted many people to scarify everything including their very lives.

The SPLA/M has terribly fallen from the right track, the airtight and the bond of loving the people which was attracting element SPLA/M used. Garang knew very well, that a leader can't succeed without loving his people and the soil, thus his vision was very admirable, inclusive of everyone. He set a high standard on discipline and concentrated in every affair touching the people he administered.

Nevertheless, people without genuine aim to remain in power, have paralyzed the nation's norms and values and smashed its strength. Currently nothing is of any importance. Everyone danced only for interest, things are in black markets, even things which were not supposed to be seen in the hands of the foreigners; it is the aliens who have accessed and possessed them now.

This system has compromised the Country, and the people are languishing and have decided to quit the Country, due to the smashed integrity. They looked for basic things which the government is supposed not to neglect or turn the blind eyes on them.

The meaning of being a Human, calls for one to know that all are equal before the Author of Creation. All deserve a blissful life,

All deserve a good diet of food, clean water, education, reliable medication from well to do hospitals. All deserve to marry and be married by anyone of their choice and make decisions concerning their lived attributes and agreements importantly help on every decision that shape their society.

Life must be enjoyed by everyone living inside the same territory not merely taken for granted by certain individuals while others are left outside to languish in unhappiness. The needs of everyone must be considered important, and his rights protected against negligence and deprivations of any types. We must pave way for every South Sudanese Citizen to enjoy the privileges and rights which are theirs including the responsibilities this nation put on our shoulders.

Therefore, to build a nation, you must consider the importance of the four above, Faith, Vision, Value and Work for they are the inseparable things that boost up the Country into quicker evolution with stability, prosperity and durability. The true faith in God yields honesty, obedience and trustworthiness. In addition, the vision of the Country can enthusiastically direct the hearts into nationalism as the right path. Whilst the values maintain the Country from being polluted by corruption. With hard working spirit, the Country could quickly progress in development.

I wish to clarify my points here: People are never what they claim, until they begin to believe in their values, custom and order of their respect to what matters according to realm of their ethical concepts. They must accept respect and build their Country upon its distinctiveness. People begin to mock themselves when they prefer the cultures of other races and embrace the traditions of other societies and change from their respective one. And it is another mockery when any leadership begins to haphazardly copy the replicas from other foreign Nations. They can investigate the cultures of their aboriginal races, those are the real residents to whom the Country is theirs forever.

That leadership whosoever, must do all her changings and adjustments based on the lay indigenous' knowledge. Any attempt in adjusting one's culture without his/her awareness, is the surest inhumanity. Let the people have their Constitution, the constitution that reflects them, and they will have no confusions as to where to adjust their life to. Thus they get a confused society. I want to redirect your eyes to this biblical phrase also, *"And ye shall know that the kingdom of God is above the kingdoms of man, yes, (and) let His will be done on earth as it is in Heaven!"* This quotation is found in the book of Prophet Daniel. But, that simple statement brought down the entire State of Babel, for when God visited the heart of Babylonian king Nabekudnazzar and found it thoroughly wicked and without the required fear of God in him. So, when you need to establish a Country on earth here, you must start it through Him who gives success. For we the mankind are just ministers helping God by executing his plans. Therefore, the Nation which can be strongly established, is the realm that understands the word 'minister' in its way or meaning. 'Minister' is a word that means 'servant' and the word servant came out from the verb 'serve'. Therefore, it refers to any Ministry that has to do with either Police, Security, Forestry, Local government,

281

Army, Civil Service, Legal Affairs, Agriculture, Communications and Information and Fire-proof. And all the rest of the Ministers 'servants' with their Ministries 'Servant-hood', they should work 'serve' harder to make their Community happy by their vital services!

They are supposed to mediate everything in honest liaison with their communities—giving them adequate services to their own mothers, fathers, brothers and sisters. Yes, these people are your own brothers and sisters, mothers and fathers : they are your own siblings. Build your mind bigger; make it accommodate all tribes of this Country! Know therefore that you are obligated to sincerely serve them with absolute heartfelt commitment and willing mind. You are not supposed to hold the Law in your hands.

Suiting my expectations Sir or Madam, I am expecting a nation whose President is the 'Chief Servant' followed in the same manner by his Ministers, Governors, Commissioners Servers. And I believe any government that is built upon the foundation of good services to her weak ones will surely grow up quickly and get released from her destitutions. It's not enough just to say tough words and void promises to your own mothers and fathers, brothers or sisters. People don't need only to accompany their leaders to the airplanes or be kept receiving their Authorities those leaning, without proper enhancement of any kind offered to them. That will surely cause the people's hearts to get dry up in complete mistrust, including myself the author of this book. People don't need to be kept dancing and praising the names of their Leaders yet those Leaders don't even dare to help the weak ones, the disabled, the orphans, the widows and the needy ones—such Leaders are realistically mocking God.

If the meaning of the 'Fire extinguisher' is well understood by the fireproof; I believe the fire-extinguishers would willingly serve the families on fire. They would even risk their lives to the extent of dying with the dying families on fire, and they will not be waiting first to be commanded by his or her boss to offer his supposed service. If the service you do does not cause your very own life, then that service is not availing and meaningless! If the fire extinguisher stands at a distance pretending to be 'helping' but not 'serving' the lives of his very own community, then there is no need for them to do that job.

If the Ministry of Communication and Information is not matching together reporting and broadcasting the disaster facing the community, or working for their services, then all is void! The Ministry of Communication is supposed to broadcast what is 'facing the residents'. And this same Ministry should mediate the problems facing the community with her government, convincing the government to work harder with devoted hearts to her poor ones, not the poor communities are forced to serve the elites.

Any government that forces her community into serving and obeying it more than serving its people and seeing to their community's needs, that leadership will end up meriting the title 'dictatorship' or 'tyrant rule'. The communities are supposed to be supported by the Ministry of Communication to 'voice out' their needs. And this Ministry is not to be held handicapped or hindered by the Security Forces or Top Political Leaders; it is supposed to operate freely for the communities of that particular nation!

If the Police don't understand that they are the eyes of the blind, legs for the lambs and the hands for the hand-less, or if they don't fathom that they are the 'life-saving' for the their poor communities, then all is void. If the police man could see two people fighting, but still sit back or walk 'away' caring not about that matter, that is a very great treason. I am very sorry sometimes to see the police allowing all things to 'go like that'. A nation whose police is 'careless' is truly domed to destruction. Police is the frequent 'live-saving' Unit, because their work is very great. A policeman is the only one who can solve the problems between the two whose matter is caused by misunderstandings or had to do with robbery, theft or any sort of agitation. Know that the cop is supposed to work harder to spare his weak ones against the offenses of their troublemakers.

It is one of the factors that can add up to redundancies or negligence in the government if the police are not exerting their moments in executing their obligated services! Because if a policeman does not face death fatalities in solving their daily encountered matters, then there is no well-done job at all. Believe my advice, subtly make everybody your friends, and be a servant to everyone including your criminals, and you will see everything subjective to your lead including the gangsters.

If the Legal Affairs allow cases to go without making scrupulous and sound solutions in it; then all is void. The word 'judge' is only meant for 'Jehovah God' therefore, this word 'judgment' is a very big word, it's meant to God alone the JUDGE of all. So, the Judge is not supposed to go against the Law and profane the meaning of which he or she has been divinely ordained to. Know therefore that the Judge is supposed to be a God-fearing man or woman and eschew injustices, and above all, he/she should be with an excellent understanding of the Law.

Understand that judiciary is a DEPARTMENT that had to do with 'justice intensively' any clumsy mistake a judge commits, that will cause your very own life. Therefore the judge is a servant of God, serving these poor people with the fear of God and accuracy. If you mesmerize with such things like kickbacks, or fear threats of any sort or ensnared by the lust for women or attacked by greediness, such that you wrongly issue unsound verdicts allowing things to go wrong with God's ordained services, then you are committing an unforgivable treason against both God and your Country abysmally. If the Judges of the nation are not committed and zealous in their services, then all is void.

Agriculture means 'cultivating' or 'planting', so if this Ministry is not working harder to make her community get an ample food at the end of her year's yielding; then all is void!

This Ministry is supposed to motivate and download in her puny-minded people to inherit the spirit of 'hard-working!' It has to stake out the optimum seasons and give the poor ones the reliable orientations of how to use their digging tools on their fertile lands. This same Ministry is supposed to have a large number of the laborers at the County or State level. If this Ministry is just sleeping allowing everything to 'go like that' then that nation will surely never get out from the strong clutches of hunger.

The Ministry of Agriculture is supposed to work harder in uniform with her poor ones to up-grade them. Sometimes if this Ministry is not careful, I am afraid to say that it will be found serving her top brass only neglecting the weak ones! But believe me, if that is the direction the nation is pushing with her Agricultural Ministry, then wait with such a nation for only seven years and you will see it with poor community and dictatorial leadership! Be careful in everything you do! For everything has a bounding ending, (and) that ending will determine either badness or worthiness not vice versa! Those rich and strong nations agriculturally do not quarrel over the power, but the poor gluttonous ones do.

Our wildlife must properly be cared for, because wildlife is the sole means for the Country to get good Customers those who come for it from Diasporas. Therefore, if this Ministry does not work hard in protecting her wildlife conserving it from daily shootings by the civilians; then that nation will get nowhere; but if they take proper care it, then that nation will get rich in an instance eventually. But if the nation doesn't have strong wildlife conservation, with a proper care to her animals—then all is void. The government is supposed to understand the situation of her soldiers; taking absolute care of the families whose fathers will be in the far Forests, leaving their children home alone. And if the government is not supporting that army, then these soldiers will eventually exit from the forest, neglecting their jobs.

Therefore, if each of the soldiers' top brass could take shrewd catering of their soldiers'such fearful eluders will in turn be convicted and challenged to change with utterance from being skeptics into defenders of their wildlife conservation enthusiastically. If the Army of the nation doesn't perceive that they are the fortress of their people, then that nation is bound to destruction.

A soldier is supposed to be a man or a woman who heartily loves his or her nation with all his heart. He or she should be very willing to work by himself or herself for her own nation's warfare! But sadly in Africa, you see the police and soldiers sometimes misunderstanding that, and they could start even exerting the poor community to yield to serve them loyally. You are called to 'protect' and 'guard' your very own people!

Don't use your gun against your own blood brothers or sisters, mothers or fathers. The killing of one's own innocent people is a greatest treason you have ever committed. Be a committed servant of the Lord God and serve your people's lives from those of their enemies. And I believe your death will be dearly to both God and the people. It is more valuable when the soldier happened to be caught in the war and live with lots of severe chastisements, but still stands firm and allows not his or her mind caught too by giving or narrating off the secrets of his or her nation; is when that soldier could be called 'hero' of our nation. We need committed soldiers not addicted drunkards! We need organized soldiers, men and women with big love to God and respect to their people. We need men and women with great zeal to humbly serve their 'community' and her 'government' with all their hearts. They are supposed to be brave and wise in whatever they could do so that they could be good examples to the next generations.

If the Security personnel don't understand that they are the 'wall' and 'solid part' of their nation, then all is void. Security is supposed to work hard to 'protect' her people from the following things precisely:

- Any sort of crafty ways the enemy may bring in distortion to either their community or government's system.
- Refuse strong intoxications from either the Leaders or poor community who are damaged by alcoholism.
- Any sort of riots or risky encountering from their enemy against their Leaders or people. For it is a great shame and treason even if your Leaders are assassinated easily while under your very guidance.
- Security is supposed to 'download' the spirit of 'hard-working' and good 'services' into her different Departments' officials!
- Security is supposed to render safety faithfully to her community and uniformly stay with her Governor or President in meditative good services to their poor communities!
- If the security of the nation stays hands folded, then that nation is truly bound to destruction! Security is supposed to 'serve' the lives of her community not watching the strong ones only properly protected against the weak!
- Any nation whose security doesn't know what to do or how to do it to her weak ones, then that security is doing no jobs at all.

- The community is puny-minded sometimes and therefore they need security with true 'mission' and 'loving-heart' in admonishing her own community!
- Security should build trust with their very own people and appear to them as 'life-saving' not protectors of the strong against their weak.
- For if the security organ acts harshly or unreasonably with his people; then give that Country only 10 years and you will see eventually her people traumatized as a result. And if you believe me or not, there will be overthrowing one after another because people will lose trust from the government or from one another. People will fight over the power because it is the 'only' means to get rich and well-protected.
- Therefore, if the government doesn't work harder—then that is the weakness of the security forces—in allowing such officials to be reluctant and redundant in serving her poor community.
- Forestry is supposed to be considered from the very beginning of our nation. And if therefore the poor community is allowed to use forestry as their basic livelihood, then that nation is really going nowhere.
- Those communities who are using the forestry as their means if they are given jobs or supported agriculturally, I believe they will cease cutting the trees of the land down.
- They need to get 'informed' not properly 'bitten' because they are from here and they had their monopoly to 'live' too! This ministry therefore is to make awareness and to open

means or jobs for these poor communities. It has to mediate the problems of the poor communities who live on forestry with the government and see to it prompted. Because many cutting axes will cause the land to have semi-desert.

- The civil service Ministries are supposed to understand themselves by their 'meaning'. Because this ministry is supposed to meet the needs of the communities not just pamper with void words.

- If the national Authorities begin to promise her community recklessly with the things that they will not be in position to do them, then that nation is worthy to be accused of unfairness.

- These people are your own relatives and no need to deceive them; you must tangibly translate all your hints down into visible actions. Let build our nation's foundation in trustworthiness, when it is not too late and let's take the bad conditions of some African, Asians and European's failures of late initiated trustworthiness! The first human needs are to provide them with such simple things as these:

- Clean and sanitized water and enough food security—good schools with truely qualified teachers—properly demarcated roads and plots for their living—up-grade them technologically—reliable hospitals with enough medical treatments— open chances for job-seekers—remember the poor in their inferior level of life and do not force them to do what they cannot afford—and provide them with reliable security— they need you to listen to their Views—provide them with adequate and attainable transports means—show them that you are working for them dearly—orient them to know how to work also for themselves—so that they become also creative, supportive, and skillful in all life aspects—so that they should not become only selfish consumers!

8.2 The Inclusivity and the Law of Prosperity

Once you skip little beginning, it'll disqualify you for life. In the truthful sense, prosperity is a thing that comes directly from the Creator himself only after sincere hard work with a focussed comittment—those nations who understood this term are now flipping on success because they quickly spread their wings and flew onto prosperity's peak! They prospered through their God-given wisdom and understanding, though they had backslidden later on fantasies. For us the South Sudanese, the difference between the past and the present is that we are looking for quicker changes such that we could be better else we will be heading to another trivials.

We should have clear and reliable objectives with a vision to enable us to have a hopeful future to reliably believe it as we start it right in our very today not vehemently expecting tomorrow. Therefore, as we have our attention drawn to the famous motto that was ever quoted by every nation inclusive of our newly coming to existence realm, the word prosperity. So, for this prosperity we sing to live, grow and yield its fruit, there must be nationalistic and scarifying hearts. We must faithfully exert another

gigantic effort to plant transparency, impartiality, humble attitudes towards accepting ourselves and analyzing the areas of our
weakness and escalate our capacities and willingly draw closer to
one another, without any selfish ulterior only. Then shall our nation 'move ahead' and succeed quickly. And the vision or values
of the nation, always are not always supposed to be kept secret.
I mean that they are not supposed to be hidden from the reach
of everyone. In fact, it must be rehearsed to everyone such that
whenever someone's temper goes against them, that it should
cause all our collective mouths to shout for silence to defy any
violations of them.

All the communities of this Country are supposed to know
scrupulously the inside-out of the direction this precious
Country of ours is heading to. It is when understanding reaches
everyone's heart and ears—that then shall the community protect their nation themselves truthfully. But any mistake of trying
to avoid the community's clear observation and allowing them
to know when, where, who, which and what, that will optimistically lead the whole land into segregation and arbitrary bickering without ceasing. A well informed community is a sign of a
bright and prosperous future. Such an acquainted and contented
community, will never hear them bought, hired or manipulated
or do bad things to their own Country because they are down-
rightly immune to any loopholes those might fail their National
Progress.

I am just trying to give my attribute. I wish that each one of
us should do the same in one good way or another. So, after my

thoughtful observation, I personally suggest why not give my hidden treasure of the little things I know, by putting it down here. The fundamental objectives those I know, though everybody knows them too, yet they are not clichéd.

There are three important things in a Country building which the entire lives revolve around them and these are;

- Family
- Land
- Jehovah

These above mentioned Objects, are the backbones which a Country should realistically observe with all her might. Above all, if Christians don't have clear and asserted standards or vision in which they wholeheartedly wished their Country to be looked like, then let them not be surprised. They will eventually be wrapped up in deterioration, in all lives' aspects in their Country. The Vision of any Country saves as the starter of the truck. Its faith saves as its driver, its speed movement saves as the work in practical, and Values saves as the Sacred the Country should be adhered to. And it is the civilized ones those who fear God alone. He, the Creator, divinely ordained them to diligently materialize proper catering of Orphans, Widows, and Disabled? Unlike the infidels, the infidel is a man or woman who ignores the existence of the living God, and he does the Jehovah God resist. No matter how willingly they try to prove themselves genuine, yet they are easily carried along by Satan and quickly deceive them and steals their hearts and minds, and drives them away from what is good or supposed to be done.

The Faithful Christain and civilized man or woman on the other hand, has the adamant virtue of a clear and valiant "Yes" or "No" wherever necessary. A faithful civilian should jeopardize those who might blaspheme their God, protect their Country against any fates, not debate it with those who would crave to spoil their dear families! Everyone who attempts to scornfully approach any sacred thing, or loot anything herein, whosoever he or she be, should clearly be warned to stop that without hesitation! And all these are the works of those who understand that 'it is their mandatory obligation to do this.

8.3 We Must Fight Away Corruption

8.4 South Sudan, The Youngest Daughter of Corrupt Mother Africa!

In those days African leaders were very well known for their purity, wisdom, honesty, integrity and acreditable characters of sound judgment. They were highly held in greater honor, and loved by both the aged and the youths. The African hands were strong in protecting his people from death—any shedding innocent blood was greatly considered sacrilegious. African leaders dominated in both the spiritual and secular lives of everyone in the community. They were very well trusted and admired by all. No one wishes to be in their stead, because they were capable and discerning any un-anticipated dilemma that could befall the society at hand. They valued character more than wealth or positions—a good name was important to them rather than silver and gold. No one suspected or doubted their selfless services to their societies—they were accountable and answerable to any mistake. They were frank and simple-hearted. Wealth and education they did not have, but integrity and character was the scepter to drawing things with.

They didn't have clothes, but they were not ashamed of nakedness because honesty was their cover. The African leadership was full of hope and peacefulness—An African leader was a symbol of hope and pride to their community. Excellent leadership systems were adopted or rather stolen from Africa. It was in Africa where one can find true leaders who were people-minded, they loved their people from the bottom of their hearts serving them with zeal and outstretched vigor. Democracy was the African culture. African eyes were sternly opened against anything that could blemish the democracy in electing any candidate. Nothing was done in Africa without it being done in honesty and fairness.

African leaderships were Chiefdoms and Kingdoms, yet everyone was satisfied under the shadow of their ideal judgments. Their sage deeds were their crowns. They did not have perfumes, but when he smiled in your face, that alone was enough to exhilarate your heart. African leaders were not called by their names, because their names were highly held in greater admiration. Africans did never accept the food of idleness. It was considered a derogatory if one is offered free food. Food was found in Africa.

To call an African a thief, was an unforgiveable sin. No one associated himself with those who had bad names. Africa was known for her beauty and original things. People came from very faraway places only to visit African landscape, animals, rivers, mountains and the sereneness of the place. Everything is not photocopy in Africa: people come here for diamonds, gold, iron and silver. If one was told not come to Africa, he would consider that as great deprivation against his desires. Africans never think to go after other cultures, Africa was true to himself and to his cultures.

Good things were taken from Africa by the near and far away nations, in order to use them wisely for their betterment. Africa deserved the respect rendered to her, had he not gone to Africa; the whites could not have invented the things he boasts on today. Nevertheless, those qualities are no more to Africans today. Nowadays African Countries are groaning or rather ailing, for African communities have nothing for which to boast about.

When one occupies the State position of leadership, then immediately what imminently becomes important is a demonstrated dignity. People will expect to see nothing from their leaders apart from honesty or integrity and any excuses said are nonsenses. So it is useless when a leader who runs this office after he or she has been entrusted by the public to lead the nation, would blindly begin to allow getting drowned in the oceans of avarice. It is a great treason!

Dignity, when the leader maintains it very well, that leader is worthy to call "wise leader". But our African leaders especially the liberationists' elites, as if they are bewitched by similar spells, after they achieve the power. They turn to ignoring the very people they once persuasively used. And eventually like before, they lose their dignity, and become traitors in power. The African revolutionists used to forget easily the objectives, values, goals and missions upon which they preciously sacrificed a lot in the battle fields.

I am a South Sudanese citizen and an African native. But Africa, is the most lucrative place in the world in terms of Agriculture. Africa has the most fertile lands and in terms of animals keeping, Africa has the world's largest forests with myriads of animals. But Africans still are backward, because African leaders lacked healthy ideal nationalism. They're poor in leadership those demanding honesty and self-less commitment. I live in Africa, yet am sick of African systems whose power abuses are wicked through and through. Sincerely speaking, after my personal thoughts, when I was trying to understand Africa situations, I saw the following:

That African soldiers have ridiculously brought down Africa. It is only in African Countries where coups used to occur concurrently. It is only in Africa, where civilians die every day because soldiers want to grasp power. African soldiers mercilessly kill his own siblings using automatic guns which he does not know how to invent. African soldiers lack military discipline. African soldiers bring disasters to their own societies. African soldiers are greedy and wicked through and through. The African soldiers don't protect their people from disasters, instead they bring turmoil to their own people. They are cursed by those who are crying and dying in Somalia, those crying and dying in Uganda, by those crying and dying in Sudan and South Sudan, by those crying and dying in Egypt and Libya, by those crying and dying in Rwanda and Nigeria, by crying and dying in Kenya and Congo.

The poor communities of Africa have nothing to hope for, because it seemed that African genes has contagion, whose cure is not in this world. For though they see how the entire world are competitively struggling to get ahead, yet Africans tend to see those people superior and worthy to be begged for supports. The African leaders are well known for proposal writing.

Africa is a Continent whose leaders are like dogs. They are like dogs to Russians or Asians, to Europeans or the Western world. African leaders have no healthy policies or love for their Citizens, believe me. The only thing I saw African leaders love most are (a) Wealth (b) power and (c) women's bodies, not with marital love that recognizes the human responsibility, but it is on gluttony, greed and avarice. Lust that is very wicked through and through. I wondered, I don't understand why our African leaders never ever get satisfied from eating delicious food of wickedness, clinging in power that ends in shedding blood and lust, those led to whoredom.

Leadership in its nature, is a job that requires somebody who is mature and his heart is tamped or weaned from committing shameful abominations. Leadership require perfection, honesty, trustworthiness and reliability without measure. A leader always is the exemplarily model for those who are aspiring to follow sage and sound rules. Any behaviors apart or different from those mentioned above, disqualifies that leadership. I am convinced and believe that no African nation under heaven whose head of State of her Country is an honest man or woman. And this gave me a slushy feeling as to whether African nations will ever accept the true change other Countries are enjoying.

The change and not changes, the change I mean here is a change that could bring about real democracy, nationalism, development, education, brotherhood and sisterhood. In those dark eras, true brotherhood and sisterhood were found in our continent, Africa.

Africans were honest sisters and brothers. Africans were hard-workers, they never ate foods of idleness. And lazy people were named in derogatory names. Africans hate to copy other peoples' cultures and names. calling an African by a name which was not his or hers traditionally, would convey plight. And their black color, to them was a sign of real beauty and when one could get even smallest white scare on one's skin, it would be considered as sign of a curse, a stigma!

White skin was considered as a curse from gods whose hearts were provoked by certain misbehaving. And bulls were slaughtered to put away such shame from the society. But nowadays, Africans hate not only their cultures, but even their beauty, the black skin. Nowadays the black skin is an unwanted type. And that (white) which was considered as a stigma or a curse, is willingly embraced and a lot of money is paid to put away the black

(African beauty) skin. African women like their men, are bleaching their bodies. African men, instead of loathing such women, they are held above those who did not bleached themselves and are given amounts of money for doing that. African leaders are real dogs to Russians, Europeans, Asians and the Western world. They don't love to stand on their own feet, but are too gullible to other men (Russians, Asians and US Head of States) and cultures, eating foods from ready tables, they love to indulge in other male privileges those that are not their own!

You can't separate slavery from African conduct, and once you attempt to take slavery from Africa, an African will be equal to zero. O God, save me. Save me O The Creator of all human beings. For I'm a human, born a human, I have the right to live equal to my being. What curse or spell has trodden this Continent?! Why are we so weak as if we are not human beings? O God, brink back what is taken away from us, O Our Creator you in who life is ordained.

When you see African Countries, especially on lands' profitability issues, we have the world's leading tourism landscapes. Our grounds are very good for Agriculture. I don't want to talk about fish or sea foods. We have replete silver, gold, diamonds, oils and trees which can be useful as medicines—yet I don't see these gigantic blisses used for African Society's profitability.

Bad leaderships had plagued the African nations by shameful thefts and crookedness. African systems have become dependent. African leaders are too weak to decide on their own, they are influenced by foreign hands. African leaderships are directed by foreign fingers. And to make matters worse, African leaders are like boys once they are let alone, they could tend to destroy their own people by using tribalistic scepter of "my clan first", thus bringing confusions on those who elected them to the public seat.

They are blind leaders. They neither find joy in being honest nor are they interested in working for the public interest. Whereas African youths run to different Countries those are not African, in order to seek job opportunities, because there are no opportunities in Africa. African land is supposed to be our collective mother, but avarice has distorted our continent. You cannot separate African politics from thefts, robberies, rapes, disasters, gluttony and demonization.

African leaders don't respect either their Society nor the God of heaven who has given them these blisses of beautiful lands and tolerable communities. And as if it is in nature, that once an African politician wishes to contest for power, he could quickly run to get evil powers in order to attain that seat, Satanism. African leaders provoked the Living God by changing their glory to another and blasphemed His Holy Nature!

African leaders are like kids, they are childish. They have grown up but still with childish love that depicts only the children's toys love. What do children love?

Children love sweet, food, sex, money, lies, dishonesty and pleasures for children don't care about holding dearly. Children don't fear any derogatory remarks, they just swallow up anything sweet, for their mouths have still fine tastes for foods. Anything is fine to a child. Children love sex, because it makes him or her feels 'enjoying'—these are childish things!

African leaders are working hard against their Societies not for their societies' wellbeing. African leaders have blinded their societies' eyes. Now even if one wished to do something good to this African society, you can't do it. These profligate African politicians had already muted this society by their corrupt leadership. Nowadays all African societies no longer care about becoming or competing for world's supremacy, because they are very well contented with their backwardness. African politicians have crippled their societies only in order to milk their societies' wealth, power and young beautiful ladies for sexual pleasures! That is why African politicians have wrongly disoriented their societies in order not to speak up for their violated human rights.

Those loves I mentioned above are what motivate African politicians to remain in power for very long time without wishing to quit the Presidential chair to those who might push the Country forward. African politicians don't have minds, and as result, they passively tend to use other men's minds. And it is only in Africa where the dangers of being betrayed or sold out or exposed to the enemy's wishes or wills are extreme in this Continent. Even the leaders, are bribed in order to do something punishable against their kin men and women or nations.

Stay far away from African politics, African politics are deadly. They are games played only by blind people, it is not a game of honest people, rather it is a game of thieves, crooks and dishonest people. Sincerely speaking, I don't see any problem with street boys, even if they steal or rap, they are just looking for food and sexual pleasure and these are normal human's basic needs.

Leading needs wisdom and properly perceived vision without which none could do anything profitable. Leadership is not at all about wealth, celebrity or being privileged with bizarre techniques, rather it is all about sound judgment—and willful scarifies done with humbler heart. Truly wise Leadership is inspired by a durable faith and born by willful stamina. However, any vision, or be it leadership, or wisdom that does not acknowledges sound values, is therefore a mess, and nothing else. Israeli wise King Solomon, alarmed at how to lead wisely, he was a novice leader, prayed to the LORD: 'Give therefore thy servant an understanding heart to judge thy people, that I may discern between good and bad: for who is able to judge the so great a people?'.

And the LORD, being pleased by such a humble and wise request, in reply said, 'because thou has asked this thing (wisdom/judgment), and has not ask for thyself long life; neither has asked riches for thyself, nor has asked the life of thine enemies; but has asked for thyself understanding to discern judgment; Behold, I have done according to thy words: lo, I have given thee a wise and an understanding heart; so that there was none like thee before thee, neither after thee shall any arise like unto thee' (See 1 kings 3: 9-12).

The true wisdom comes from above, where the treasures of wisdom are. The wise Apostle, convinced on this, recited this to his Colossians students, 'in whom are hid all the treasures of wisdom and knowledge' (see Col 2:3). Therefore, sage leadership is the one that has insight-search and analyze anything deeply and patiently. We can see this in his wise book titled 'Fooled By Randomness', Nassim Nicholas paved his writing by this story. Croesus, king of Lydia, was considered to be the richest man of his time. To this day Romance languages use the expression 'rich as Croesus' to describe a person of excessive wealth. He was said to be visited by Solon, the Greek legislator known for his dignity, reserve, upright morals, humility, frugality, wisdom, intelligence and courage. Solon did not display the smallest surprise at the wealth and splendor surrounding his host, nor tiniest admiration for their owner.

Croesus was so irked by the manifest lack of impression on the part of this illustrious visitor that he attempted to extract from him some acknowledgement. He asked him if he had known a happier man than him. But Solon cited the life of a man who led a noble existence and died while in battle. Prodded for more, he gave similar examples of heroic but terminated lives, until Croesus, irate, asked him point-blank if he was not to be considered the happiest man of all. Solon answered: 'The observation of the numerous misfortunes that attend all conditions forbids us to grow insolent upon our present enjoyments, or to admit a man's happiness that may yet, in course of time, suffer change. For the uncertain future has yet to come, with all variety of future; and him only to whom the divinity (God) has (guaranteed) continued happiness until the end, we may call happy'.

You see, Solon admired not privileges the King of Romance

had—but he saw stupidity on the king judgments touching life. That is how any wise man sees life. Therefore, to give deeper explanations: "wisdom and Vision of Leadership is the art of putting the right Candidates into the right positions" again, "Leadership is the ability of realizing the best way of 'how to do something', and 'when' and 'why' you do that". It considers 'where to place 'what' with 'whom' or 'which' item is worthy-picking first with whom?" You must understand that "leadership demands stern eyes, integrity, heart to serve others, a will to sacrifice, and the strength to stand alone when necessary."

My main problem is with these crooked profligates who refused to join street life but tend to occupy our public offices, and have pushed our Countries backwards, but not forward.

And above all, we must fight Corruption, actually there is nowhere in the world said to be thoroughly virgin of corruption. Tell me if you know one! Corruption is everywhere, in any community i.e. in the Parliament, Churches, Mosques, Army, civil societies, private sectors, judiciary, NGOs it is found in any Country living under the heavens! According to the book titled "The Case Against Corruption" which was written in 2006 by Bhare el Ghazal University in collaboration with Fredric Ebert Foundation—it has stated that 'Greed and avarice' the inordinate and insatiable desires for acquiring and hoarding wealth and other forms of material possessions may be considered the driving force behind corruption. Adding that the influence of the relatives, friends and political associates whose hidden motives are to benefit through employment and other forms of favoritism.'

Fearing to be nicknamed 'unhelpful' by close relatives and friends thus the corrupt leaders succumb to such influences, forgetting the moral injunction which says, 'do unto others as you would them have do unto you'. According to University of Bhar el Ghazal of The Case against Corruption, the corruption types are classified as "grand corruption" which involves senior officials such as judges, under-secretaries, ministers and heads of states and Governments; and "petty or parochial corruption", which entails junior employees such as nurses, clerks, immigration offi-cials, custom clerks and traffic police (Moody-Stuart, 1996).

They properly explained the forms of corruptions i.e. brib-ery, extortion; promotion of monopolies; nepotism, cronyism, si-necures, tribalism and discrimination; tax fraud and accounting tricks; mismanagement of natural resources; and rigging of elec-tions. Adding under monopoly that C= M+D-A meaning cor-ruption (C) equals Monopoly (M) plus Discretion (D) minus Accountability (A) as it was described by Robert Klitgaard in his book titled 'Corruption as a System' (March 1998 Washington). Let me put this clearly, in any corrupt regime governments, if you can analyze properly, you will detect that the most affected, victimized and vulnerable are women. Because all those powers of greed and avarice that these regimes are inhumanly wield-ed against girls and fair young women. Though they are not in-volved in governing or getting privileged in the high positions like men, yet they face intolerable abuses! Optimistically saying, corruption tears any government down no matter that it alleges to remain in power. It neglects to retain minds that all humanity is created equal, no matter what befell the other or privileged another.

Still we are equal and the same in appearance, heart beats, ambitions and almost wanting to become something important all of us too! Moreover, this is the root of every legacy or let me say dignity. We aren't created like: Donkeys, Human and Master human, NO! Therefore, when we talk about this subject, I would like the reader to consider and focus on it diligently because humans are created naturally deceptive, responsive, and offensive, including also the spirit of generosity and natural love of one to another. Therefore, if we long for a zero Corrupted Country; we must nourish the right path and be good examples to demonstrate in our respective companies, organizations, public offices, good governance.

I say this before we are corrupted and end up disappointed. I wish to say that any people who yearn to protect our Country from future plights should not guide its presidential position by military strength, nor lower it upon the tree of tribalism. For in doing that, you should not boast that your Country would be spared from rampant civil wars. It may have a respite peace time but still war after war will enfold us. Be informed of this, that everybody will raise their long sticks with hockey-like ends to try pull it down, knowing that once he possesses it, he will wield it against anyone. And change any rules and directs the State wherever he or she wishes to, for as long as he or is sure that once he or she gets into power, that he or she will definitely never be held accountable by anyone.

That is why I wish to advise that the only durable and ever-lasting State peace is by making access to this position simplified, but still strongly regulated by Country Laws and Regulations which stipulate clear qualifications. Properly affiliated by strongly independent people and immune to any illegal sorts of kickbacks, well monitored law enforcements organs. I dare say, let the Electoral Commission be reliable and trusted by all such that no one doubts its liability, virginity and accuracy, allowing not any suspicions against the electoral Commission to adduce that votes might be rigged. So, to avoid all these plights, it does not call to kill the people, rather eliminate Corruption whereabouts methodically. Study its initiators and look for relevant and possible ways to expose it out first then tackle it scrupulously by setting shrewd mechanisms, such that when everyone is brought to book, he or she should acquaintedly come to himself or herself that he or she is wrong. Sometimes you must accept your weakness but strengthen your weak part by studying other Countries' both strengths and weaknesses then take those relevant things out and utilize them, there's nothing bad in doing that! I prefer you use these few methods suggested to prevent sabotages:

- Restrict, constitute and somewhat regulate the bankrolls and Banking systems—and money taken out of your Country.
- Restrict, constitute and somewhat regulate foreign entry in the Country, and establish boundaries to foreign currencies.
- Restrict, constitute and somewhat regulate buying and selling of commodities.
- Restrict, constitute and somewhat regulate salary payment

mechanisms, and put boundary to the use of money by any politicians.

- Restrict, constitute and somewhat regulate donations which are flowing into your Country.
- Restrict, constitute and somewhat regulate hospitals,sick accommodation –and the entire health facilitations.
- Restrict, constitute and somewhat regulate roads construction—and people movements.
- Restrict, constitute and somewhat regulate marriages dowry and parties expenditures.
- Restrict, constitute and somewhat regulate celebrations for budget amounts.
- Restrict, constitute and somewhat regulate rallies, types and their expenditures.
- Restrict, constitute and somewhat regulate any type of recreation's expenditures.
- Restrict, constitute and somewhat regulate employment and its qualifications and put boundaries to promotions and awards.
- Restrict, constitute and somewhat regulate the child bearing.
- Restrict, constitute and somewhat regulate entering of lodges of men and women who are illegal and without wedlock.
- Restrict, constitute and somewhat regulate the duration of foreigners' entry into the Country without clear documents and projects—those without their wives or husbands. Waste no time once you have been endowed with a lucrative Country by your Creator—start straight away by setting out

reliable barriers to help establish, stablize and escalate your land in a quicker ways possible. Knowing that any impartiality made in the Country based on the regulations will hinder its going ahead (and) it will echo right back badly—by inspiring sabotages (and) it will destroy the State eventually without any other remedy!

8.5 The Utilization of National Recreations

Instead of holding the National recreations as something meant solely for playing, why should it not be used as income generating tools? The youths shall have activities those we will support up through the Ministry concerned. Therefore I prefer that the following should be a beneficial flow as below:

i.   It shall be an obligation of the government to provide the needed equipment for the good performance of games; those that are wanted for the games' better enjoyments and entertainments. Such that each game could attract those watching it and be paid by money as well for its developments.

ii. Footballers, tense, belle ball, karate, wrestlers, races of running, drivers or swimmers, government should invest in them by availing courses and trainings such that the athletes could be energetic and well prepared. And have them given access to go even beyond the Country for international competitions whereby they could generate money for the Country and themselves as well. I encourage that, because in my own view, I can see that is also one way into prosperity, civilization, security and better future building.

iii. Technology is another means for the Country to extend her wing also to prosperity and better future achieving—once we could open privileges for our youths and children to be properly trained, equipped and enhanced to properly know enough from technological system such that nothing the advanced Country does without our awareness.

iv. By having strong technological systems, we will be able even to participate in international advertisements and fundraisings through technologies.

v. We shall work harder to get modernized in technology and advanced industrializations such that our next generations will be more and more invested into technologically as well, and eradicate technological illiteracy from our Country!

8.6 The Utility of Rivers

Instead for our rivers to stay useless and harmful to us in flooding seasons, I propose that why not open dams and channels for the irrigations of crops in dry months.

i. New rivers will be initiated in some waterless places to help the Country eradicate droughts and semi-deserting of some dry areas

ii. Big pools and entertaining of swims' relaxing should be also made to let citizens reap water entertainments and enjoyments those that brought about in water utility.

iii. We should open electrical energy from water and use it for electricity, beside also we are going to build modernized and internationalized hotels and restaurants alongside rivers; this plan will cause our Country to be one of the best Countries in the world's hotels and restaurants decorators.

iv. We must plant edible trees alongside rivers and streams those dug from big rivers, this will help make our land rich with fruits and decorate the Country by making it green.

8.7 Detach Military from Politics

It is wise to separate the military organ from political parties, because if we need a committed, tribe-less and organized military, those who can fight tirelessly without any redundancies, then let's separate this organ and make it independently far from political parties! This is for our safety and the advancing of wellbeing, and for our national development process. I am speaking about this not because I wish to demoralize the military, but I am advising this as adduce of preventing our precious Country from frequent entangling at the hands of the armed officers. Whose notions of their hearts state: 'now that I have fought in the Sudanese People Liberation Movement, so don't I deserve to rule this Country? We might end up concluding, of course yes! 'Then he or she may begin his lobbing inside the barracks.

Our innocent army will eventually be bewildered and some might be lured into sabotages. In addition, he/she might end our Country up in devastating mutinies. Because a liberation struggle should not be used as the virtue of getting into power for such position to be retained, it needs qualifications such as thinking, intellectuality, creativity, global vision and stamina to execute plans which can prosper the entire Country. And if we don't want to misuse our Country's power which is the army, then let's be faithful enough to willingly stay away from confusions made by our own selfish ambitions. We need a nationalistic army whose sole agenda is to protect this Country, and stick to the militarily prescribed regulations, disciplines and orders only. And if anyone wishes to join politics, he or she should totally be disconnected from his military back-bone such that he could not be tempted to use the gun against his opponent in case the land will fall into chaos and tragedies.

Let's separate the army from politics—let's have a pure national army which does not involve in political propaganda. Let's have a national army which is not belonging to a particular party. One day, I heard so many times our SPLM members shrieking jubilantly quoting, "SPLM is the party and the SPLA is its military wing" in this he believed that by doing so, that it will spare them from the threats of other South Sudanese parties and independent candidates who might be contesting for power. It is to avail precaution against those who might get strong back-ups from the communities.

Thus they might win if the political arena is safely left open for every non SPLM contestants, so that the SPLM members will risk lose the long fought for Country eventually. However, my people don't understand that the issue of SPLA/M has become historical right now, for every hour holds its own different history contrary to the past one. The strength of SPLM/A initiative is ineffective now at the current moment. What regaled it those days was that the allegation was against the Islamic government of Khartoum it was not South-South wars. Now the issue is completely very different and if we don't separate the Army from politics it will be all of us who will have nowhere to put our feet for rest.

In addition, because this army you see now will always break away with whosoever would call himself or herself an SPLM member. Those renegades with their tribal allegations, will lure this innocent community into aimless bickering due to their unquenchable quest. For not being given what it thinks it merits, such are the dilemmas we will always face until our Country will totally be destabilized. Every tribe will be persuaded to align to their SPLM generals and they will blindly fight for the rights of their sons who are not equally endowed with fair takings. True to say it, some will automatically misquote my personal advice saying that it is because this young lad might not be an SPLA/M member thus he is opposing it. No! No! No! I am an SPLA/M son, SPLM is my mother and SPLA is my father. SPLA/M is my true backbone! I am only speaking this out of discernment—am sparing our SPLA/M dignity.

I wish to maintain our eventful historical struggle to remain clean and pure from getting blemished by those who are defaming its noteworthiness because of their personal ulterior motives. Do not also undermine that in the first time before SPLA/M members mingled into this title, that it caused many politicians

to lower down their political parties—(and) joined into one title "SPLA/M" and if you don't know this historical perspective,
then you should go and read the movement's hence. I personally realized this: those different parties have seen the same threats
which SPLM thought to have seen it first at the contrast. In addition, are mobilizing young men in the army to align to them—
such that they could have enough militarists who would also be
loyal to their parties. This they suggested in order for their voices
to be escalated so it could be loudly heard. Moreover, since the
SPLM has ruled it out that the entire National Army as its own
party-wing! In addition, any attempt from either of the South
Sudanese parties to jubilantly wish the South Sudanese presidential position, such a party would easily be hindered by subtle
military strength! So my sibling, why do we flippantly encourage
such internal tensions by fueling it ignorantly?

Therefore, I am admonishing you my people that any Country
whose army is gullibly loyal to the political parties, that nation
has nothing to hope for such a nation has no future either! It'll
remain backward until such unlearning estate separates the arm
willfully from political influences. I am saying this in order to let
it be clear that if we love our Country, then we should see to this
advice accepted and faithfully adopted.

1) Let's consider the records of the soldier how he was relieved
   from his military service and appreciation she/she obtained
   as merits from his commander or boss.
2) Let's see the soldier's commitment first and how much he or
   she loves his or her Country, through his or her deeds.

3) Let's see to what extent a civilized soldier has academic qualifications, those would take him to be elected for civil responsibilities.

4) Let's understand his or her mood about what he or she alleges to do, before he could deceive the people and get into power.

5) Let's first wait to hear his or her whereabouts before he or she could be assigned.

6) Finally, let's consider the able, qualified and visional men and women who have their nationalistic hearts to their Country.

8.8 The Prison Utilization

Our prisoners shall not only be taken to strangling as execution of capital punishment. We end up merely feeding death; rather we will take them to cultivate areas for agricultural improvement, thus we would feed prosperity and have our economy enhanced. There will be

i. strong and reliable mechanisms for the prisoners to abide by it, such that there won't be any escape for them.

ii. The prisoners will work hard all day in all agriculture's different farms such as vegetation's, Dura growing in its different wheat's productions.

iii. We will have good-yielding from our prison department such that instead of calling it just "prison" we will cease from that name and give it another vital name such as "greater asset for the Country's prosperity"

316

iv. There must be secluded places for the prisoners such that there won't be arbitrary visitations of parents whose family members have been sentenced to capital punishments: [b] because their arrested family members are no longer theirs rather they are government's tools for works.

v. Nonetheless the prisoners have their full rights of proper feeding, health care, trainings of any necessary things that they might need.

vi. The underage (teenagers) will never be allowed to go in jails because we believe that jails can correct the erring adults, but it does the opposite to the teneagers' conduct.

vii. Inside the prison there must be proper monitoring from any violence of any sort. We must be preventive aganist other disasters such as killings or abuses inside our prisions.

8.9 Enhancement of Public Services

Let's give the disabled opportunities to generate their business and open up to enhance them. Let's equip and orient all the disabled to attained some skillful crafts for generating livelihood for themselves. And let's not allow beggary in this rich and full of different assets Country.

i. To empower women's businesses and provide to them with the relevant tools those could make them generate more cash for their livelihoods.

ii. We shall make conducive access for job seekers quickly because his request for jobs will not be seen as something simple, rather in fact we should strengthen this process with a bill of rights such that everyone must have a job accordingly.

iii. A student in the University should have a half salary from the government until the time he or she will be graduated, where he or she could eventually be received to his or her career.

iv. Education must be thoroughly enhanced herein such that no child will be taken to the Diasporas for schooling.

v. Everyone must be going to school. The government will be behind everyone by giving a salary to those who are schooling in obedience to the decree. Those who refuse will never get that opportunity of getting free money.

vi. Our youth must see to it that they should respect themselves and be responsible—and it shall be zero tolerance to youths to drink alcohol or drugs publicly, because we consider them as our next future.

vii. Nevertheless they have their full rights to have good clubs where they freely discuss or debate moral or social things therein

viii. Security organs must be provided to the civilians such that the citizens feel that this is their Country belonging to them but not only to those who think themselves as the elites alone.

ix. A soldier in the army must have his or her salary received on time and receive other incentives and allowances once he or she has been commissioned to any another mission to carry it out.

x. Security personnel must have his or her military

preparation—such that he should lack nothing of the equipment needed for any job he or she could be carrying it out.

xi. Their salary should not be the meagre one, rather they must receive enough money to moralize their committments in performing good missions.

xii. We must maintain our traditions, customs, sacred places and names.

xiii.To encourage many civic educations to every village where there are no urban awareness of hygenic knowledge.

xiv.Any bad cultures which are not from this Country, we will discourage herein and that will be a work of police and security organs.

xv. Any other aggressive languages or dances, or activities which are not from this Country background, we will stop it and have it punished.

xvi.Any Nation that will not respect our rules, decrees and laws those that govern us, shall never have a long-lasting relationship with our Country.

xvii.   There must be army deployed all around our territories to protect the Country against any insecurity.

xviii.   We will protect the Country from diseases or any epidemic disasters, for we believe God is for protection beside that efforts of ours, in anything, He is in control.

8.10 The Trade Runnings

Our traders must also comply with our national decrees and

accept plans laid down for them by government, such that when they face any bankruptcies they could find loans redemption from their government.

i. We could recognize a trader as National trader not when he or she robs or cheats these poor communities of our Country (this is meant to all traders including foreigners) rather, we will consider him as our trader once he or she cares for his or her community. And that shall be detected in the way of how he or she is selling her or his goods, and what types of the commodity he brings to the market.

ii. He or she must have first good background records i.e. we meant that realistically for those who will attempt to cheat the Country's public money on basis of his or being a trader and has the right to be enhanced.

iii. Ministry of Health shall see to it that everything in the markets are hygienically edible and clean and are two year secured from the date of their expiry. Local government shall monitor marketing to execute that health law and trade organizations.

iv. The Country is obligated to protect their property and take careful care of what might loot or steal or any other disasters those who would attempt to jeopardize their treasures.

v. Anything they could seal or bring sin, the public must properly be seen to it that they are not an expired commodity.

vi. All the prices must be discussed and regulated preliminarily by the Legislative Assembly and Ministry of Commerce and Industry. Then shall the price of any commodity be permitted to go the market.

vii. The traders will borrow from the governmental banks only when they could qualify the requirement and return the debts to banks accordingly.

8.11 Strict Laws to Govern Aliens

In the first place, we want to be clear that we love our foreigners visitors or investors and we should make "hospitality" our ultimate motto, but keep an eye on their movements.

i. The foreigners who come as traders must first and foremost come themselves by themselves rather then attaching themselves as partners to the natives—following the legally National procedures of entry.

ii. Any foreign investors those who will be coming for investment here in this Country must be guided by laws. Requirements, those govern investor's jobs and qualifications those standardized for that title.

iii. Instead for the foreigners to use the citizens for their selfish quests, we will set a proper mechanism for them to stay peacefully and well protected also. Because there is no violence against our foreigners allowed. If the citizens would be found haranguing the foreigners, he or she can be arrested for that.

iv. Nevertheless any single person whether he or she, they are not allowed to use any citizens of this Country as their guides, house-keepers, watching their clothes, clean their waste of any type. Rather the foreigners are the ones going to be used. We believe these foreigners have come to work here; therefore they are the ones to work for the South Sudanese communities and themselves.

v. For it is forbidden for the strangers to enslave the natives of this Country! If the foreigner is found violating this regulation he or she shall be confiscated and banished from this Country immediately without mercy.

vi. [a] No foreigner is allowed to come in to the Country without proper or reasonable purposes or while he or she has no proper documentations [b]; and he or she must come also with his wife or husband aligned to one another properly.

vii. It is forbidden for the foreigner to come here in this Country and begin to enjoy sexual abuse with the ladies or gentlemen of this Nation; and if somebody from either here or a foreigner wanted to have wife or husbands from one another, there must legal procedures opened and followed.

viii.For if we will detect some foreigners violating this law, he or she will be arrested until he or she pays the least coin for her freedom. Likewise to the natives of this Nation, they will be arrested on same basis and they will also be asked to vacate from such deeds!

ix. We are a peace-loving Country, and it is our priority to have so many relationships and International deals in which we don't wish to be selfish by receiving gifts and aids from others and end up idle. Therefore we will give as well as other due to us.

x. We will respect and admire those who will sincerely honor our National friends those who will respect our status those which govern our relationships with other Countries.

xi. We will have strong Diplomacy that will surpass other Countries which shall be guided by reliable methods.

8.12 Yes for South Sudanese Identity

We as a Country would not just assume that the citizens of our Country will just work or do their things without our national viewpoints, to assert how the true nationalist should look like. Always it is our joined duty to see one another and how our deeds prove that we sincerely love this Country. It will not be just a song to be sung, the ways we are redirecting our Country. We must altogether demonstrate true responsibility and concern in our heatrs towards our beloved Country. Therefore the true citizens are recognized in responsibilities, those which each one of our Country members do, regardless of his or her racism not to internal segregations. It is believed that any kingdom divided against itself will doubtlessly fall. Therefore, we as South Sudanese Citizens should work tirelessly towards cultivating a race-less and intermingled Country, whereby our motto shuold be "shoulder to shoulder in brotherhood". We shall subdue our differences with the following also:

i. Encourage intermarriage i.e. enhance marriages amongst our different tribes in line with the law.

ii. No Dinka—no Baria—no Nuer—no Lou—there is only

South Sudanese Citizenship!.

iii. All ladies are accessible to all men from any tribes; the government will be behind their marriage by supporting their wedding in one way or another.

iv. No one is allowed to refuse his or her daughters in marriage to somebody she loves on the basis of their tribal segregations.

v. No one from the job seekers could stick to one area; rather everyone has to be transfered elsewhere in the South Sudanese states such he or she could know his or her communities inclusive counterparts in other States.

vi. This transferring statement is meant forev eryone i.e. elected governors for governorship, Commissioners, Teachers, Administrators, Directors, nurses and doctors you are obligated to go to any state or county once you will be sent there. You have no choice to fail your transfer.

vii. All the Southerners have the right to own lands and properties in any state as long as it is inside this Country's territories.

8.13 Our Wildelife Preservation

Let it in the first place be understood that the lives of animals are assigned by God into the hands of mankind to begin with, therefore it is a responsibility endowed to man by the Creator Himself.

Anything we do against our both tame and wild animals God

will hold us accountable to each misdemeanor; whether we like or not, the Lord can inspire the hearts of His innocent creatures to depart from such irresponsible hands. I am not preaching, rather I am retrieving complete truth. I want the ignorant man and woman to get to know how far the agenda of our wildlife is so important even to God Himself to be honest.In as much as we must take strict care of our animals because they are massive asset to our Country. If any system in the country wishes always to build genius security for her wild people, let them neglect nay to employ everybody. Let them assign security personels all over monitoring who is still jobless. Invest somewhat on developing more than just and relying on mere security neworks.

Let all the citizens get jobs—such that everyone should be busy working. Because if you just think that your Country is merely secure due to your deployed security forces, then you are making a clumsy mistake! For those who are jobless—will do you no less then becoming your internal fades! Make scrupulously sure that every citizen members are collectively busy working, and by doing that, you are sparing the entire Country from savage sabotages and theft of any types. Make sure that in every morning all the legs are scurrying to their working places! That is the best security arrangement I know! The mechanism we should use will be as follow;

i.   We should have a very strong Law to maintain and protect the welfare of our animals.

ii. There must not be any misuse of the animals for any personal desire, concepts or examinations.

iii. Our forest must properly be protected from any territorial misuse and lootings.

iv. It is forbidden to bring any type of our wild animal without any legal approval from department concerned.

v. It is forbidden to arbitrarily kill the animal without any risk it has caused, you are only allowed to immediately report that issue to the department concerned.

vi. There must be fundraising for our animals' increasing.

vii. We will use its rich asset for our Country's prosperity and development.

viii. Our kids must be taught both in schools, churches, the importance of their wild animals.

ix. There must be fundraising for our animals' increasing.

x. We will use it rich asset for our Country's development.

xi. Our children must be taught both schools, churches the importance of their wild animals.

8.14 I Love this Land of Mine!

Yes, I Love my Motherland with all the heart that I have!!!!

I love her wild natural fruits and the Fragrances of her flowers therein!

I love her waters those overflowing from her Niles, the water that runs down from the Ghazal River—I love the water that goes down from the Lol River joining itself with river Jurr!

I love the water that moves teemingly from the White and Blue Nile Rivers—and the water that flows from the Red Sea! I love to drink from the Blue Nile;

I like drinking the water from those Niles flowing with abundances!

I love all my low lands and those thick Forests with trees and long papyrus, which can hide even the great beasts of the land!

I love the lilies even roses, the sunflowers, yellow and red flowers. I enjoy the flowers of my forests' sweet fragrances!

I love all my high lands even those sandy grounds, I like walking in my jungles which are full of our wild animals!

I like looking at the papyrus even those grassy-looking forests standing by the Rivers sides!

I yearn to walk upon our mountains' peaks, those of Marra, Immatong, Lainya and all my huge and beautiful hills!

I love those happy-giving aspects of my wild trees, I enjoy the way Jehovah God of heaven designed them all!

Do you wish me to be your friend of peace? Do well to my Motherland, and I will love and serve you even with trembling!

Do you wish to be my forever enemy? Why wish an early death?

If you just speak ill of my Motherland or look at it with contempt, or let your fingertip point at it either;

I will gush your eyes out, I will cut off your tongue and break your one fingertip that pointed at it!

Consider me your real enemy because you will never find favor within me henceforth. The love I have for my Motherland will quickly consume you! Take your tapping away from nearby it, so that you will be spared from the flaming heat of my jealousy those dashes!

I promise my Mother that you are my Land; I promise my Land that you are my Mother. I swear to protect you! Promises lick souls and drinks bloods, therefore let us make a reliable Covenant my Motherland;

Promise me that as long as I am on your hands, that you will never let me down;

And I promise you that as long as my feet are holding upon your hands I will protect your dignity to the last breath of my soul!

I call upon the heavens and the Hades to witness this Covenant, and I command all eyes to honor it!

I am commissioned by the Lord Himself; I am assigned with a covenant that I will never violate "the Covenant to love my Motherland and defend it".

I am predicting that this nation will one day be led by leaders who are God-fearing. I am predicting that this Country will one day know the 'Jehovah God' as their only God to serve! I am predicting that this Land will have faithful Leaders whose biggest agenda is to serve their weak ones!

I am yearning for a nation that will follow God faithfully knowing that the Almighty Yahweh is a God of all mankind including them.

I am praying for a Country whose faith is in the true God the 'only'

One who created the heavens and earth.

I am longing for a nation who will settle properly with her people in green pastures of justices and righteousness allowed to walk to and fro with not even one to hinder her spreading wings!

I am longing for a nation who will mingle her decrees with the sound Laws of the Jehovah God which is the true wisdom and understanding—Amen!!!!

Chapter Nine

9.1 The Gained Wisdom

9.1.1 Learning Makes A Difference

I am saying that 'learning makes a difference' because I am a life student. I used to learn everyday! So beware, there are other dangers yet to come! You know, it is not enough just to fight your rooted adversary in one way and then 'go to bed to rest!' Mark this, always in any nation whose Leaders are not alert against their shrewd enemies—or those with hidden agenda foes who might turn against them—are every now and then entangled in the same facades! There were some leftover stalemates from those sent men of the Khartoum government.

The Khartoum Army who came to South Sudan here without their wives in those civil war, but have harshly turned onto the Southerners' women! And those soldiers abused even underage young girls—as a result, there is an increasing rate of prostitution and crimes in the land! This also if not purged, will lead the whole land into upheaval prostitution! And people will eventually be infected with ugly and incurable diseases. The same in Arab traders who were sent to do different businesses here, but the truth was, they were security spies who were technically doing businesses like:bookshops, cement shops, goods shops, chewing-men, wheel-barrows men, soft-drink places, renting houses nearby the top Leaders' homes, playing football inclusively, selling vehicles, motor bikes, helping the top leaders in lending them freely.

They cunningly go into your offices and spy and deceptively promise the leading bodies! They still go as far as enticing young women with their money for sex and retrieve enough information, in order to report them back to their Islamic governments. This too, is a big tragedy waiting for us. The Muslims' agenda with this land is not yet through. I was tempted to mentoned the names of some people or the place in which they sat for their Islamic meeting, but for prudence sake I hang up. So, to mention but few, it was in May of 2009, where secret symposium meetings for the South Sudan were laid down with very strong strategies for the Islamization to these people. Their plans were not just for now, rather future plans for 20 to 50 years to come! They trusted their Islamic tactics, also in the passive nature of these communities!

• They agreed that they are going to marry from the top families whose positions are highly observed by all people, and are well feared, but they are not going to allow their daughters to be married by infidels, South Sudanese as they termed them, except to lead as an alternative of gaining strong loopholes.

• They agreed that they are going to take absolute control of the markets all over the South Sudan areas. They are going to collect zakah taxes and use this for spurring down the Leaders.

• They agreed that they are going to stand with the government of the South Sudan in all her financial needs with an ulterior motive of gaining trust such that no one could detect what they will be looking for.

• They agreed that they will convince whosoever in order for them to arrive to the goals of building mosques in all the ten States of South Sudan.

• They agreed that they are going to enter into the parliamentary organ and audubly ask for forming an Islamic party such that they will manage to change everything in the long run. They will adopt an Islamic government to take over the leadership of this land from kufaar, meaning wicked non-Muslims.

• They agreed that they will take their children to English schools and equip them such they could be able to rival over everything that belongs to the South Sudanese Country.

• They agreed that they will open strong Islamic companies connecting their companies with the Arab world. Because they believe this project is not their own rather it is for the whole Muslims wolrd wide.

• They agreed that they are going to let their well committed Muslim sons enter into police i.e. CID, army, national security, and drive buses. In these they believe that they will control everything because they will have easy access to doing anything.

•   They agreed that this pledge should be done tactically by grasping the favors of the ruling authorities, and by possessing liable documents, stating that they will legalize their request by quoting this conducive 'Article 25 of 2008 that permit freedoms of worship' for anyone to exercise one's own religion.

•   They agreed that they are going to unite with Somalia's Muslim brothers in achieving their security wellbeing—they believe by saying this because if somebody from the Christian's leaders attempts to interfere with their progress, that he could be transfered to his creator (get killed) that is. Their concepts of them in wanting to do all those I believe they are not new things to us, because we know the whys and whats for. So, to make my point clearer, I want to say 'be watchful'. Save yourselves from Muslim communities! Have a clear agenda and distinctive side! Do not be tempted to say in your hearts that you are able to play games with Muslims once again!

9.2 My Own Proverbs

I like proverbs and riddles; my reasoning is simple, because it was said that long ago, great leaders are those who easily understand the language of proverbs and interpret riddles. It was strongly believed, that any leader who did not master proverbs, guess ridlles and play chessare worthy nay called 'leaders' since they don't play games of wisdom! Therefore, play with me in these few proverbs!

- *Yes, heavy jets do surly lean on strongly cemented ground.*
- *Give me my tomorrow, and I will give you my today.*
- What are those chameleons doing as they walk to and fro sir? These reptiles are said to be risky, I don't know how? Tell me if you know its remedy!!
- *He who is aiming for a long journey, should sleep little, wake much and walk much.*
- You have not done it well, until to the point of "the well done" and when you quit, have it owed to the next to come. Is it not true Sir?
- What are those poisonous snakes which bite deadly from both sides near your ankles please tell me, if you know where they're exactly from!
- Your legs! Your legs! There is a deep pit in the ground there that is said to be swallowing you all! For if it could swallow you, how will you make it out?
- There are some deadly hooks laid ready to catch the innocent fish somewhere here. I don't really know where? Please tell me if you had already known the way!
- There are some sweets said to bring stomach problems. I don't know why? Please get me its answer if you know!
- Many are the people who listen to a call, sit and eat, than the call sit and read….Am I wrong sir?
- Sorry! Sorry! Sorry even for this fault! Says someone who did faults after he was told not to do faults…Am I wrong sir?
- The rich greet themselves sumptuously—whilst the poor ones glue in one another hug and kiss in heartfelt harmony!

Am I wrong sir?

- Your real enemy is not that enemy but dread the enemy who lurks inside your siblings and refuse to tell you that he is an enemy!...Am I wrong sir?

- Lavish food is openly exposed, sincere heartfelt helpful promises come after the poor man who is already dying—than in the time when he is striving with life, what bad luck!....Am I wrong sir?

- The same things dwell in one heart, "crime" and "innocence"and it is the owner of the same organ responsible which one to nourish!...Am I wrong sir?

- Like controlling the desert storms, is an intervention made to an idiot ruler!...Am I wrong?

- Like honey offered to a dog is a word of love uttered to a woman who has private lovers!...Am I wrong sir?

- I tried to sleep on my bed—yet I found myself bitten by deadly scorpions three times at a go! Wow! Wow! I cried, but no one is there to help me!

- Some loving foreigner happened to have whispered to my ears that there is siding road herebut I don't know where it could be exactly?

- I dreamt as if someone came in my house in the night and put his feet in my shoes and walked away with them totally and never returned! What a great misery, but I don't understand why!

- As I came back home from hunting, I smelt the wolves' incense, but when I asked my own kids, 'what is this smelling I smelt?' they both responded back in Arabic, 'mafi haja hini ya Abui' (there was nothing here father) that is!

- My friendships are getting weaker and weaker each day since I became a friend to that shop-keeper!

- I heard the sounds of gangsters knocking at my door saying secretly, 'let's get in and plunder all his properties,' so I girded myself well and jumped to my feet. As I walked outside, I opened the door, I found out that they were those towelled neighbors of ours standing outside with craving-eyes as if they are looking for my properties!

- One day we were in the sitting-room with my best friend from my own native village suddenly he told me,' excused me Muonyjang, I am going for a short call, I will come soon' he therefore stayed outside for a long time, and when I went outside to see him worried to what might had overtaken him, he was already gone!

- I was bathing and the soap covered my face all over, and as I was still cleansing it off I heard tapping sounds, "thud! Thud! Thud! So I hurried up in clearing my face from the soap and when I finished, I found everything had already been taken; my keys, money with all silver and gold in my clothing; those which were for the feeding of my kids' forthcoming days were all stolen!

- Every time my mum warns us to get in earlier as soon as it becomes dark. So one day my elder brothers refused to; they stayed outside till their bodies become wet in the mid night and soaked up by the dew of the cool. So they finally decided to go inunfortunately a bizarre thing grasped them by their necks and gored them to death!

- One day I was struggling with my own object which I could hardly handle, fortunately I saw a caravan of camel-men passing by. I went to them and asked one of them to help me; I saw his cheeks moving up and down slightly in a silent grin, and he said, bring it, let me 'see it from close' and repair its broken 'parts', when I gave it to him. He took it and ran away with it!

- Always in the nights times I used to hear bizarre sounds like, 'biim! Biim! Biim! In the dark! So one day I decided saying, 'I am going to see what is happening every time there'. And when I reached the place, I could not see properly, but I just heard something sounding, 'thud! Thud! Thud! So I went closer and closer, and to my surprise, I found torn apart dead bodies. My next stranger who is neighboring us here, is an ogre, he drinks the blood of men!!

- I am a new driver and I could hardly drive well so some kind of stranger came and asked me cunningly to 'help me' but when I gave him my new car to he drove it too adventurously till I was about to get shipwrecked into a bottomless sea; so I call for help loudly, 'help! Help! Help! But all my brothers were in deep conversation!

- More are they who come in one's death day, than those pleading and laboring in telling her mother to deliver him! Am I wrong sir?

- What a victim! A poor and unlearned man going to a house

of a traitor and says, "I want to tell you this secret friend, but keep it between us" not knowing that his death awaits him there!....Am I wrong sir?

- How are you beautiful woman? What is your name? "My name is Miss Fortune" said the seductive woman as she gently dangles her lure. Wow! What a beautiful name! exclaimed the poor unwarned young man; but her true name was really "Misfortune"—he came to learnt that name later on when he was already confinded between two walls by her husband!...Am I wrong sir?

- Like attempting to ride on untamed mule, is a good status made to govern an aggressive and senseless community...Am I wrong sir?

- The world is a place of testing minds and there is some One behind it keenly watching it, for what the crazy humans are doing!

- All those scenarios are kept for another history still to be born: generations shall pass by, times strictly ordered. People run and follow after the life's cunning mirage; dangling its promises of "tomorrow will be much better than today", but when the tomorrow arrives she says, 'it is not with me, maybe it is with the day after tomorrow!"

- And when somebody warns on this, he would be reputed with the nickname as 'man of interruptions', so, try your level best to the best of your level, afterwards, see if you have really made it! For the never-leaning figures perish! If you wish to hearken to my notion, make God your only hope, and you will survive it all!

- I heard that the sons of Loowloow refused to till their gardens last year; and in the next month, they gathered themselves questioning what would their children eat next year? What a silly talk!

- Give me, I will reward you back, say the law of nature, but Mr. Adak-rot refused and said, "I am a son of a hero, my father's credit will sustain me!" I came to hear it later on that his teeth were knocked outwhen he was struggling with Mr Austerity!

- Without knowing its risk, Muc-kuc-kang married a foreign woman, saying with great enthusiastic, "I will marry from such as this, because they are uniquely pretty", but in a short while; I heard that all his properties were smuggled off by his " very, very beautiful wife".

- Correct a wrong doer once, twice give him your counsel but in the third time, let his own fault teach him its algebra!

- Happy are the children whose father is wise, they frequently drink dignity and fill their mouth with fruits of integrity, what a good meal!

- In the house of the just, every day is a day for celebration, and feastings for new honey moons!

- Richness is good, even the wealthy men are well respected for their big achievement—but how honesty brings with it countless credit to those who are glued to her!

- Eat your food in the day light, before the dark comes, it will spare you from those who recline at same table in condemning you for consuming the delicious part!

- When there is a thinker in a Country, that Land is truly lucky, luckier only if his counsels are accepted and observed diligently;
- The true leader makes heaven on earth, he is enough for the making of the impossible things possible. Just be patient with him, let him pick it from the sides he wishes to, you will be more astonished to see the reality of his magical ability!
- When the Country wishes to prosper, let them not neglect education, let them invest into educating their children in advance and they will be surprised to see the reality of the things those they have never thought of, easily unfold by their children!
- Live, live but don't live just to leave, but leave something behind, because in this arena, you're supposed to live and leave something behind and once they are offered to wrong figures still that is no thanks at all!
- Happy are the eyes which see the truth from wrong and the heart that fondles the right paths!
- Commit no tragedy against your own land or a brother once you found yourself doing that, put your hands on your mouth and say to yourself "stop it".
- Live in the bush, but do not be bushy live in the dark but do not be darkness!

Chapter Ten

10.1 The Woman, The Center of All Arguments

10.1.1 The Woman in South Sudanese Society

The woman is the glory of any society living under heaven. And it is supposed for any society or leadership to make it their premier duty to protect women, and develop their capacity. Because woman is the mother of the nation—and once she is provided to, protected and developed, she will give birth to greater leaders. But sorry to say this, being a woman in the Dinka community is not something easy at all. I always feel okay once I see myself created a man in our society. Becoming a woman even in your youngest age, you are expected to get prepared for hard work. Woman are only 'workers' in our society. They are victimized in an endless childbearing, bearing children to men they didn't chose by themselves, but chosen for them by their fathers, or uncles, or brothers, woman has no absolute right over herself. She has no right to choose on her own even if she is a mature woman. The girl can be given to a man older (old man) than her age just because that man has got many cows. On the other hand, men, their counterpart, have absolute power, they marry and continue marrying until one is satisfied but women are culturally crippled.

The woman is the anchor of any nation living under heaven. Nevertheless, many Generations failed to perceive their wisdom and art of doing things. Our South Sudanese women marked to me a great note worthiness to be appreciated, they contributed into the making of our freedom. They were the ones who enabled the attained Country South Sudan tangibly! Without their heroic contribution, all the exerted efforts would have being in void. You see, though our women were not doing all these either knowingly or unknowingly, yet they contributed so much.

Unfortunately in many generations, it took many nations by surprise to understand and believe the importance of the lady in their own community. Especially in our Jieng communities, women are merely meant for dowry, they are seen as marketable elements! And if somebody bears a baby daughter, he doesn't feel so happy, because they are considered half-beings! She is not allowed to be amongst men or even say something as her attribute, because "there is no room for a woman amongst men of Jeing community". They are merely used for self-pleasures, relations on friendship building, such that an old man can gives his 14 years old daughter to his or her best friend in marriage i.e. it is another forced marital relation which the Dinka community called it later on as "an agreed marriage".

Our Dinka elders don't see that errors though through women, numberless men died. It we were supposed to do something good to our women in our Country at large, we supposed to start giving something out of true heart for compensating their neglected rights, it should be a continuous spirit. My Mum one day retorted our conversation on "taking many cows for myself talk" she said, "Real men are valued by what they give, not by what they take away.it is weakling when you are at the side that takes away, for the strong man is him who gives much, not him who takes away". She continued, 'it is the distinct weakling Folks habit always, they like to take away anything that fall on their ways, they are crazy opportunists" she concluded. At first I defiantly disregarded her words, but with enough time spent, I came to realize that she was not only right, but I got the logic behind her reasoning!

Hence, I decided "not to be at the side that takes away", for I have fully gotten what it means to be "a take aways folk". I understood the smart credit and joy that one feel especially when you give what you have sweated for it, to your own siblings and Soil. It engenders impeccable joy and peace that will continue to swell the heart. I have understood that it is only those who give what they toiled for; that they are the only ones who get that immeasurable joy. This is what many of us, the South Sudanese folks lucked. For we did not give to this Country something, we did not shown her respect, loyalty, honesty, responsibility, sacrifices, equity and above all, love and hard work. My mother taught all these important lessons. Therefore, if I could question somebody on the basis of death retaliations whether it's happened because women are valueless or is it because that woman are valuable? Of course, the answer would be that it's because women are most valuable! Therefore, if her importance takes the life of man, then that mean the important person is woman, not the man, let's be sincere! Therefore, accept alsothat women are more gifted mysteriously. In fact, the history admits that she was the first person who perceived the meaning of life! She can work, talk, and walk while she could be thinking with full concentrationand still she can derive sage answers to something!

They have gigantic ability of thoughts and tireless memory. Thus whenever we fail to understand her importance, the lives turn worst in that particular community or in those times they lived with women. People began to face lot of failures, groaning and so many different frustrations in their selfish lives those they lived. And it is because life is meant to be meaningful when it is lived together. For after my long, long time on logical thoughts, I came to understand that the reasons challenging every man and woman are based on their capacity of thinking and acting out abilities. I realized that one logical reason as to why we men are still alive and continue to live, is because of women. You can analyze a woman's thoughts that they are completely disorganized, full of doubts, fears for unknown, hatred, revenge, resentment and shyness that continue to disturb her emotionally. And when she is angry, she looks as if she is going to blow off soon some times, but the amazing part of her ability is the power to control herself from doing something stupid.

A woman is more focused on doing good deeds, because she knows that what matters more are deeds in whatsoever. Because she understands that the more alarming part of everything is an acted out deeds. She understands that the effects those deeds can do to others are the ones more damaging and un-repairable than mere thoughts and feelings. Therefore, despite the mess that comes into her mind, she can still do well in serving others, care for others and speaking out something of good morals for all. Sometimes when we can see two women disputing, it is easy to get reconciled, no matter how big the problem might be, you can still manage to reconcile them. In actions, women are strongly focused in doing something morally fantastic, responsible, realistic and reliable. A man on the other hand, his thoughts are distorted by his contradicting deeds.

Though he has gotten capacity on well-arranged ideas, organizational ability on how to execute or act out his vital agendas. Yet when it comes for him acting out his thoughts, he is completely erroneous and evil-driven. He (man) brings hazards and woes to the people whom he was supposed to be helping, protecting and pleasing. So many great women appeared in the history of the Holy Bible such as Deborah who fought against her foes and returned with great loots of triumphher name was remarkably awed. Not forgetting Queen Esther whose quotation remained to this day in which she said with courage, "I will go to the King though it is against the Law, if I perish, let me perish"; remember also Delilah who brought the great Israeli giant Samson in chains of victory to her coward people whom Samson was slaying everyday. Her quotation remained remarkable in history as she says, "to every hard question, it has got an answer, to every complicated riddle, there is its interpretation". Our culture believed that woman should not talk in the meetings those belonged to men—because that they are thoughtless. Our culture see to it as completely wrong for a woman to ride on a bicycle, or drive a car, or even sit on a mule—traditionally we believed that a woman cannot be a fighter, to fight in wars those could be fought by men! But now, the story proved the opposite—they are found even now in the hostlest frontline with men! Do not forget, through woman we have got a Savior! I believe firmly that any community which does not respect and develop up their women is bound to go nowhere else!

One day, I visited the prisoners in our Aweil East county Wanyjok, as I entered, I saw young drunk men in chains, and as I turned and looked at the other corner of the compound jail, I saw old men also badly suffering in chains! And with twinkling of agitation on my face I questioned the prison police, "why are these old men here?" He replied, "their in-laws had them jailed" I stammered saying, "but...but...but why?" The prison police replied, "because they gave their daughters in marriage—but the ladies escaped to their other unknown beloved men" Then.... then what is the fault of these old men here seeing that the ladies were the ones who did escape? He smiled at me and said, "their in-laws want their dowries those cows they paid back, but none of these old men still has any of the cows left". I said, "are they from one area?" No, they were brought from different localities, he replied. And before I could ask another question, I heard one of them swearing, "I will never, never do such a thing again, if her dowry will be the only food left for me to feed on, I will prefer death but I will never take any of my daughters' dowry again, let each one of them be free to do what she desired on her own!"

So here, I was quieted. I looked down for a short while, then I took a deep breath, convinced of this issue, I nodded my head saying, "My fathers refused to perceive this, that if God did not made them rich on their own, their daughters' dowries won't make them rich either". And now they are paying the price of their dull understanding, until they will percieve that no need to look at their daughters as marketable properties. Therefore, any communities who merely use their ladies for sale, and approach their ladies with contempt and triviality—because that they don't see their importance, are truly unthinkable! And for sure, they are on their ways to destruction! Do not misquote me sir, I don't mean to hurt your dignity, rather I am opening your eyes into a better and wiser Community!

Your young girl is as important as your son—both of them descended from your same blood! Therefore if you are convinced to fully willingly serve your boy, then what about your girl? Do you want to be reminded that she is your child too! It is therefore, valuable to see into it that you should appreciate their importance because they are the back bone of our Nations. And they are the very ones who taught us the language we all speak now and the way we behave took them stern concentration to make us who we are right now! Therefore, the Arabic parables that says, "A foolish mother produces a foolish Nation" And another parable says also, "by a milk of foolishness, the woman brought forth a foolish-minded son!" So it is something acknowledgeable that women are the ones who suffered in catering for the children, they held us in their wombs for 9 months and whenever we got sick, they are the ones too much worried about the child's illness more than the men {this is sincerely speaking}. All we do whether bad or worst, their hearts remained tender and forgiving—something that man lacked! They taught even the great kings to walk and admonish him how to eat his bread with respectfulness in a modest manner! Women are the ones concerned in child management—even the perilous hours, woman will never leave her child away and escape with her life, that fear is unthinkable! Ladies are a blessing to us in all that we need –their love is completely unique and it has its own importance that surpasses that of a man. The love of a woman is binding and it has a very strong toughness –because women are already naturally created that way. In the streets of the wise woman you cannot see many street boys or girls, because she knows how to handle her own house tactfully and with hard-working hands she managed her family well. She has no fear of anything. All her families have got plenty of food, clothes and covering made from Egyptian's. Her husband is highly respected, wow!

In AMURT International organization that was building a girls' primary school, I went there to one of their girls' college in Mabil at Wanyjok, Aweil East County. And I found ladies in class 3, and I asked them: 'how are the lessons girls? "No bad, said one of the ladies in answering to my question nonchalantly" and she continued saying, "but there are no boys herein this college". She continued, we would have learned faster! She said this statement in a heartfelt regret. And to my surprise they all stood to their feet and reiterated the same! Some even added saying, "Our minds alone without the mixture of boys is not attractive in learning!". So the ladies need us and we men needed them too. Despite that some people are looking to one another for other ulterior such as mere selfish reasons such as haste lusts. You have now seen how I talked for a long time with long and meaningful words, those which identified her beauty, goodness, importance and all that sweetness she has! And that is why I said that women are very important in our lives.

I could also remember in 1995 when I was coming from Muglad to Senar, and I ran short of money before I could even reach El Nihoud. I starved badly. I found no food for the three days of my travel from El Nihoud up to El Rahad. I suffered badly—and when that lorry reached El Rahad I could not even stand it any longer, because of the fourth days I spent also without food. So I was just sitting under a certain platform ten meters away from where men were sitting and conversing. And after almost 30 minute later, a lady who was sitting behind those men saw me and asked the men saying,' what is wrong with that young boy?' But the men answered saying,' he might be tired and wanted to rest'. But the lady insisted worriedly,' but that young boy is totally in real fervent fever, he looked also so hungry with signs of malaria infections?" she then got up and came to where I was lying down on the dust halfway. And she asked me,' young man, where did you come from?" I am from Muglad, I answered her halfway sobbing. As she was still talking to me, I felt cared for—I wished if she could keep speaking to me longer! I longed if she could remain besides me, but she cannot make it because she had been making tea. She made for me a drink from lemon—I found myself relief, may God bless her!

I was completely convinced of the motherly love and concern the ladies have! The way she said with concern,' fever of malaria, hungry and so forth, exactly that was why I was fainting! I believe firmly that it was even through wise ladies that the princes, kings, presidents, business men, high-ranking in the army, were able to manage, rule and led kingdoms with every thing else! And if corruption prevailed in the nation, women would be obligated as of greater factor who promoted such ugly and extravagant habits because the ladies are very influential in so many ways! I seconded also that if gluttony prevailed either, it would also be the ladies who were the ones boosting it through so many complaints—and men are easy to give either in or up into corruption since it is what causes her happiness! But if the woman can accept to be simple-hearted, I believed firmly that we will not hear anything such extravagant corruptions happening so often.

Because women are the ones with audibility to ask their husbands questions of how, where and when you afforded, attained and earned all these? The real advisers of the presidents and big business men are their women! She is not denied of anything she asks for from her husband, even if she inquires the annihilation of her figures she disliked! And I said therefore that ladies have powers more than even those men who think they can make it! It is therefore, true that through corrupted lady a nation becomes corrupted and eventually becomes poor—through her few and simple statements she can bring down the whole kingdom! But if she is an encouraging wise lady, surely the entire nation will eventually become strong with ample food! That is why I said also that, it is through the wishes of unfaithful lady that wrong behaviors such as bad styles of dressing and dancing are downloaded and encouraged! Because men are obligated to do merely what a lady recommends as something good and joy-giving! I am sure that even it is only through the wishes of the simplest lady in the community, that we can lose our focus and the visions at the national level! Even in the happiest families, it would be her exerted momentum which can cause that family to adopt rest and peace in the family's lives! It is only through the desires of the lady, might the life of her husband be either ruined or remain firmly secured! She is helpful, she is meaningful and sweet! Our lives are determined by the ladies we have adopted as partners!

Therefore, when it comes time to the love initiative, beware not to introduce your relationship one to another in a haste sex. Because some ladies think that their young men will not love them deeply if 'they don't give their bodies for sex as tying bond'. It is also the same with other young men; they wished to have sexual relationship more before marriage which will eventually result into boringness when they get married later! Listen to this sage counsel of mine, "be sober and gentle, and perceive one another first". Because by doing it that way—it has caused many engagements ending up with hurts and bitter disappointments. Therefore do not expose your bodies before marriage—please I urge you to wait for ululations and laughter's joyous days! I wish you could understand that by having hasty sex before marriage will cause the whole of your lives in marriage full of doubts, faithlessness, disrespectfulness and eventually you will end up insulting one another with heinous words those that are not supposed to be heard between a newly married couple!

Being a civilized or educated lady you need to know that the way you dress determines who you really are. And some failed to fathom that moderate dressing is better off—be responsible and encourage modesty to win in our community. Do not just take those western styles of dressing. Please I urge all my age-mates to behave in a responsible manner—because soon we are going to remain with everything in our catering. And if we behave recklessly, remember that our sons and daughters will eventually behave too much worse! I love women because they are responsibleonce they put that to heart, and that is why I want to encourage all my age-mates young men to never stagger in to marrying outside appearance ladies, do not spouse (make a partner) a reckless woman as your wife, no!

Because the way she behaves will determine the future of

your whole household life later on! And I encourage ladies also, do not be duped by those radical and irresponsible guys- those who only love your bodies but actually do not love you by who you are. It is in the time when you are in love engagement that you need to discuss all matters partnering marriage in detail and frankness. I encourage you ladies to talk everything inside-out all strictly and in full details, because once that time is gone, you will never, never find it again! So, let us express our love to them as I heard a certain story told of two birds' singing to one another, the male one was singing to its darling female bird, "I love you! I love you! I love you!" But the female bird also sang back to him saying, "Show it! Show it! Show it!! Therefore, I, Longbany, am going to show it to the woman of my Country and to all ladies over the world to whom this hymn will vitally count.

10.2 You Darling African Black-Woman of Mine!

You, my black woman of Africa, I love you my lady; I love this black-skinned woman of my earth (Country)!

I love to look at her round-black cheeks!

Her twin breasts are like well-fed gazelles! I like her bosoms, I love that shy-looking eyes! Don't look at me, for your eyes thoroughly over-whelm me! I am captivated by your only even one glance!

You made me merry by your white teeth those matching together as army in uniform! Your back is dangerously bending up—and with a soft and smooth voice you have totally enthralled me! You are amazing!

And with your unique nature of God's creative hand you surpassed thousands of the world women in beauty!

You have your own beauty—your bosom is likening unto that thin-backed butterfly!

You have a neck that is tall and straight up—your lips are sweeter than the honey-comb; you are beautiful by nature!

Your beautiful laps are like well-built pillars of the temple, your laps are leveled lovely altogether! Those women who use charms to win the heart. Hearts are nothing to your natural beauty—you are a unique being! I desire you day after another, for you are sweeter than the honey-comb!

Your fragrance is so sweet that deliberately evokes real love because you are a virgin!

Your embrace worms the body of him who hugged you! You are just clean by nature!

Your thigh is widely matching together like a City gate that has been well built for the King to enter; your waist is like a path that leads high on the hill-peak,

Your body is skillfully made—your framework is alluring even to the king!

You win even the heart of the Prince—for you are a manipulative being!

You hindered my heart to never love other beings; for you caught all my sensibility and robbed me of my own attention—I am your lovesick!

You made me look crassly at your natural beauty; you bind me to glance at you eagerly and so often—yet never I satisfied to peer at your seductive eyes even now!

You are a very important woman; your black-skin has a big space in my heart!

Your exquisite beauty is gripping like gravity of an iron!

You throw your King into great confusions—you held the prince captivated and caused the Emir to be sent into jail!

You captured the eye of him who saw you—and harden his heart so that he could not dare an accidental death fate from your own brother!

You are like a strong charm whose fortunes cannot be thwarted—your God had designed you truly well!

Please I beg you, hug me, allow me to embrace and huddle myself in your arms—and my heart will be relented and relieved from my longstanding frustrations and wounding of an old.

You look dreadful and a war victim—your face is still afraid from your enemy;

but comfort—comfort!

Be not afraid and dreading again, for the Jehovah LORD has released you from agony and sighing—He has sheltered you and me with abundant peace!

The LORD promised you saying;

from now on, I will not forgive those who will try to plunder you again!

I will not let go of those who will attempt to mock you—but I will fight them mercilessly;

I will break the neck of an elephant that attempts to approach you with triviality and contempt—I will smash the skins of the hard crocodile—I will not sit back and wait or even hesitate!

Oh LORD! Thank you for the beautiful woman you gave me—at first, I did not consider it, but when I open my eye-lids at her; I saw her impressive beauty!

You, my black woman of Africa! You cook all tasty and good—you are skillful in all that you do! You shrewdly manage your own house well!

Being with you is more important than in the King's Palace—to dwell beside you is more exhilarating than even in the Castle!

You black woman! You are more beautiful than even an angle—your eyes are completely white and sharp like a sharpened dagger! You made me reeled and fell back from your radiant eyes—I am seriously wounded in the heart by reason of your lovely glances!

Your fragrance is naturally sweeter than sweet and pure perfume made from an expensive nave! I like your sweet and fantastic fragrances—yes I like it, I like to smell it!

I don't care even if your own brother accused me of being unfair with you—I will not be afraid or shy to hold you by your hands even in the eyes of your own mother! I love you, I love you my Queen! Without you the world is a hell of fire to me!

I fervently prefer you above everything the LORD our God has made! Do not bother to emblazon yourself in human attire;

By putting on anything that will make you disguised from your natural being—for your natural body is liken a canopy of a Queen—yes, like even the lilies of the fields!

You confused and made me babble with words I don't even understand once I see your prettiest face!

You kept me all night awake and awaiting for the new sun to rise;

So that I could go to the highland where you live with your own mother in an intention to see you again—days without you I hated them all!

My body wetted from the cold of early morning dews as I stood waiting for you in your father's own shrubs!

I am poor and without even one cow—so your parents charged me with more cows those dowries I could not afford or even attain—and they thought by charging me costly that it will make me fear and shy away eventually so that I could not have you as my own;

but believe me, I won't leave or even stay away from her—for she is my all-joy!

Forgive me my darling—for at first, I did not perceive you;

at first, I did not consider it; please, let go of my sills of the past and let's begin even now! Let's take the love-life in our hearts not by our hands!

Let's be sincerely and live together as Royal family! Let the world remain outside as maids and bodyguards stay outdoors from the presence of their masters!

Let the beloved ones lie in their remote and greenish pastures with no even one to interfere in their love! Stay far away you women of the world! Do not interfere in our love; for her love is a real amusement even to my heart—you are a pleasing being!

I promise you do not worry—for your husband is a brave man, he will do it all!

I promise you!!

Just walk to and fro freely, for your husband is behind you girded— he is a real warrior!

You, my black woman of Africa! You give birth to great Champions— your womb brings forth heroes whose hearts know no fear!

Your breasts feed only Queens and Princes of the world! Your beau is a hidden treasure—you are not even now tasted; your sweetness give joy to the heart of the Noble of the City.

Your beautiful cheeks are like newly found honey-comb—you allure even the Chief of the Royal palace into hiding places—you are a beautiful being!

You, my black woman of Africa, Speak! Speak! For your words sustain me and surround me like a well-built wall;

your words heal my wounds those which had been in my heart for long time!

Hold my hand, let me walk down with you in the greenish trees shadow's places;

I am yours and you are mine, walk with me for one of your trip counts!

Allow me to lie on your bosom and rest on your twin breasts—let me drink pure wine from your virgin-well till I get drunk!

You, my black woman of Africa! You are like a hook that catches the great sea monitor; your black skin has totally bewitched my heart hastily!

You, my black woman of Africa! You kept me giggling excitedly because you seized all my heart with deep love!

You are amazing! You enticed me into rectifying your beau outpouringly—yet I am never acquainted to say it again, still even now!

For you have lifted my head up and crowned me with regalia of a King!

May the LORD God of heavens bless your very womb, may your children call you 'woman of excellence'!

May your name be highly honored by the Kings, and highly spoken well of even in the entire World—amen!! Come along—come along my darling my Princess, let's walk away!

Pictures of siblings and leaders

Rev. Malong Bak

Debora Adut Tong

Dut Deng & Dut Bak

Debora & grand daughter

Dut Bak

His Great Hero Saint
Wol Athian (Makuei-alany)
1854 He destroyed slavery camps
established in Rumbek 1838, after
He made Allies with Atuot & Nuer
under the leadership of Teny
Wol died in 1948 at the age of 118
in Pakam Area

1

His Divine Prophet:
Ngundeeng-bong - 1906

His Great Seer Prophet:
Rukpa Bakuparang-ga

Great Azande King:
Gbudue Bazingbi - 1905

2

His Divine Grace:
Prophet Ariath-makuel

His Divine Prophet:
Pita-lugar - 1949

His Divine Prophet:
Ali Abdalatif (Tok-mac)

Fr. Saturino Lohore
1955

3

William Deng Nhial
Founder:
Sudan African National Union (SANU)

His Great Hero & Revolutionary
Dr. Gorang-de-Mabior
**Commander & Founding Father
The Republic of South Sudan**

Commander
Karbino Kuanyin Bol

4

Commander
William Nyuon Bany

Pan-Madhol Hamite Heroes & Saints of South Sudan Freedom

In Conclusion, A Word to My Kids

Dear son, let me quote you the wise sayings of King David's Son which goes; hearken unto your father that begotten you, and despise not your mother when she is old. Buy the truth, and sell it nay; also wisdom, and instruction, and understanding. The father of the righteous (son) shall greatly rejoice: and he that begets a wise child shall have joy in him. Your father and your mother shall be glad, and she that bore you shall rejoice. My son gives me your heart, and let your eyes observe my ways! My son, I would not like to keep you uninformed, for that is a killjoy to me! I did not rejoice before I could put down my pen and precisely narrate the whole history of our slavery, the deprivations and the destitutions those we went through. These words I have already written to you are still boiling inside my heart—they burned and ran me down by giving me a sluggard feeling!

Thus I want you to take my warning, to the heart, and keep it shrwedly—grasp these sage instructions tiedly and leave it nay! There is a great reason to be scrupulous my beloved kids; there is a need to arm yourselves continuously against your adversaries. Do not be reluctance and redundant my kids, for you have a nearby enemy! You have a foe that was here from an old! He deceived our grandfathers and entered our land! He had become co-existing with us decievely. His aims are never for your good. He massacred both men and females in myriad number. He kidnapped thousands of innocent Dinka children of which I also was one. He captured and lured some of our Chiefs into an unexpected slavery, looting many lands and possessed them to date. He colonized many tribes of the Southerners into adopting his customs by using the bait of Islamic religion which is only but illusion!

He ravished thousands of young women and underage girls from these victimized tribes of the South. He robbed all their livelihoods such as cows, goats, sheep, wheat products, petroleum, and good trees' productions and utilized their gums and logs! He had had military genius and deceptive avenues which paralyzed our fathers into his gullible subjects! Beware my kid! Your enemy is a disaster-making one even from an old! He is a robber—he is a killer even a murderer of souls—beware my lad! Beware my child! Be shrwed and tactful! Don't sleep before he does—open your eyes wider and plan scrupulously—knowing that is beside you. And tenaciously hold to God, be built and rooted in Him, believing Him for a sure help. And delightfully and willfully align to His life-giving word!

And do not be lured to other bad cultures, to inherit foreign practices—is a sin my lads! Never leave thine Creator; never abandon the God of your father—for His is your father's both Father, friend and his protector! For I was a castaway.

About the Author

- Malong the "Longbany" Baak Malong Diing Mou, was born in 25th of May, 1982.
- Longbany is from NBG Aweil.
- Longbany is a brother, uncle and a father of a family.
- 1997-2003, Longbany attended primary and secondary education at Maridi County, Western Equatoria.
- 12/2009 to 06/2010, Longbany obtained an Advance Certificate on Teaching Methodology on Children Ministry, Emmanuel Christians' Institute in collaboration with Petra College in South Africa, at Yei River County (Goli College).

- Longbany experienced 10 years volunteer as Senior Teacher at Aweil East.
- 2015-2019, Longbany worked as an Assist. Inspector for Social Welfare NBGS in Aweil.
- January-July 2006, Longbany worked for Tearfund as Livelihood Senior Supervisor in Malual-kon field.
- 22nd May, 2004, Longbany became the Founder of Aweil Town Pentecostal Churches in (NBG) Aweil.
- 2017-2018, Longbany has been awarded three (3) Diplomas, for Online Courses i.e. (Teaching Skills for Educators, Law and Sociology).
- February 2009, Longbany become a Co-Founder of Northern Bhar El Ghazal Aweil Inter-Churches' Committee (NBG-ICC).
- 2016, Again, Co-Founder of Pastors' Union of called "Aweil Pastors' Fellowship".
- Longbany is an Activist on: Human Rights violations, and a voice for good governance.

Website: **malongbaak.blogspot.com**
Tel: +211911243360 / ++211922635522
longbany2015@gmail.com
Copyright © Malong Baak 2021

CPSIA information can be obtained
at www.ICGtesting.com
Printed in the USA
LVHW021139090322
712797LV00003B/214